STUDY GUIDE TO ACCOMPANY
STANTON · ETZEL · WALKER

Fundamentals of Marketing

TENTH EDITION

Thomas J. Adams

Sacramento City College

McGRAW-HILL, INC.

New York   St. Louis   San Francisco   Auckland   Bogotá
Caracas   Lisbon   London   Madrid   Mexico City
Milan   Montreal   New Delhi   San Juan
Singapore   Sydney   Tokyo   Toronto

The editors were Bonnie K. Binkert, Lee Medoff, and Peggy Rehberger;

the production supervisor was Elizabeth Strange.

Malloy Lithographing, Inc., was printer and binder.

To the memory

of an immigrant who believed in the

promise of the American market--

my father, JAMES T. ADAMS

CONTENTS

What This Study Guide Will Do for You   vii

PART ONE: MODERN MARKETING AND ITS ENVIRONMENT 1
 1 The Field of Marketing 3
 2 The Changing Marketing Environment   17
 3 Strategic Planning and Forecasting 31
 4 Marketing Research and Information 47

PART TWO: TARGET MARKETS 65
 5 Market Segmentation and Target-Market Strategies 67
 6 Consumer Buying Behavior 85
 7 The Business Market 102

PART THREE: PRODUCT 117
 8 Product Planning and Development 119
 9 Product-Mix Strategies 137
10 Brands, Packaging, and Other Product Features 151

PART FOUR: PRICE 167
11 Price Determination 169
   APPENDIX B: Marketing Math 188
12 Pricing Strategies 192

PART FIVE: DISTRIBUTION 209
13 Channels of Distribution 211
14 Retailing 228
15 Wholesaling and Physical Distribution 246

PART SIX: PROMOTION 267
16 The Promotional Program 269
17 Personal Selling and Sales Management 285
18 Advertising, Sales Promotion, and Public Relations 301

PART SEVEN: MARKETING IN SPECIAL FIELDS 319
19 Services Marketing by For-Profit and Nonprofit Organizations 321
20 International Marketing 338

PART EIGHT: MANAGING THE MARKETING EFFORT 355
21 Marketing Implementation and Evaluation 357
22 Marketing: Appraisal and Prospects 374

WHAT THIS STUDY GUIDE WILL DO FOR YOU

Educational psychologists tell us that one of the keys to learning is reinforcement. This Study Guide is designed to reinforce the book of Professors Stanton, Etzel, and Walker in spades. You will be guided through a set of varied exercises that examine and reexamine the textual material again and again from many points of view. Our goal is an ambitious one--we want you not only to know marketing, but to know you know it. In short, we want you to understand it.

Each Study Guide chapter is divided into ten parts--material designed to reinforce the corresponding chapter of the textbook.

Part A lists the Chapter Goals. Note that these are worded exactly as they appear at the beginning of each of the text chapters. This is a listing of the major elements in the chapter we hope you will come to understand.

Part B, Key Terms and Concepts, is simply a listing, in order of their appearance in the text, of the chapter's key terms and concepts. The numbers refer you to the text page where the term or concept first appears.

Part C, Summary, briefly reviews the essential elements of the text chapters, highlighting the general meaning of the text subjects you should remember. Note that the Summary in the Study Guide is worded differently from the Summary in the text. Read them both, since they summarize the same material using different words (reinforcement again). Text page references are also provided.

Part D, Completion, gives you an opportunity to test your comprehension of the major topics in the text by completing an abbreviated outline. This is one of the most valuable tools in the Study Guide since it calls largely for self-testing your knowledge of the textual material.

Parts E, F, and G, True-False, Multiple Choice, and Matching Questions, not only help you to measure how well you have mastered the fundamentals of marketing in the text, but give you a leg up on the kinds of questions that may be asked on examinations. The answers to questions for Parts D through G appear in **Part J, Answers to Questions**, which appear at the end of each Study Guide chapter.

Part H, Problems and Applications, allows you to put your understanding of marketing into practice. Realistic situations are provided that allow you to experience both the difficulties and rewards of putting your ideas into action. Some questions require you to do additional research through library reading or field work.

Part I, Exercise, will help you bridge the gap between knowledge and experience. If it is to have any use to society at all, marketing must be an applied discipline. The attempt in this section is to put into practice the theory and knowledge introduced in the chapter. Some of the exercises are group efforts; others, individual efforts. All, however, are reasonable approximations of what you are likely to find marketing to be outside the classroom.

Short readings are presented in **Part J, A Real World Case**. They are taken from many general and specialized periodicals you might encounter in the field of marketing. Although we have tried to select each so as to underscore the key ideas in the chapter, you will note that other, seemingly extraneous ideas also come into play. But this is the way the real world of marketing works--not with crisp precision, but in a halting, buzzing, vibrating, even brawling and intimidating fashion. A few multiple choice questions test your comprehension of the case. Think of these readings as a mere antipasto to the genuine entree you will find on your own in the Real World of Marketing.

There is no magic procedure for you to follow in using this Study Guide. This is not to say that you shouldn't establish some pattern of study for yourself. For example, you may wish to alternate between the Study Guide and the text, reading the Summaries and then the corresponding text chapters, reading the lists of key terms and concepts and then rereading the text for meaning, finishing the Completion section as the text is being reread, and so forth. Sample these approaches and find the pattern that works best for you.

A NOTE OF THANKS

It is an author's happiest task upon the completion of a book to acknowledge his debt to those who helped bring it to life: to Professor William J. Stanton for making the many years we have worked on these projects happy and rewarding; to Professor Michael J. Etzel of the University of Notre Dame and Dean Bruce J. Walker of the University of Missouri, Columbia, for their cooperation and helpful suggestions; to Lee Medoff, my editor at McGraw-Hill, Inc., for his promptness, enthusiasm, and professionalism; to Shirle Baumgartner, an uncommon proofreader, for explaining the difference between a dangling participle and a split infinitive; and finally, to my marketing students at Sacramento City College who taught me so much, and without whom--let's face it--this work would be unnecessary.

Sacramento, California   Thomas J. Adams

PART ONE

**MODERN MARKETING
AND ITS ENVIRONMENT**

CHAPTER 1

THE FIELD OF MARKETING

PART 1A: Chapter Goals

After studying this chapter, you should be able to explain:

- The relationship between exchange and marketing
- How marketing applies to business and nonbusiness situations
- The difference between selling and marketing
- Marketing's evolution in the U.S.
- The marketing concept
- The impact of ethics and quality management in marketing
- Marketing's role in the global economy, in the American socioeconomic system, in an individual organization, and in your life

PART 1B: **Key Terms and Concepts**

1. Marketers	[5]	12. Societal marketing concept	[11]
2. Market	[5]	13. Ethics	[12]
3. Exchange	[5]	14. Quality	[15]
4. Marketing	[6]	15. Customer satisfaction	[15]
5. Products	[6]	16. Utility	[20]
6. Customers	[6]	17. Form utility	[20]
7. Consumers	[6]	18. Information utility	[20]
8. Production-orientation stage	[7]	19. Image utility	[20]
9. Sales-orientation stage	[8]	20. Place utility	[20]
10. Marketing-orientation stage	[9]	21. Time utility	[20]
11. Marketing concept	[10]	22. Possession utility	[20]

PART 1C: Summary

Marketing has many meanings. Among these are a broad meaning of marketing and a business meaning, the less broad interpretation. The broad meaning refers to marketing as an exchange relationship that aims to satisfy human needs and wants. Within this broad perspective there is great variety as regards (1) who the marketers are, (2) what they are marketing, and (3) to whom they are appealing [4].

In the narrower business sense, marketing is defined as a total system of business activities designed to plan, price, promote, and distribute want-satisfying products to target markets in order to achieve organizational objectives [6].

Marketing did not arrive full-blown--it developed over many years. Marketing evolved through three stages: (a) production-orientation (just build the product and we'll worry about selling it later); (b) sales-orientation (sure we'll build it, but we have to push it hard too); and (c) marketing-orientation (first, let's find out the consumer's needs, then we'll build the product) [7-10].

With the growing realization that marketing is central to the success of an individual firm, a

4

philosophy of business, the marketing concept, came into being. It is built on the belief that: (a) firms should be consumer-oriented, (b) all marketing activities in an organization should be coordinated, and (c) these two factors are essential to meeting an organization's performance objectives [10-11. Recently, this philosophy has been taken a step further to include society in general. It is not enough that a firm satisfy its customers. It must do so without harming society in general. In other words, it should be done ethically--with the standards of behavior generally accepted by a society. The main job of marketing management is to breathe life into this philosophy and make it a reality [11].

There is an increasing emphasis on quality in the American economy. For marketers, the best measure of quality is customer satisfaction. To maintain quality, marketers must (1) ensure that all marketing activities contribute to creating reasonable expectations on the part of the customer, and (2) eliminate variations in customers' experiences in buying and consuming the product [15].

Marketing is important globally [16], in the American socioeconomic system (the American system employs between one-fourth and one-third of the civilian labor force and accounts for approximately half of every dollar we spend at the retail level) [19], and in the individual firm (goods- and service-dominated profit-seeking firms, and also nonprofit organizations) [19-20]. In all these arenas, marketing creates value--what economists call utility, or the attribute an item has that makes it possible to satisfy human wants. Marketing creates four types of utility: time, place, possession, and information (image), and plays a supporting role in the creation of form utility [20-21].

PART 1D: Completion

1. Generally speaking, marketing is considered a(n) _____ performed by business firms.

2. It can also be carried out by other _____ and even _____.

3. Within the broad dimensions of marketing, three elements are analyzed: (1) _____ , (2) what is _____, and (3) their _____.

4. _____ are people and organizations that wish to make exchanges.

5. A(n) _____ is considered to be an individual or organization that has an existing or potential exchange relationship with someone or something else.

6. Since marketing is a(n) _____ , it consists of all activities designed to generate and facilitate that exchange which is intended to satisfy human _____.

7. There are three ways to satisfy a want: (1) _____ for yourself, (2) _____ production from someone else, and (3) voluntary _____.

8. Marketing is defined as the total _____ of business activities designed to plan, price, promote, and distribute _____ products to _____ markets in order to achieve _____.

9. This definition implies that marketing must be _____ and that a marketing program should start with an idea about a new _____ and should not end until the customer is _____.

10. In the text, _____ will be used generically to denote a good, service, idea, person, or place.

11. Customers and consumers are not the same thing. _____ make buying decisions, while _____ are individuals or organizations that use or consume a product.

12. Selling and marketing are also not the same. In _____ , a firm makes a product and then convinces customers to buy it. In _____ , the firm first finds out what the _____ wants and then develops the product that will satisfy the <u>need</u> and still yield a satisfactory profit.

13. The three stages of the evolution of marketing are _____ stage, _____ stage, and _____ stage.

14. Manufacturers in the first stage were _____.

15. The _____-orientation stage is the "hard sell" stage.

16. In the marketing-orientation stage, attention shifts from selling to _____.

17. A key to effective marketing is a(n) _____ on the part of the company's top executives.

18. The marketing concept is based on three fundamental beliefs: (1) all company actions should be oriented toward the _____ , (2) marketing activities should be _____ , and (3) both of these are essential for achieving the organization's _____.

19. The _____ marketing concept recognizes that in implementing its marketing program, _____ might be adversely affected.

20. A firm's marketing concept and its social responsibility are _____ so long as it strives over the long run to: (1) satisfy the wants of its product-buying _____ , (2) meet the _____ needs of others affected by the firm's activities, and (3) meet the firm's _____.

21. _____ are the rules or standards of behavior generally accepted by a society.

22. _____ is the absence of variation in products.

23. Product quality is the responsibility of every _____.

24. For marketers, the best measure of quality is _____ satisfaction.

25. Marketing plays an important role in the _____ economy, in the American _____ system, and in an individual _____.

26. Most countries today recognize the importance of _____ beyond their own national borders.

27. Aggressive, effective marketing has been largely responsible for the _____ _____ in the United States.

28. Between _____ and _____ of the civilian labor force is engaged in marketing.

29. About ___ cents out of every dollar we spend as consumers goes to cover marketing costs.

30. A measure of the importance of marketing in our socioeconomic system is its creation of _____ , that is, the attribute in an item that makes it capable of satisfying human _____.

31. Marketing creates four types of value: _____ , _____ , _____ or _____ utility, and _____ utility, and plays a supporting role in creating _____ utility.

32. _____ account for over two-thirds of the nation's gross national product.

33. Three reasons for studying marketing are: (1) it plays a large part in our _____ , (2) its makes us _____ consumers, and (3) it may tie in with our _____ goals.

PART 1E: True-False Questions

If the statement is true, circle "T"; if false, circle "F."

T F   1. Whenever you attempt to persuade someone to do something, you are engaged in marketing.

T F   2. The idea of quality in marketing is simple--simply build the best product you can and people will buy it.

T F   3. The marketing concept emphasizes customer orientation and profitable sales volume.

T F   4. Central to the idea of marketing is the concept of exchange.

T F   5. The marketing concept means that marketing executives should run the company.

T F   6. Over one-half of the civilian labor force is engaged in marketing.

T F   7. As a philosophy, the marketing concept is meaningless unless it is translated into effective action.

T F   8. The newest interpretation of the marketing concept reaffirms the idea that marketers should concentrate on a single group only--the customer.

T F   9. Ethics are the standards of behavior generally accepted by a society.

T F 10. Marketing is limited to business organizations. Organizations such as churches, museums, symphony orchestras, hospitals, and universities derive little or no benefit from marketing.

T F 11. The "hard sell" stage in the development of the marketing concept began with the end of the Vietnam War.

T F 12. Selling and marketing mean the same thing.

T F 13. When a company bends its supply to the will of consumer demand, it is applying the marketing concept in its business.

T F 14. An example of the creation of form utility is a baker mixing the appropriate ingredients to make bread.

T F 15. An example of exchange is a robber growling his offer of: "Your money or your life."

PART 1F: Multiple Choice Questions

In the space provided write the letter of the answer that best fits the statement.

____ 1. Of the total amount spent for all products in the United States in a year, about what percentage of sales goes to cover marketing costs?
A. 20.   B. 25.   C. 33-1/3.   D. 50.   E. 70.

___ 2. Which of the following statements regarding ethics is correct?
   A. Ethics are the rules we play by.
   B. Ethics are the standards of behavior accepted by a society.
   C. Ethical standards must be communicated to employees.
   D. Ethics is a cornerstone of business success.
   E. All of the statements are correct.

___ 3. Which of the following is marketing?
   A. Two candidates are debating in public for the same political office.
   B. The U.S. Postal Service encourages stamp collecting.
   C. A first-round draft choice is negotiating his first contract.
   D. The government sponsors a "Say NO to drugs" campaign.
   E. All of the above.

___ 4. Which pair of terms best describes the marketing concept?
   A. Problem solving and decision making.
   B. Increasing sales and better management.
   C. Building quality products and reducing prices.
   D. Customer orientation and profitable sales volume.
   E. Lower prices and better service.

___ 5. The definition of marketing includes all the following elements EXCEPT:
   A. Profit maximization.   D. Public benefit.
   B. A system of business activities.   E. Target markets.
   C. The creation of value.

___ 6. Marketing emphasizes:
   A. Products.   C. Customers' wants.   E. Needs of the seller.
   B. Sales volume.   D. The short term.

___ 7. The societal marketing concept emphasizes:
   A. The long run.
   B. A broad definition of "customers."
   C. Consumer satisfaction.
   D. The company's performance objectives.
   E. All of the above.

___ 8. Which of the following statements regarding quality is correct?
   A. Quality is the absence of variation.
   B. Quality must be the responsibility of every employee.
   C. For marketers, the best measure of quality is customer satisfaction.
   D. Product quality cannot be delegated to one department in an organization.
   E. All of the above are correct.

_____ 9. For exchange to take place, all of the following must be present EXCEPT:
    A. Self-sufficiency.
    B. Unsatisfied needs.
    C. Communication between the parties.
    D. Each party must have something to exchange.
    E. Noncoercion.

_____10. When McDonald's can get children to associate its food with Ronald McDonald it has
    created _____ utility.
    A. Time   B. Possession   C. Form   D. Information   E. Place

_____11. Current marketing emphasizes all of the following EXCEPT:
    A. Consumer wants.   C. Market needs.   E.   Buyers' needs.
    B. Societal needs.   D. Sellers' needs.

_____12. The "hard sell" stage in the evolution of marketing was the:
    A. Production-orientation stage.   D. Societal-marketing stage.
    B. Sales-orientation stage.   E. None of the above.
    C. Marketing-orientation stage.

_____13. In the evolutionary development of marketing, the first stage emphasizes:
    A. Marketing.   B. Advertising.   C. Production.   D. Sales.   E. Customer orientation.

_____14. Consumers are viewed as the target of all business activities under the _____ concept.
    A. Production   B. Marketing   C. Social   D. Segmentation   E. Consumer

_____15. What is being marketed could include:
    A. Goods.   B. Services.   C. Ideas.   D. Places.   E. All of the above.

PART 1G: Matching Questions

In the space provided write the number of the word or expression from column 1 that best fits the
description in column 2.

	1		2
1.	Consumers	____	a. Utility created through manufacturing.
2.	Customers	____	b. Utility created by storage.
3.	Ethics	____	c. Standards of behavior generally accepted by society.

4. Exchange   ____   d. The total system of business activities designed to plan, price, promote, and distribute want-satisfying goods, services, and ideas to target markets to achieve organizational objectives.

5. Form utility

6. Image utility

                ____   e. The last stage in the evolution of marketing management.

7. Information utility

8. Market   ____   f. The "hard sell" stage.

9. Marketing   ____   g. Utility created by taking title.

10. Marketing concept   ____   h. A transaction intended to satisfy human wants and needs.

11. Marketing-orientation stage

                ____   i. The individuals or organizations making the buying decision.

12. Place utility

13. Possession utility

14. Production-orientation stage

15. Quality

16. Sales-orientation stage

17. Societal marketing concept

18. Time utility

PART 1H: Problems and Applications

1.   Interview the director of public relations for your college or university. In what stage of the evolution of marketing would you place his or her program? To which target markets are appeals being made? Do you believe they will be successful? Why?

2.   In your opinion, why should the marketing manager, rather than the production manager, make decisions regarding packaging, labeling, design, and color of a product?

3.   Give the meaning of the following statement: "A marketing philosophy should be introduced at the beginning rather than at the end of a production cycle."

11

4.   Describe a hospital or the Boy or Girl Scouts in marketing terms, making use of the broader dimensions of marketing.

5.   In a way, marketing people are agents of change. Based on your present knowledge and some library research, what do you think marketing in our society will be like in the year 2000? Make a list of two large corporations and two small companies that are known to you. Comment on how you think they will change by the year 2000 in terms of:
    A. The products they make and sell.
    B. How they will distribute their products.
    C. How they will advertise and sell their products.
    D. The prices they will charge for their products.

6.   How do dictionary definitions of marketing differ from the definitions used in this chapter?

7.   In your own words summarize:
    A. The relationship of modern marketing to global marketing.
    B. The meaning of the broader dimensions of marketing.

8.   The marketing concept is often described as a "way of thinking" about organized activity. How do you explain this?

PART 1I: Exercise

The keystone idea in this book is the marketing concept. The entire work is built around it. To help you better identify marketing concept orientation, read the following ten pairs of statements. Write "MCO" beside the firms having the marketing concept orientation.

1.   Firm A   "I'll give them any color car they want so long as it's black."
      Firm B   "I'll give them any color car they want."

2.   Firm A   "By adding plastic carrying handles, we can make it give better service."
      Firm B   "By adding plastic carrying handles we can cut our costs."

3.   Firm A   "If we can get you to sign this contract today, we can easily fit it into our factory schedule."
      Firm B   "If we can get you to sign this contract today, you can get the products in time to meet your sales goals."

4.   Firm A   "We offer you a means for gathering, processing, and analyzing business data."
      Firm B   "We make computers."

5. Firm A "We make pumps."
   Firm B "We deliver usable water into people's homes at the right pressure and in the right volume."

6. Firm A "The first product my grandfather made when he started this furniture factory is this Shaker love seat. We'll always make it."
   Firm B "The simplicity of this classic Shaker furniture design is continuing to enjoy wide acceptance."

7. Firm A "Please donate blood. Your hospital needs it."
   Firm B "Please donate blood. You will never know when you or one of your loved ones will need it."

8. Firm A "Perhaps we had better get back to taking Visa cards. A lot of customers seem to be using them."
   Firm B "We'll continue with MasterCard as long as they give us a better deal than Visa."

9. Firm A "Profits are down. Let's look around to see if we can do a better job of meeting the needs of our customers."
   Firm B "Profits are down. Let's initiate a cost-reduction program."

10. Firm A "No way I'm going into that new shopping center. The rents are outrageous."
    Firm B "No way I'm going into that new shopping center. Our customers are better served if we stay right here."

PART 1J: A Real World Case: Listening to the Market

Washington--It's about five years into the fax revolution, and here comes the U.S Postal Service with plans to equip some of its post offices with coin-operated versions of the wonderful machines. Can it be that the post office has mastered a fundamental lesson--that it's not in the business of moving the mails, it's in the communications business?

Better late than never, of course, and it must be acknowledged that the Postal Service is moving faster on fax than it has on other advanced technologies. Electronic scales that weigh the goods and calculate price were long commonplace in grocery stores before they supplanted medieval weighing devices in the nation's post offices. Up to the time of the change, not too many years ago, Postmaster Ben Franklin would have been right at home behind the counter.

Copying machines, another essential of modern communications, are now standard in post offices, though they are frequently out of order, as are stamp vending machines. (And, needless to say, change is not ordinarily available for using these machines.)

What ails the post office and why has the comedians' model of government service gone sour? The usual answer is that increasingly crushing volumes of mail are overwhelming the mails worldwide, and that compared to other countries, the United States is faring quite well in postage costs and delivery time. Maybe so, but that's still a poor excuse for the horrendous service that postal customers frequently experience. That it's worse elsewhere is no comfort.

With annual revenues of $45 billion, the Postal Service is one of America's biggest industries, about four-fifths the size of IBM, double the size of Chrysler and five times the size of General Dynamics. Yet, when it comes to spending money to find new and better ways to accomplish its tasks, the Postal Service is a pygmy of industry, spending only $90 million, or 0.2 percent of sales, on research.

Like other low-tech, labor-intensive industries, the Postal Service follows a tradition of performing relatively little research. But adherence to that tradition is a formula for continuing disaster, since it provides no better ways to cope with the growing avalanche of mail.

In research spending, the contrast with other industries is striking. The automotive industry averages about 3 percent of sales on research; electronics, 5 percent. Housing and construction, notorious laggards in research, devote 1.8 percent of sales to that purpose--nine times the percentage allotted by the Postal Service.

The reality of the mails is that fewer and fewer people will entrust valuable materials to the vagaries of the U.S. Postal Service. Hence, the prosperity of commercial express services and fax. That the Postal Service is increasingly sensitive to this competition is evident in its catchup offerings for these services.

Another sign is in a remarkable three-year contract that it has just signed for clocking the reliability of first-class mail delivery. At a cost of $23.4 million, the accounting firm of Price Waterhouse will mail a million letters a year to addresses in 86 cities and log the delivery times. It's reassuring to find that the Postal Service cares enough to expand its research horizons. But in the research business, you can't call it research when you already know the outcome. The Postal Service can be confident that deliveries in the 86 cities will be found to be somewhere between slow and lethargic.

The money could be more profitably spent on more letter carriers. Or, even better, on serious research about the real business of the Postal Service. Remember, it's communications, not just moving paper.

Source: Daniel S. Greenberg, "Postal Service Isn't Just for Mail Anymore," *Sacramento Bee*, February 13, 1990, p. B7. Reprinted by permission of Science and Government Report.

____ 1. Although he does not say it, the author is suggesting that the Postal Service move into the
_____ -orientation stage of the evolutionary development of marketing.
   A. Marketing   C. Production   E. Manufacturing
   B. Sales   D. Advertising

____ 2. The Postal Service produces which of the following economic utilities?
   a. Time.   b. Place.   c. Possession.   d. Image.   e. Form.
   A. e only.   B. ab only.   C. abe only.   D. abcd only.   E. abcde.

____ 3. The authors would probably maintain that the Postal Service is in the _____
   -orientation stage of the evolutionary development of marketing.
   A. Marketing   C. Production   E. Societal
   B. Sales   D. Advertising

PART 1K: **Answers to Questions**

PART 1D: Completion

1. activity
2. organizations/individuals
3. marketers/marketed/potential market
4. Marketers
5. market
6. exchange/needs or wants
7. produce/steal/exchange
8. system/want-satisfying/target/ organizational objectives
9. consumer oriented/product/satisfied
10. product
11. Customers/consumers
12. selling/marketing/customer/need
13. production-orientation/sales-orientation/ marketing-orientation
14. production-driven
15. sales
16. marketing
17. favorable attitude
18. customer/coordinated/objectives
19. societal/society
20. compatible/customers/societal/performance objectives
21. Ethics
22. Quality
23. employee
24. customer
25. global/socioeconomic/organization
26. marketing
27. high standard of living
28. one-fourth/one-third
29. 50
30. utility/wants
31. place/time/information/image/possession/ form
32. Services
33. daily activities/better informed/career

PART 1E: True-False Questions

1. T   2. F   3. T   4. T   5. F   6. F
7. T   8. F   9. T   10. F   11. F   12. F
13. T   14. T   15. F

PART 1F: Multiple Choice Questions

1. D   2. E   3. E   4. D   5. A   6. C
7. E   8. E   9. A   10. D   11. D   12. B
13. C   14. B   15. E

PART 1G: Matching Questions

a. 5   b. 18   c. 3   d. 9   e. 11   f. 16
g. 13   h. 4   i. 2

CHAPTER 2

THE CHANGING MARKETING ENVIRONMENT

PART 2A: Chapter Goals

After studying this chapter, you should be able to explain:

- The concept of environmental monitoring (environmental scanning)
- How external environmental factors such as demography, economic conditions and social and cultural forces can affect an organization's marketing
- The difference between selling and marketing
- How external factors such as suppliers and intermediaries that are specific to as given firm can affect that firm's marketing
- How the nonmarketing resources within a firm can influence its marketing

PART 2B: Key Terms and Concepts

1. Environmental monitoring [42]
2. Environmental scanning [42]
3. Demography [43]
4. Economic environment: [44]
   a. Business cycle [45]
   b. Inflation [46]
   c. Interest rates [46]
5. Types of competition [46
6. Social and cultural forces [47]
7. Political and legal forces [50]
8. Technology [50]
9. The market [53]
10. Suppliers [53]
11. Marketing intermediaries [54]

PART 2C: Summary

A firm operates its marketing effort within a framework of ever-changing forces that constitute the system's environment. Some of the forces--external macroenvironmental factors--are broad, external variables that generally are beyond the control of the executives in a firm [42]. Changing demographic conditions are one of these forces [43]. Another is economic elements such as the business cycle, inflation, and interest rates [44-46]. Other macroenvironmental factors include competition, social and cultural forces, political and legal forces, and changing technology [46-53]. Management should develop a means of monitoring all these external environmental factors.

Another set of environmental factors--suppliers, marketing intermediaries, and the market itself--are also external to the firm [53-54]. But since these factors are part of the firm's marketing system, the company can to some extent influence them.

The final set of factors that influence the firm's marketing system are the nonmarketing resources within the firm [54-55]. These factors include the company's production facilities, financial capability, human resources, location, R & D capability, and image. These variables generally are controllable by management, as are the environmental elements within the marketing department.

PART 2D: Completion

1. Environmental _____ (environmental _____) is the process of (1) gathering _____ regarding a company's external environment, (2) _____ it, and (3) _____ the effect of whatever trends the analysis suggests.

18

2. A firm operates within an _____ environment that it generally _____ control.

3. The _____ forces are divided into two groups: _____ influences such as demographics, laws, and economic conditions, and the _____ influences, which include _____ , _____ , and _____ .

4. There are six interrelated macroenvironmental forces that influence a firm's marketing system: (a) _____ , (b) _____ conditions, (c) _____ , (d) social and _____ forces, (e) _____ and legal forces, and (f) _____ .

5. _____ is the statistical study of human population and its distribution characteristics.

6. The _____ is a significant force that affects the marketing system of just about any organization.

7. It is affected especially by such economic considerations as the current stage of the _____ , _____ , and _____ .

8. As opposed to times past, we now think of a(n) _____ business cycle: _____ , _____ , and _____ .

9. _____ , which is defined as a rise in the prices of goods and services, presents real challenges in the management of a marketing program--especially in the areas of _____ and _____ .

10. A firm's _____ environment is a major influence shaping its marketing system.

11. Competition comes from three sources: (1) _____ competition from competitors selling similar products, (2) competition from _____ products, and (3) competition for the customer's _____ .

12. Some _____ and _____ affecting marketing are emphasis on the _____ _____ (the greening of America), changing _____ and _____ , changing attitudes toward _____ and _____ , _____ buying, and desire for _____ .

13. Five examples of political-legal forces are: (1) _____ policies, (2) social _____ and _____ , (3) governmental relationships with _____ , (4) marketing _____ , and (5) government as a source of _____ and buyer of _____ .

14. Technology is a major environmental influence on marketing because it so crucially affects consumers' <u>life-styles</u> , <u>consumption patterns</u> , and <u>economic</u> well-being.

15. Three forces making up the external microenvironment are: (1) the firm's _____ , (2)

19

_____ , and (3) _____.

16. The _____ is the focal point of all marketing decisions in an organization.

17. It is defined as people or organizations with _____ to satisfy, _____ to spend, and the willingness to _____.

18. _____ begin to be really appreciated during periods of shortages.

19. _____ are independent business organizations that directly aid in the flow of products and services between a(n) _____ and its _____.

20. Marketing intermediaries include two types of institutions, _____ such as _____ and _____, and various _____ organizations (transporters, warehousers, financiers) needed to complete exchanges between buyers and sellers.

21. The intermediaries are also part of what we call _____.

22. The firm's _____ is also shaped by internal forces that are largely controllable by _____.

23. The firm's internal nonmarketing resources include its _____, _____, and _____ activities.

24. Other nonmarketing forces are the firm's _____, its _____ and _____, and the overall _____ the firm projects to the public.

PART 2E: True-False Questions

If the statement is true, circle "T"; if false, circle "F."

T F   1. Since people make a market, the more people, the bigger the market.

T F   2. If one were to depict the external macroenvironment of a firm's marketing system as a series of concentric circles, the innermost circle would be labeled "The Company's Marketing Program."

T F   3. It is impossible for a marketer to influence the political-legal environment.

T F   4. Technology is a two-edged sword--it brings benefits; it creates problems.

T F   5. Marketing intermediaries are independent business organizations which directly aid in the flow of products and services between a marketing organization and its markets.

T F   6. A demographer studies, among other things, the migration patterns of people.

T F   7. A good marketing executive will use the internal controllable forces at his or her disposal in order to adapt to the uncontrollable external environment.

T F   8. When prices rise at a faster rate than personal incomes, there is a decline in consumer purchasing power.

T F   9. Increasingly, the consuming public is less interested in environmental issues.

T F 10. Offering a below-market interest rate as an inducement to buy is a form of price cut.

T F 11. Economies in times past went through business cycles that had three phases. Now these cycles go through four phases.

T F 12. In order to better meet international competition, American firms are merging with foreign firms to form international alliances.

T F 13. It is necessary for marketing executives to monitor only one of the marketing mix elements: promotion.

T F 14. A firm's financial capability is part of its internal nonmarketing resources.

T F 15. The only types of competition are brand competition and competition between substitute products.

PART 2F: Multiple Choice Questions

In the space provided write the letter of the answer that best fits the statement.

____1. Which of the following is an external macroenvironmental factor affecting a company's decision making?
   A. Caliber of the executives in a firm.
   B. Nature of the product.
   C. Price of the product.
   D. Federal legislation.
   E. Financial condition of the firm.

___ 2. All of the following are laws primarily intended to protect consumers EXCEPT:
A. Pure Food and Drug Act.
B. Sherman Antitrust Act.
C. Consumer Product Safety Act.
D. Consumer Product Warranty Act.
E. Consumer Credit Protection Act.

___ 3. The economic stage that represents a period of retrenchment is called:
A. Prosperity. B. Recession. C. Recovery. D. Inflation. E. None of the above.

___ 4. All of the following are internal nonmarketing resources EXCEPT:
A. Production facilities.　　　　D. Financial capability.
B. Human resources.　　　　　　E. Company's location.
C. Federal legislation.

___ 5. All of the following are external macroenvironmental forces that affect a firm's marketing system EXCEPT:
A. Demography.　　　　　　　　D. Economic conditions.
B. Competition.　　　　　　　　E. Social and cultural forces.
C. R & D capability.

___ 6. A market is:
A. A place where buyers and sellers meet.
B. The demand made by a certain group of potential buyers for a good or service.
C. People of organizations with wants to satisfy, money to spend, and the willingness to spend it.
D. All of the above.
E. None of the above.

___ 7. Demography would normally be interested in which of the following topics?
A. The rate at which the population is aging.
B. Migratory patterns of the population.
C. Birth and death rates of the population.
D. The ratio of specific minorities to total population.
E. All of the above.

___ 8. Today business cycles are thought to go through the following steps:
A. Recession, prosperity, depression, recovery.
B. Prosperity, recession, depression, recovery.
C. Recession, depression, recession, recovery.
D. Recession, prosperity, recovery.
E. Prosperity, recession, recovery.

22

___ 9. Markets include:
   A. People with needs.
   B. People with money to spend.
   C. People willing to spend.
   D. All of the above.
   E. None of the above.

___10. Marketing intermediaries include all of the following EXCEPT:
   A. Wholesalers. B. Transporters. C. Bankers. D. Retailers. E. Warehousers.

___11. "When a couple decides to buy a home for the first time, producers of Hawaii vacations, Colorado ski trips, and romantic 'Love Boat' tours lose out." This statement recognizes _____ competition.
   A. Brand B. Substitute product C. Customer buying power D. Cutthroat E. Unfair

___12. When a restaurant competes with a vending machine dispensing food, the competition is called:
   A. Brand competition.
   B. Substitute product competition.
   C. Competition for the consumer's buying power.
   D. All of the above.
   E. None of the above.

___13. Which of the following are social and cultural macroenvironmental forces?
   A. Emphasis on quality of life.
   B. Changing attitudes toward impulse buying.
   C. Changing attitudes toward fitness.
   D. Changing roles of men and women.
   E. All of the above.

___14. All of the following are laws to regulate and maintain competition EXCEPT:
   A. Federal Trade Commission Act.
   B. Clayton Antitrust Act.
   C. Fair Packaging and Labeling Act.
   D. Robinson-Patman Act.
   E. Consumer Goods Pricing Act.

___15. All of the following are political-legal influences on marketing EXCEPT:
   A. Regulatory agencies.
   B. Monetary policy.
   C. Fiscal policy.
   D. Governmental relationships.
   E. Competition.

PART 2G: Matching Questions

In the space provided write the number of the word or expression from column 1 that best fits the description in column 2.

1		2
1. Business cycle	____	a. The statistical study of human population and its distribution characteristics.
2. Competition	____	b. A period of generally rising prices.
3. Demography		
4. Economic conditions	____	c. People or organizations with wants, money to spend, and the willingness to spend it.
5. Environmental monitoring	____	d. Economic stages that pass from prosperity to recession to recovery.
6. External macroenvironment		
7. External microenvironment	____	e. Brand is an example of this.
8. Inflation	____	f. This includes the firm's production facilities, location, image, and R & D capability.
9. Interest rates	____	g. Includes middlemen and various facilitating organizations.
10. Internal nonmarketing resources		
11. Markets	____	h. Forces largely not controllable by management.
12. Marketing intermediaries		
13. Political and legal forces		
14. Social and cultural forces		
15. Suppliers		
16. Technology		

PART 2H: Problems and Applications

1. Interview someone such as a scientist, a manufacturer, a sales executive, or a possible customer in an area of highly rapid technological change. This may be in an off-campus business

24

setting or in a biology, chemistry, or computer laboratory on campus. Write a report to your instructor explaining:

    A. The new technology.

    B. How the new technology will have a positive and/or negative effect on the market for existing products.

    C. What the likely response will be from existing competition.

2.   Interest rates are expected to fall during the 1990s. How will this likely affect the sale of:

    A. Houses?

    B. Automobiles?

    C. Videocassette recorders?

3.   If the price of gasoline and other petroleum products begins to rise dramatically in the 1990s, how will this likely affect the sale of:

    A. Airline tickets?

    B. Motor homes?

    C. Automobiles?

4.   The traditional American family is changing. With about half of all first marriages ending in divorce, there is a rise in what some sociologists call "blended families." A blended family is one that results from two or more previous marriages. Do some library research on blended families, paying particular attention to the implications for food, furniture, and housing.

5.   In 1978, the airline industry began a series of steps that ultimately led to deregulation. In fact, in 1985, the regulatory agency in charge of regulating routes and rates for airlines (the CAB) was abolished. Write a report to your instructor on the effects this has had on the number of carriers, the economic health of these carriers, the price of tickets, and the mix of services.

6.   In the 1980s, one began to hear of a demographic group called "YUPPIES" or "YUMPIES." These are usually defined as young upwardly-mobile professional people. Comedians such as Jay Leno had so much fun with this group that it almost became an insult to call someone a yuppie to his face.

    A. Define a yuppie.

    B. What social, economic, and political forces helped to create yuppies?

    C. What are typical yuppie products and services?

    D. Are yuppies for real, and if so, how long do you think this phenomenon will last?

7.   As a follow-up to question 6, interview five people you perceive to be yuppies and five non-yuppies of the same age group regarding their shopping behavior. How do the two groups differ in what they buy, when they buy, how they pay (cash or credit), and how they decide what to buy?

8.   Demographers have been criticized as being good bean counters and number crunchers

but poor forecasters. For example, they failed to forecast: (1) the movement of large segments of the population to the Sunbelt, (2) the surge in the number of women, both single and married, seeking work, (3) the increase in single households, and (4) the trend among women to delay marriage and babies. Write a report to your instructor explaining what you think causes this inability to forecast by demographers.

9. Assume you have been hired by a shopping center developer to advise him on the major demographic trends of a city known to you with a population of at least 50,000. Trace the major demographic trends you foresee for this city. Hint: Consult the latest editions of the *Census of Population* and *Sales and Marketing Management*'s "Survey of Buying Power."

PART 2I: Exercise

The text defined demography as "the statistical study of human population and its distribution." Statistics may include items such as sex, race, age, education, income, national origin, occupation, marital status, family size, and housing status. These data are easily and cheaply available through the Census Bureau, Bureau of Labor Statistics, Bureau of Economic Analysis, and such private organizations as the Conference Board and the Population Reference Bureau.

There are a number of trends that will have a massive effect on marketing. Some of the more important trends are: (1) an increasingly older population, (2) an increasing number of women in the labor force, (3) an increasing number of college graduates, and (4) an increasing trend toward smaller families.

You are to predict the positive and negative effects of these trends on the following three industries: food, clothing, and automobiles.

1. The food industry:
   a. Effects of an increasingly older population.

   b. Effects of an increasing number of women in the labor force.

   c. Effects of an increasing number of college graduates.

   d. Effects of an increasing trend toward smaller families.

26

2.   The clothing industry:
   a.   Effects of an increasingly older population.

   b.   Effects of an increasing number of women in the labor force.

   c.   Effects of an increasing number of college graduates.

   d.   Effects of an increasing trend toward smaller families.

3.   The automobile industry:
   a.   Effects of an increasingly older population.

   b.   Effects of an increasing number of women in the labor force.

   c.   Effects of an increasing number of college graduates.

   d.   Effects of an increasing trend toward smaller families.

PART 2J: **A Real World Case: Old and Proud**

The aging marketplace won't catch Lucky Stores by surprise. The supermarket chain has just completed a two-year pilot study to make its store environments and merchandise more friendly and accessible to older shoppers.

"The project was undertaken to determine how Lucky could better serve the needs of its 'fifty plus' customers," says Judy Decker, communications manager, Lucky Stores. The Santa

27

Ana-based chain is a division of American Stores.

The study is a joint venture of Lucky, 15 food producers (ranging from Campbell Soup Co. to Nabisco Brands) and Age Wave, a consulting firm based in Emeryville, Calif. Geared to improving Lucky's competitive advantage with customers 50-plus-year-old, it is believed to be the most comprehensive study of older consumers' shopping habits ever undertaken.

"Based on the information gained from this study, we hope to make the shopping experience more tailored to the specific needs of older consumers," adds Decker.

Lucky is now in the process of defining exactly what adjustments or refinements it will make to existing stores or incorporate into new store construction. Among the expected design changes, says Decker, are better lighting, rest rooms up front, lower shelves, wider aisles, and benches for tired shoppers. Larger type will be used on shelf signing as well as other signage throughout the store.

"We are also looking at shopping carts that are easier to turn and move about," adds Decker.

New training program: The supermarket chain is rolling out a new training program designed to sensitize store employees to older shoppers. Some 35,000 Lucky employees, ranging from store managers to baggers, will participate.

"We have found that service ranks as the most important consideration for older customers in determining store preference," says Ken Dychtwald, president and ceo of Age Wave, which is developing the training program. "It makes sense from a business point of view that retailers make a special effort to reach out to these customers."

Dychtwald says that when Age Wave asked older individuals why they shopped at Lucky, the overwhelming response was "Because they treat me well." The training program, he adds, will reinforce the warm relationship Lucky enjoys with senior consumers.

"We want employees to become active participants in helping older shoppers," says Russ Patera, senior vp of training and development, Age Wave. "Our aim is make the employees alert to the needs of the older shopper from the time the customer enters the store."

The program emphasizes communication skills and appropriate employee behavior when dealing with older customers. All of the videos were filmed in the stores using Lucky employees.

"We show good and bad examples of customer-employee interactions in very believable situations that employees can easily relate to," Patera says.

As part of their training, employees receive what Patera calls a "life experience kit." Articles in the kit enable Lucky employees to experience some of the most common ailments that plague

28

older shoppers. Sunglasses coated with silicone, for example, simulate cataracts. Other chronic conditions, including reduced hearing and lung capacity, are similarly simulated.

"It is important that employees understand that older people are not invalids, but that some do suffer from chronic conditions that can impair their ability to find an item, get in the correct line, etc.," Patera explains. "The more familiar an employee is with these conditions, the more understanding and accommodating he or she is likely to be with the affected customer."

Patera also recommends that retailers make a special effort to train and hire older adults. Senior workers, he adds, can help bridge the huge age gap that exists between older shoppers and service-givers.

"But don't put older people in demeaning positions," he adds. "Give them a job where they can make a contribution. Lucky has already made inroads in this area. The senior greeter is a very valuable concept which Lucky is in the process of implementing."

Lucky has not revealed the cost of the two-year study. But the chain is confident that the project will give it a competitive advantage in years to come.

"The 'fifty-plus' group, which is going to represent a very significant portion of our population in the near future, is already an important segment of our customer base," says Decker. "Our participation in this project will put Lucky ahead of the pack in our ability to sell to the mature customer. We feel we are on the cutting-edge of the shifting marketplace."

Source: Reprinted by permission from Chain Store Age Executive (July, 1991). Copyright Lebhar-Friedman, Inc., 425 Park Avenue, New York, NY 10022. "Lucky Targets Older Shoppers," *Chain Store Age Executive*, July, 1991, p. 33.

_____ 1. The article deals mainly with:
   A. Inflation.
   B. Interest rates.
   C. The business cycle.
   D. Legal issues.
   E. Demographic issues.

_____ 2. The major thrust of the article deals with which of the following macroenvironmental factors?
   A. Economic conditions.
   B. Competition.
   C. Legal forces.
   D. Social and cultural forces.
   E. Technology.

PART 2K: **Answers to Questions**

PART 2D: Completion

1. monitoring/scanning/information/
   analyzing/forecasting
2. external/cannot
3. external/macro/micro/suppliers/marketing
   intermediaries/customers
4. demography/economic/competition/
   cultural/political/technology
5. Demography
6. economic environment
7. business cycle/inflation/interest rates
8. three-stage/prosperity/recession/recovery
9. Inflation/pricing/cost control
10. competitive
11. brand/substitute/limited buying power
12. social/cultural forces/quality of life/
    role of men/women/health/fitness/impulse/
    convenience
13. monetary and fiscal/legislation/regulation/
    industries/legislation/information/products
14. life-styles/consumption patterns/economic
15. market/suppliers/marketing intermediaries
16. market
17. needs/money/spend it
18. Suppliers
19. Marketing intermediaries/marketing
    organization/markets
20. middlemen/retailers/wholesalers/facilitating
21. channels of distribution
22. marketing system/management
23. production/financial/personnel
24. location/research/development/image

PART 2E: True-False Questions
1. F 2. T 3. F 4. T 5. T 6. T
7. T 8. T 9. F 10. T 11. F 12. T
13. F 14. T 15. F

PART 2F: Multiple Choice Questions
1. D 2. B 3. B 4. C 5. C 6. D
7. E 8. E 9. D 10. C 11. C 12. B
13. E 14. C 15. E

PART 2G: Matching Questions
a. 3 b. 8 c. 11 d. 1 e. 2 f. 10
g. 12 h. 6

CHAPTER 3

STRATEGIC PLANNING AND FORECASTING

PART 3A: Chapter Goals

After studying this chapter, you should be able to explain:

- The nature and scope of planning and how it fits within the management process
- Similarities and differences among mission, objectives, strategies, and tactics
- The essential difference between strategic planning and strategic marketing planning
- The steps involved in strategic marketing planning
- The purpose and contents of an annual marketing plan
- Similarities and differences as well as weaknesses and strengths across several models used in strategic planning
- The nature of demand forecasting in marketing
- Major methods used in forecasting market demand

PART 3B: Key Terms and Concepts

1. Planning [61]
2. Strategic planning [61]
3. Mission [61]
4. Objective [62]
5. Strategy [62]
6. Tactic [62]
7. Strategic company planning [63]
8. Situation analysis [64]
9. Organizational strategies [65]
10. Strategic marketing planning [65]
11. SWOT assessment [65]
12. Positioning [66]
13. Differential advantage [67]
14. Differential disadvantage [67]
15. Marketing mix [68]
16. Annual marketing plan [70]
17. Boston Consulting Group screen [72]
18. Stars [73]
19. Cash cows [73]
20. Question marks [73]
21. Dogs [73]
22. General Electric business screen [74]
23. Invest strategy [75]
24. Protect strategy [75]
25. Divest strategy [75]
26. Harvest strategy [75]
27. Porter's Generic-strategies [76]
28. Overall cost leadership [76]
29. Differentiation [76]
30. Focus [76]
31. Product-market growth matrix [77]
32. Market penetration [77]
33. Market development [77]
34. Product development [77]
35. Diversification [77]
36. Demand forecasting [79]
37. Market factor [79]
38. Market index [79]
39. Market potential [79]
40. Sales potential [79]
41. Market share [80]
42. Sales forecast [80]

43. Market-factor analysis   [82]

44. Direct-derivation methods   [82]

45. Correlation analysis   [82]

46. Survey of buyer intentions   [83]

47. Test marketing   [83]

48. Past sales analysis   [83]

49. Trend analysis   [83]

50. Sales-force composite   [84]

51. Executive judgment   [84]

52. Delphi method   [84]

PART 3C: Summary

The management process consists of planning, implementation, and evaluation. The first job of management is to prepare a strategic plan for the company, from which strategic plans for marketing can be developed [61].

A firm's marketing effort is more likely to be successful if it engages in strategic marketing planning. Marketing planning should be done within the context of strategic planning for the entire company and for each strategic business unit (SBU) in the firm. Strategic company planning is the process of matching an organization's resources with its marketing opportunities over the long run [61]. This planning process involves: (1) defining the organization's mission, (2) analyzing the situation, (3) setting organizational objectives, and (4) designing organizational strategies to achieve the objectives [64].

Strategic marketing planning should be done within the context of the organization's overall strategic planning. The strategic marketing planning process consists of: (1) conducting a situation analysis, (2) setting marketing objectives, (3) determining positioning and differential advantages, (4) selecting target markets, and (5) designing a strategic marketing mix to satisfy those markets and achieve those goals [65].

Before deciding on a target market, the company should forecast the demand in the total market and in each segment they have targeted [79]. Demand forecasting involves measuring the industry's market potential, then determining the company's sales potential or market share, and finally preparing a sales forecast. The sales forecast is one of the most important documents developed in business [80]. It is the foundation for all budgeting and operational planning in all major departments of a company. There are two basic methods available for forecasting market demand: "top-down" and "bottom-up" [81]. Specific methods used to forecast sales are market-factor analysis, survey of buyer intentions, test marketing, past sales and trend analysis, sales-force composite, and executive judgment. Each method has its strengths and weaknesses [81]. It is management's challenge to select the technique that is appropriate in a particular situation and is most likely to provide an accurate forecast.

PART 3D: Completion

1. The management process, as applied to marketing, consists basically of (1) _____ a marketing program, (2) _____ it, and (3) _____ its performance.

2. Management first has to decide what it seeks to accomplish as a business and develop a(n) _____ to achieve it.

3. In strategic planning, managers match an organization's _____ with its market opportunities over the _____.

4. An organization's _____ states what customers it serves, what needs it satisfies, and what types of products it offers.

5. The mission statement should not be too _____ and _____ nor too _____ and _____.

6. A(n) _____ is a desired outcome.

7. A(n) _____ is a broad plan of action by which an organization intends to reach its objectives.

8. A(n) _____ is a means by which a strategy is implemented. It is more _____ and _____ than is a strategy.

9. Defining an organization's mission means answering the question, "what _____?"

10. _____ planning (from 3 to 25 years in length) usually involves _____ and a special _____.

11. _____ planning is for 1 year or less and is the responsibility of _____ and _____ executives.

12. The planning activities of a company may be conducted on the following levels: (1) _____ planning, (2) _____ planning, and (3) _____ planning.

13. Strategic marketing planning includes: (1) defining the organization's _____ , (2) analyzing the situation, (3) setting organizational _____ , and (4) selecting appropriate _____ so as to achieve the firm's objectives.

14. Defining organizational _____ is the first step and this influences all subsequent _____.

34

15. The second step is conducting a situation _____.

16. The next step in the _____ process is for management to decide upon a set of _____ that will guide the organization in accomplishing its _____.

17. The last step is to select appropriate _____ which indicate where the firm wants to go.

18. Strategic marketing planning involves five steps: (1) conduct a(n) _____ , (2) develop _____ , (3) determine _____ and _____ advantages, (4) select _____ and measure market _____ , and (5) design a strategic _____.

19. Situation analysis involves analyzing where the firm's marketing program _____ , how it has _____ , and what it is _____ in the years ahead.

20. In doing this, many firms conduct a SWOT assessment: what are its _____ , _____ , _____ , and _____?

21. Company _____ often translate into marketing _____.

22. After the product is positioned, a(n) _____ must be identified--that is, any features of an organization or brand perceived by customers to be desirable and different from competitors.

23. Target markets must be identified on the basis of _____.

24. Finally, the firm designs a(n) _____--that is, the combination of a product and how it is distributed, promoted, and priced.

25. The _____ is the master blueprint for a year's marketing activity for a specified organizational division or major product.

26. The exact contents of an annual marketing plan should be determined by an organization's _____.

27. In an annual marketing plan, more attention can be devoted to _____ than is feasible in other levels of planning.

28. In order to foster better planning and because some companies are so large and diversified, the total organization should be divided into major product or market divisions called _____ or _____.

29. To be identified as a(n) _____ , a unit should have the following characteristics: (1) it is a

35

separately identifiable _____ , (2) it has its own distinct _____ , (3) it has its own _____ , and (4) it has its own _____ with _____ .

30. The four planning models discussed in the chapter are: (1) the Boston Consulting Group _____ , (2) the G.E. _____ , (3) Porter's _____ Model, and (4) Product-Market _____ Matrix.

31. The Boston Consulting Group Matrix classifies SBUs according to two factors: market _____ and growth _____. This yields four categories: _____ , _____ , _____ , and _____ .

32. The G.E. Business Screen classifies its SBUs according to two other factors: market _____ and business _____. This yields four categories: _____ , _____ , _____ , and _____ .

33. Porter's Generic-Strategies Model classifies its SBUs according to two factors: scope of _____ and _____. This yields three alternatives: overall cost _____ , _____ , and _____ .

34. The Product-Market Growth Matrix also considers two factors: _____ and _____. This yields four strategies: market _____ , market _____ , product _____ , and _____ .

35. An important part of successful marketing planning is _____ --estimating the sales of a product during some _____ time period.

36. A(n) _____ is an element which exists in a market, which can be measured quantitatively, and which is related to the demand for a product or service.

37. A(n) _____ is a market factor expressed as a percentage or some other mathematical term.

38. The market potential for a product is the expected _____ for all sellers of that product during a stated period of time in specific _____ .

39. The _____ of a product is the share of a market potential that an individual company expects to achieve.

40. _____ refers to the proportion of total sales of a product during a stated time period in a specific market that is captured by a(n) _____ .

41. A(n) _____ is an estimate of probable sales during some specified future time period and under a predetermined market plan of the firm.

42. The most common period for a sales forecast is _____.

43. Short-term forecasts may be made for one _____ or one _____.

44. Before a firm can make an effective sales forecast, it must have predetermined marketing _____ and _____.

45. The completed _____ serves as the key controlling factor in operational planning throughout the company.

46. Using the top-down method of forecasting sales, a company would take the following steps: (1) it would forecast general _____ conditions; (2) it would determine the _____ _____ ; (3) it would measure the firm's _____ ; and (4) it would forecast the firm's _____ of the product.

47. In contrast, the bottom-up technique estimates the future demand in various _____ of the market from various _____ in the company.

48. Individual _____ are _____ into one total forecast.

49. The _____ analysis method involves determining the relationship between a selected factor and the market demand for the product.

50. The _____ method is simple, inexpensive, and requires little statistical analysis.

51. Correlation-analysis techniques spell out the degree of association between _____ of the product and the _____.

52. A major problem with a survey of buyer intentions is that consumers may not _____ buy as they said they _____ to buy.

53. In test marketing, a company estimates the sales potential of a product by marketing the product in a(n) _____ geographical area and then _____ the data to a(n) _____.

54. Forecasts based upon _____ and _____ are very common since they are simple and easy to produce.

55. However, they may be highly _____.

56. The sales-force composite method of forecasting is a popular _____.

57. Forecasting by executive judgment alone is very risky, since, in some instances, it is based on

_____ or _____.

58. A refinement of executive judgment is the Delphi _____.

PART 3E: True-False Questions

If the statement is true, circle "T"; if false, circle "F."

T F 1. Organizational strategies are the detailed operational means by which a strategic plan is to be implemented.

T F 2. Strategic planning is the managerial process of matching an organization's resources with its marketing opportunities over the long run.

T F 3. Strategic planning is a long-run concept.

T F 4. SBUs are "small business underwriters," that is, insurance specialists.

T F 5. "Stars," "dogs," "cash cows," and "question marks" are categories in the Boston Consulting Group Matrix.

T F 6. An organization's mission means answering the question: "What business are you in?"

T F 7. The last step in strategic company planning is to select strategies to achieve the organization's objectives.

T F 8. The executive judgment method of sales forecasting should not be used at all.

T F 9. Surveys of consumer buying intentions generally are an inflated measure of a product's potential.

T F 10. The sales potential is an estimate of the total industry potential for the company's product in the target market.

T F 11. "Sales potential" and "sales forecast" mean the same thing.

T F 12. One of the best methods of sales forecasting is to base the estimate entirely on past sales.

T F 13. The completed sales forecast serves as the key controlling factor in operational planning throughout the company.

T F 14. In strategic marketing planning, the first step is to conduct a situation analysis.

38

T F 15. There are two basic methods for forecasting demand: a "top-down" and a "bottom-up" approach.

PART 3F: Multiple Choice Questions

In the space provided write the letter of the answer that best fits the statement.

____1. The planning activities of a company include:
   A. Strategic company planning.
   B. Strategic business unit (SBU) planning.
   C. Strategic marketing planning.
   D. Annual marketing planning.
   E. All of the above.

____2. In order to be identified as an SBU, a unit should have the following characteristic:
   A. It is a separately identifiable business.
   B. It has its own distinct mission.
   C. It has its own competitors.
   D. It has its own executives and profit responsibility.
   E. All of the above.

____3. Which of the following is a method for forecasting demand?
   A. Market-factor analysis.   D. Trend analysis.
   B. Survey of buyer intentions.   E. Any of the above.
   C. Test marketing.

____4. The process of strategic company planning consists of the following steps:
   1. Selecting appropriate strategies to achieve the organization's objectives.
   2. Situation analysis.
   3. Setting organizational objectives.
   4. Defining the organization's mission.
   A. 1423   B. 3421   C. 4321   D. 4312   E. 4231

____5. A market factor expressed as a percentage is known as a:
   A. Market index.   D. Market potential.
   B. Sales potential.   E. Market forecast.
   C. Sales index.

____6. A _____ is an element which exists in a market, which can be measured quantitatively, and which is related to the demand for a product or service.
   A. Market factor   D. Sales potential
   B. Market index   E. Sales forecast
   C. Market potential

____7. The strategic marketing planning process consists of all of the following EXCEPT:
   A. Conduct a situation analysis.
   B. Establish strategic business units.
   C. Design a strategy to achieve the objectives.
   D. Set the organizational objectives.
   E. Define the organizational mission.

____8. The share of total industry sales which one firm should get in a stated market during a given period of time is that firm's:
   A. Market potential.   D. Sales potential.
   B. Sales budget.   E. None of the above.
   C. Sales forecast.

____9. Market potential is most closely related to:
   A. Sales potential.   D. What industry sales will be next year.
   B. Market index.   E. Last year's sales.
   C. Market share.

____10. The strategy of selling more of its present products to its present market is called:
   A. Market penetration.   D. Diversification.
   B. Market development.   E. None of the above.
   C. Product development.

____11. A review of the firm's existing marketing program is called:
   A. An annual marketing plan. D. Sales potential.
   B. Market potential.   E. Sales forecast.
   C. Situation analysis.

____12. A cornerstone of successful marketing planning is:
   A. A market index.   D. An annual marketing plan.
   B. Demand forecasting.   E. The marketing mix.
   C. The marketing concept.

____13. According to the Boston Consulting Group Matrix, if the industry growth rate is high and the firm's market share is also high, the product is a:
   A. Star.   B. Question mark.   C. Cash cow.   D. Dog.   E. Turkey

____14. Planning activities that determine marketing strategy in a firm may be conducted on the following level:
   A. Strategic company planning.   D. Any of the above.
   B. Strategic marketing planning. E. None of the above.
   C. Annual marketing planning.

____15. According to the product-market growth matrix, the strategy of developing new products to sell to new markets is called:

  A. Market penetration.
  B. Market development.
  C. Product development.
  D. Diversification.
  E. None of the above.

PART 3G: Matching Questions

In the space provided write the number of the word or expression from column 1 that best fits the description in column 2.

1	2
1. Correlation analysis	a. The process of setting goals and selecting strategies and tactics.
2. Delphi method	
3. Demand forecasting	b. A broad plan of action by which an organization intends to reach its objectives.
4. Direct-derivation method	c. That portion of marketing potential a firm can expect to achieve.
5. Market factor	
6. Market-factor analysis	d. A market factor expressed as a percentage or some other mathematical term.
7. Market index	e. The expected combined sales volume for all sellers of a product during a stated period of time in a stated market.
8. Market potential	
9. Market share	f. The ratio of a firm's sales to total industry sales on either an actual or potential basis.
10. Mission	
11. Objective	g. Using a group of experts individually and anonymously to assess future sales.
12. Planning	h. A statistical refinement of the direct-derivation method of demand forecasting.
13. Sales forecast	
14. Sales potential	i. Cornerstone of successful marketing planning.
15. Strategic planning	j. States what customers it serves, what needs it satisfies, and what types of products it offers.

41

16. Strategy

17. Survey of buyer intentions

18. Tactic

19. Test marketing

20. Trend analysis

PART 3H: Problems and Applications

1.   Develop a strategic marketing plan for the campus bookstore. How could it reach a larger, off-campus market? Would there be any constraints to this expansion off-campus?

2.   What is the risk and uncertainty that is inherent in any high-level marketing decision? Give an illustration.

3.   Make a list of the policies adhered to in your school's cafeteria.

4.   Your authors suggest that in defining the organization's mission, the question "What business are you in?" must be asked. Give the marketing-oriented answer for each of the following businesses:
   a. Columbia Pictures (VCR movies).   d. Head skis.
   b. Disneyland.   e. Campbell Soup.
   c. Word Perfect program.   f. Sheraton Hotels.

5.   The product/market expansion strategies analyze entering new markets or developing new products. There are four strategic alternatives: market penetration, market development, product development, and diversification. One way companies quickly achieve one of these strategic alternatives is through merger. Consult *Business Week*, *Forbes*, or *Fortune* magazines. All have editions devoted to the top mergers of each year. See also *Mergers & Acquisitions* magazine. Report to your instructor on four mergers, each of which resulted in one of the strategic alternatives.

6.   Assume you must estimate sales in your company for the following products: electric blenders, locking gas caps, and a new type of ski wax. What market factors will you need to know to make an effective forecast? Which method(s) of forecasting would you use and why? Prepare a report for your instructor.

7.   Using the buying-power index found in the latest edition of "Survey of Buying Power" (published by *Sales & Marketing Management*), allocate the sales potential for a product on a

regional basis. Assume the product's national sales potential is 1,750,000 units.

8.   *Business Week* regularly publishes the findings of surveys of consumer buying intentions, such as the buying of new automobiles. For some recent time period, compare one of these reports on consumer intentions to buy automobiles with actual car sales as reported in *Business Week*.

9.   Interview a local executive of a wholesaling company. Does he or she use executive judgment when making sales forecasts? Is more than one method of sales forecasting used? Why? Which does he or she prefer? Write a report to your instructor on your findings.

10.   You have just been asked by your boss, sales manager for an irrigation pump manufacturer, to develop a sales forecast procedure for the company. Write him or her a memo presenting your procedure for doing so.

PART 3I: Exercise

A group of wealthy doctors and lawyers have formed a limited partnership and bought 640 acres of prime vineyards in California's San Joaquin Valley. Their plan is to begin bottling wine in two years. You are marketing vice-president.

Given the following information, define your target market and then settle on an appropriate marketing mix strategy.

1.   Women buy 60 percent of all wine sold in the United States.
2.   White wine outsells red wine by a margin of 2 to 1.
3.   Wine drinkers generally are either college educated or ethnic.
4.   Wine drinkers are in middle-, upper-middle, to upper-income brackets.
5.   Table wine consumption has quadrupled in the past 20 years.
6.   It is expected the table wine market will continue to grow at a 3 percent annual rate for the next ten years.
7.   There has been a shift from sweet dessert wines to dry, light table wines.

A.   Target market

B.   Product planning

C.   Price structure

D.   Distribution system

E.   Promotional program

PART 3J: A Real World Case: Scanning the Market

Half the money I spend on advertising is wasted, and the trouble is, I don't know which half.
William H. Lever, founder of Lever Brothers Ltd.

What makes a shopper buy a particular brand of dog food or detergent? It seems like a simple enough question. Yet, despite billions of dollars spent every year to advertise and promote packaged goods, companies have never been entirely sure how effective each marketing tool really is.

That's finally beginning to change. The installation of checkout scanners in most of the nation's supermarkets has brought an avalanche of data, more timely and specific than any available before. Though most marketers are only beginning to exploit this information, they are getting a better feel for exactly what a price cut, coupon blitz, store display, or discount to the retailer actually does for sales and profits.

WEEKLY REPORTS. Instead of receiving monthly or bimonthly reports with at best a regional breakdown of how a brand is doing in its category, marketers now get weekly data for every item and size, sometimes down to the individual store. This creates endless possibilities for investigation. How often should a coupon be used, and does it work better in Des Moines than in Dallas? Is one size easier to sell to retailers than another?

So far marketers have gotten furthest in examining the effectiveness of promotions such as displays and newspaper ads. The three sellers of scanner data--Control Data's SAMI, Dun & Bradstreet's A. C. Neilsen, and Information Resources Inc.--all track such information along with product sales. Nestle Foods Corp. learned that a combination of store displays and newspaper ads resulted in huge volume increases for its Quik chocolate drink.

Warner-Lambert Co. found that in some instances, store displays were far more effective than newspaper ads or price promotions, and its sales force now focuses on persuading supermarkets

44

to provide such displays. Ore-Ida Foods, Inc. priced a frozen-food brand below a key rival's, but it turned out that retailers were pocketing the difference and providing the competition with more merchandising support. When weekly chain-by-chain scanner and promotion data revealed the problem, Ore-Ida decided to boost its prices and use the extra margin to pay for promotional efforts such a bigger newspaper ads.

FRUSTRATION. Most marketers haven't gotten as far using scanner data to analyze the effects of TV advertising and consumer promotions such as coupons. Nielsen, SAMI, and IRI all supply some of that data. But a system to provide reliable nationwide information linking which TV ads individual households watch with what they buy is still under construction. Eventually, packaged-goods companies hope such "single source" data will allow them to hone their marketing even more finely. If they know how effective specific commercials or coupon programs are, they can decide whether they are worth the trouble and expense.

In the meantime, they are trying to figure out how to make better use of the reams of information they already have. After some early optimism, most big manufacturers are frustrated by their slow progress. The data still have glitches, and there's not enough software available for analyzing ©them. "The information preceded clients' ability to handle it," says SAMI head Steven A. Wilson. "They can't absorb the amount of information we're imposing on them." Adds Brian M. Shea, Ore-Ida's marketing research manager: "The promise is there to do all this linking, but I haven't seen it yet."

Still, that hasn't stopped packaged-goods marketers from continuing their push to use scanner data. If that information ultimately gives them the answer to Lever's conundrum, it will be worth the wait.

_____

Source: "Thanks to the Checkout Scanner, Marketing Is Losing Some Mystery," *Business Week*, August 28, 1989, p. 57. Reprinted from August 28, 1989, issue of Business Week by special permission, copyright © 1989 by McGraw-Hill, Inc.

_____

_____ 1. In what step of the strategy marketing planning process does this article fit?
A. Conduct a situation analysis.
B. Determine marketing objectives.
C. Select target markets and measure market demand.
D. Design a strategic marketing mix.
E. All of the above.

_____ 2. After gathering scanner data, the forecaster would use which of the following procedures   to forecast market demand?
A. Top-down approach   B. Bottom-up approach   C. Either approach

PART 3K: Answers to Questions

PART 3D: Completion

1. planning/implementing/evaluating
2. strategic plan
3. resources/long run
4. mission
5. broad/vague/narrow/specific
6. objective
7. strategy
8. tactic/specific/detailed
9. what business are you in
10. Strategic/top management/planning staff
11. Short-term/lower-/middle-level
12. strategic company/strategic marketing/ annual marketing
13. mission/objectives/strategies
14. mission/planning
15. analysis
16. strategic planning/objectives/ mission
17. strategies
18. situation analysis/marketing objectives/ positioning/differential/target markets/ demand/marketing mix
19. has been/been doing/likely to face
20. strengths/weaknesses/opportunities/threats
21. strategies/goals
22. differential advantage
23. opportunities
24. marketing mix
25. annual marketing plan
26. circumstances
27. tactical details
28. strategic business units/SBUs
29. SBU/business/mission/competitors/ executive group/profit responsibility
30. Matrix/Business Screen/ Generic-Strategies/Growth
31. share/rate/stars/question marks/cash cows/dogs
32. attractiveness/position/invest/ protect/harvest/divest
33. target market/differential advantage/ leadership/differentiation/focus

34. markets/products/penetration/ development/development/diversification
35. demand forecasting/future
36. market factor
37. market index
38. sales volume/markets
39. sales potential
40. Market share/single firm
41. sales forecast
42. one year
43. month/quarter
44. goals/broad strategies
45. sales forecast
46. economic/market potential/share of the market/sales
47. segments/organizational units
48. estimates/added
49. market-factor
50. direct derivation
51. potential sales/market factor
52. actually/intended
53. limited/projects/larger area
54. past sales/trend analysis
55. unreliable
56. buildup technique
57. intuition/guess-work
58. method

PART 3E: True-False Questions

1. F 2. T 3. T 4. F 5. T 6. T
7. T 8. F 9. T 10. F 11. F 12. F
13. T 14. F 15. T

PART 3F: Multiple Choice

1. E 2. E 3. E 4. E 5. A 6. A
7. B 8. D 9. D 10. A 11. C 12. B
13. A 14. D 15. D

PART 3G: Matching Questions

a. 12 b. 16 c. 14 d. 7 e. 8 f. 9
g. 2 h. 1 i. 3 j. 10

46

CHAPTER 4

MARKETING RESEARCH
AND INFORMATION

PART 4A: Chapter Goals

After studying this chapter, you should be able to explain:

- What marketing research is and the role it play in improving marketing decision making
- The systems that have been developed to increase the usefulness of data
- The appropriate way to conduct a marketing research project
- How to gather and use information about competitors
- Who actually does marketing research
- The current status of marketing research

PART 4B: Key Terms and Concepts

1. Marketing information system (MkIS) [91]
2. Decision support systems (DSS) [93]
3. Data bases [94]
4. Single-source data [95]
5. Marketing research [96]
6. Situation analysis [96]
7. Hypothesis [96]
8. Informal investigation [97]
9. Primary data [98]
10. Secondary data [98]
11. Survey [100]
12. Personal interview [101]
13. Mall intercept [101]
14. Focus group [101]
15. Telephone survey [101]
16. Mail survey [102]
17. Observational method [102]
18. Personal observation [102]
19. Mechanical observation [102]
20. Experiment [103]
21. Laboratory experiment [103]
22. Field experiment [103]
23. Test marketing [104]
24. Simulated test market [104]
25. Random sample [106]
26. Convenience sample [106]
27. Competitive intelligence [107]

PART 4C: Summary

Today's business person cannot afford to make decisions based solely on insight, intuition, or guesswork. There are too many factors in today's dynamic environment that make it imperative for all firms, large and small, to learn to manage the constant flow of information. Three tools used in research are marketing information systems, decision support systems, and the research project.

A marketing information system tends to concentrate on the future to solve and prevent problems, and is a broader and more inclusive activity than marketing research, which is focused on the past. It includes determining and specifying data needs. It further includes the generation of this information by means of marketing research and the processing of these data [91]. The decision support system differs for a marketing information system in that the manager, using a personal

48

computer, can directly interact with the data [92].

The benefits flowing from a marketing information system are many, and they depend, to a large extent, on the support management gives to the development and operation of the system. Broadly stated, the benefits of the marketing information system lie in the fact that it is designed to generate and process an information flow to aid managerial decision making in a company's marketing program. A marketing information system has many areas of informational input to help it function effectively, not the least of which is marketing research.

Marketing research, by its very nature of solving problems on a project-by-project basis, can provide information that is used to set objectives, control direction, evaluate courses of action, and make an exhaustive search for and study of facts relevant to any problem in the field of marketing [96]. Research is a key management tool because it presents an accurate, critical, objective, and continuing investigation of a problem, an alternative course of action, or a hypothesis [96]. The most common activities of marketing research are studies of industries, measurement of market trends, and market share analyses [96].

A marketing research investigation involves the following steps: (1) defining the objective, (2) situation analysis, (3) an informal investigation, (4) a formal investigation, (5) analysis of the data and preparation of a written report, and (6) a follow-up of the study [96-107].

The two sources of information in marketing research are primary sources and secondary sources [98]. The three most widely used methods of gathering primary data are by survey, by observation, and by experimentation [100-105]. The funds available will often be the deciding factor in which of the three interviewing methods--personal, telephone, mail--to use [100]. The observation method requires that data be collected by observing some action of the respondent; the experimental method involves the establishment of a scale model or controlled experiment which simulates the real market situation as much as possible [103].

Sampling is at the heart of marketing research. Just as we judge a glass of beer from a sample, the researcher is required to make judgments on consumer attitudes, expectations, needs, wants, and values on the basis of a sample, the best being a random sample [106]. Random sampling has a big advantage--it is the only method that allows one to make generalizations to a universe [106].

Marketing research has had less than universal acceptance [110]. It is not a substitute for good judgment nor are its predictions always free from error. Also, inadequate communication between the researcher and management has been the cause for much misunderstanding of the goals of marketing research [110].

PART 4D: Completion

1. Management in any organization needs _____ about potential <u>markets</u>   and

49

_____ to develop successful strategic marketing _____ , and to respond to _____ in the marketplace.

2. _____ is the development, interpretation, and communication of decision-oriented information to be used in the strategic marketing process.

3. Marketing managers rely on two primary sources of information: (1) the nonrecurring _____ , conducted by a company's own marketing research staff or an independent research firm, to answer a specific question, and (2) using regularly scheduled reports called _____ .

4. A marketing information system (MkIS) may be defined as a(n) _____ , _____ procedure to _____ , _____ , _____ , _____ , and later _____ information for use in making _____ .

5. A well-designed MkIS can provide a continuous flow of information for management _____ .

6. The value of an MkIS is dependent upon three factors: (1) the nature and quality of the _____ it works on, (2) the ways in which the data are processed to provide _____ , and (3) the ability of the operators of the MkIS and the managers who will use the output to _____ .

7. Centrally managed international organizations must be informed about what is happening _____ .

8. When a MkIS does not work, it may be because: (1) it is not always obvious what information is needed to make _____ , (2) it is _____ , and (3) it is not well suited to the solution of _____ .

9. A(n) _____ (DSS) is a procedure that allows a manager to interact with data and methods of analysis to gather, analyze, and interpret information.

10. The DSS adds _____ and _____ to the MkIS by making the manager an active part of the research process.

11. Data organized, stored, and updated in a computer are called a(n) _____ .

12. Am important data source for data bases is the _____ , the electronic device at retail checkouts that reads the bar code for each item bought.

13. _____ data are a means by which household _____ can be matched to television _____ exposure and _____ .

14. The most common activities of marketing research departments are studies of _____ , _____ , and _____ .

15. The six-step marketing research program suggested comprises the following actions: (1) define the _____ of the project, (2) conduct a(n) _____ analysis, (3) conduct a(n) _____ investigation, (4) plan and conduct a(n) _____ investigation, (5) analyze the _____ and prepare a(n) _____ , and (6) make a(n) _____ .

16. Situation analysis involves getting acquainted with the _____ and its business _____ by means of _____ research and extensive interviewing of _____ _____ .

17. A research hypothesis is a tentative _____-- a possible solution to a problem.

18. An informal investigation consists in talking to people _____ and _____ the company. These people outside the company may be middlemen, _____ , advertising agencies, and _____ .

19. The importance of the _____ in a research project will often be to determine whether further study is necessary.

20. The steps involved in a formal investigation are as follows: (1) select the sources of _____ , (2) find sources of _____ , (3) determine the methods of gathering _____ data, (4) prepare forms for gathering _____ , (5) plan the _____ , (6) collect the _____ , (7) _____ the data and prepare a(n) _____ , and (8) conduct a(n) _____ .

21. Primary data are original data gathered specifically for the _____ .

22. The sources of secondary data are: (1) _____ ; (2) _____ ; (3) trade, _____ , and _____ associations; (4) private _____ firms; (5) _____ media; and (6) university _____ organizations.

23. Company sales people, middlemen, or customers are sources from whom _____ can be gathered.

24. Three widely used methods of gathering primary data are _____ , _____ , and _____ .

25. A survey consists of gathering data by interviewing _____ .

26. Interviewing and data gathering in a survey may be done by the researcher in three ways: in _ _____ , by _____ , and by _____ .

27. An advantage of the personal interview is its _____.

28. Rising costs and other problems associated with door-to-door interviewing have fostered a trend for interviewing in a(n) _____. This technique is called the _____ _____ method of interviewing.

29. _____ are 4-10 people who meet with an interviewer face-to-face and freely discuss topics of interest.

30. In a(n) _____ , the respondent is approached by telephone, and the interview completed at that time.

31. _____ involve mailing a questionnaire to potential respondents and having them return the completed form by mail.

32. In the _____ , no interviews are involved. The data are collected by observing the _____ of the respondent.

33. In the _____ , a controlled experiment is established that simulates the real market situation as much as possible by changing one variable while holding all others constant.

34. In _____ , the researcher duplicates real market conditions in a small geographical area in order to measure consumers' responses to a strategy before committing to a major _____.

35. Because of its limitations, the use of traditional test marketing is declining _____, as less _____ alternatives are being developed.

36. One method that has evolved to overcome the disadvantages of traditional test marketing is the _____.

37. Several fundamental considerations in preparing a data gathering form include: (1) the _____ of questions, (2) _____ format, (3) _____ layout, and (4) _____ .

38. Random sampling has one big advantage--it is possible to make generalizations to a(n) _____.

39. One common question regarding random sampling is,"How large should the _____ be?"

40. Collecting _____ by interviewing, observation, or both is often the weakest link in the research process.

41. The end productsof the investigation are the researcher's _____ and _____.

42. Researchers should _____ their studies to determine whether their results and recommendations are being used.

43. _____ is the process of gathering and analyzing publicly available information about the activities and plans of competitors.

44. _____ are the primary internal sources of competitive data.

45. A firm wishing to undertake a research project can get the job done with the _____ and by a(n) _____.

46. There are several factors that account for the less-than-universal acceptance of marketing research: (1) _____ are difficult; (2) predictions of the future can be _____ ; (3) researchers become too focused on _____ and forget their major goal is to help management make _____ ; (4) researchers fail to adequately _____ with management; and (4) management is reluctant to treat marketing research as a(n) _____ process.

PART 4E: True-False Questions

If the statement is true, circle "T"; if false, circle "F."

T F 1. Simulated test marketing is faster and less expensive than test marketing.

T F 2. Employees, particularly sales people, are the primary source of competitive data.

T F 3. A marketing information system suggests a process while marketing research is more concerned with techniques.

T F 4. The best plan is to first set up some means of collecting primary data and then investigate secondary sources.

T F 5. It is obvious that large marketing organizations need a marketing information system. It is just as obvious that small firms do not.

T F 6. A marketing information system is consistent with the marketing concept.

T F 7. Marketing information systems were developed and used many years before the advent of marketing research.

T F 8. "Random sampling" means that the investigators are haphazard and sloppy in their questioning of research subjects.

T F 9. Marketing research makes very little use of the scientific method.

T F 10. Properly conducted, marketing research can serve as a substitute for executive judgment.

T F 11. Often a marketing research project will be dropped after the completion of the informal investigation stage.

T F 12. One criticism of the experimental method of gathering primary data is that the setting is often unnatural.

T F 13. Ordinarily, secondary data can be gathered faster and at less expense than primary data.

T F 14. Personal interviews usually are less expensive than mail or telephone interviews.

T F 15. For a sample to be statistically reliable, sample size is critical in the design of the sample.

PART 4F: Multiple Choice Questions

In the space provided write the letter of the answer that best fits the statement.

_____ 1. All of the following are sources of primary data EXCEPT:
   A. Company sales.   C. Public libraries.   E. Retailers.
   B. Customers.   D. Wholesalers.

_____ 2. Marketing research may be defined as:
   A. A means of generating, evaluating, and communicating information.
   B. A careful survey of all potential markets.
   C. The scientific method applied to the study of business institutions and functions in marketing.
   D. A careful analysis of all published data pertinent to a given marketing problem.
   E. Surveys of consumer behavior.

_____ 3. Which of the following is a correct statement regarding the objective of a marketing research project?
   A. The objective is always to solve a problem.
   B. The objective should not be determined finally until plans have been set.
   C. The objective may be only to determine if a problem actually exists.
   D. The objective is always to define the problem.
   E. None of the above is correct.

54

____ 4. The largest single source of marketing data in the country is:
   A.   The federal government.
   B.   Universities.
   C.   Company records.
   D.   Advertising media.
   E.   Public libraries.

____ 5. Which of the following is a source of primary data for a marketing research person in a steel company?
   A.   Census of business.
   B.   Trade associations.
   C.   Interviews with company salespeople.
   D.   A company's internal records.
   E.   A university's Bureau of Business Research.

____ 6. In the data-gathering stage of a marketing research project, experts usually recommend you:
   A.   Gather primary data.
   B.   Collect secondary data only.
   C.   Collect secondary data first, then gather primary data as needed.
   D.   Hire an outside firm that specializes in data gathering.
   E.   Gather the two types of data at the same time.

____ 7. All of the following are characteristics of a marketing information system EXCEPT:
   A.   Emphasis is on handling external information.
   B.   Is concerned with preventing as well as solving problems.
   C.   Operates continuously as a system.
   D.   Tends to be future-oriented.
   E.   Is a computer-based process.

____ 8. The advantage of a marketing information system is:
   A.   A faster information flow.
   B.   A more complete information flow.
   C.   The potential of continuous monitoring.
   D.   All of the above.
   E.   None of the above.

____ 9. All of the following are advantages of interviewing by mail EXCEPT:
   A.   Less interviewer bias than shopping mall intercept method.
   B.   Less expensive than personal interviews.
   C.   The possibility that truer answers will be given.
   D.   The ease of compiling a good mailing list.
   E.   Less trouble managing interviewers.

____10. Generally, the most timely method of gathering primary data is the:
   A.   Survey method.
   B.   Focus group.
   C.   Personal interview.
   D.   Telephone survey.
   E.   Mail questionnaire.

___11. The ideal marketing information system has the ability to:
   A. Generate reports as needed.
   B. Integrate data to provide information updates.
   C. Analyze data using mathematical models that represent the real world.
   D. Allow managers to get answers to "what if" questions.
   E. All of the above.

___12. The potential benefits of simulated test marketing include:
   A. Lower costs than traditional test marketing.   D. All of the above.
   B. Speed in getting results.   E. None of the above.
   C. The possibility of keeping the process secret.

___13. The advantage of field experiments over laboratory experiments is:
   A. Their expense.
   B. Their realism.
   C. Consumer responses may be more influenced by the situation.
   D. The possibility of their being unnatural.
   E. The researcher's ability to control the situation.

___14. Marketing research can be carried out by:
   A. The company's marketing research department.
   B. Outside firms with large data bases.
   C. Outside firms with large data sources.
   D. Outside firms that collect, process, and analyze survey data.
   E. All of the above.

___15. Marketing research is not accepted by everyone because it:
   A. Cannot be measured in direct terms of the organization.
   B. Often cannot predict future marketing behavior.
   C. Often does a poor job of communicating with management.
   D. Is not treated as a continuous process by management.
   E. All of the above.

PART 4G: Matching Questions

In the space provided write the number of the word or expression from column 1 that best fits the description in column 2.

            1   2

1. Competitive intelligence   ____ a. An example of this observation method uses
                                              scanners in supermarkets to record purchases.

2. Data bases

3. Decision support system

4. Field experiment

5. Focus group

6. Hypothesis

7. Informal investigation

8. Laboratory experiment

9. Mail questionnaire

10. Mall intercept

11. Marketing information system

12. Marketing research

13. Mechanical observation

14. Personal interview

15. Personal observation

16. Primary data

17. Random sample

18. Secondary data

19. Simulated test market

20. Situation analysis

21. Survey

22. Telephone survey

23. Test marketing

_____ b. A tentative supposition or a possible solution to a problem.

_____ c. Original data collected specifically for the project at hand.

_____ d. Government provides the greatest source of these data.

_____ e. A research method consisting of data-gathering by interviewing a limited but representative number of people.

_____ f. A small number of items chosen at random from a larger number of items.

_____ g. When researchers try to define the problem more clearly and develop hypotheses for further testing.

_____ h. Another name for test marketing.

_____ i. Consists of talking to people outside the company such as middlemen, competitors, advertising agencies, and customers.

_____ j. Open-ended questions asked of a group of 4-10 face-to-face.

_____ k. The process of gathering and analyzing publicly available information about the activities and plans of competitors.

PART 4H: Problems and Applications

1.   Why is a marketing information system of any benefit to a small company (75 employees)?

2.   "A marketing information system isn't really necessary for all companies." Defend your agreement or disagreement with this statement in a report to your instructor.

3.   In today's business setting, a company needs to add a new dimension to its information management--one that is predicated on the systems approach to marketing management. Do you agree? Why?

4.   Assume you have the responsibility for setting up a marketing information system. What type of information do you want to process and store for: a wholesale lumber company, a pottery manufacturer, or a chain of hotels or restaurants? Each business has over 500 employees, many of whom are outside sales people. Each firm also conducts business throughout the United States.

5.   Explain why it is important to clearly state objectives and problems in a research investigation.

6.   What is the difference between an informal investigation and a situation analysis?

7.   Assume you have completed a situation analysis and an informal investigation on the lift-truck business in Atlanta, Georgia, and Jacksonville, Florida. Your dealer in Jacksonville argues that industrial customers south of Columbus and Savannah, Georgia, tend to look to Jacksonville when they buy industrial goods and supplies; therefore, he would like to have these regions assigned to his dealership as his area of primary responsibility. This market area currently has a volume of $8 million annually. What recommendations would you make for a formal investigation if the research question is: "Where do industrial buyers in southern Georgia tend to go when buying industrial goods and supplies, Atlanta or Jacksonville?" Report your research plan in memo form to your instructor.

8.   What are some possible uses of the observation methods? List some advantages and limitations for mechanical and personal observation methods.

9.   What procedure would you recommend be followed in preparing a questionnaire? Prepare a memo to your instructor on this subject. Hint: It may be helpful to consult a standard text on market research to complete this assignment, such as Robert Ferber (ed.), *Handbook of Marketing Research* (New York: McGraw-Hill, 1974).

10.   Why are huge increases in sample size needed to produce small increases in the statistical reliability of the sample? Explain in statistical terms.

11.   If we wished to use a random sample to determine fast food preferences among people in Denver, why would we need an accurate and complete listing of all people within the city limits? Prepare a report on this subject.

12.   Design a short questionnaire (not more than five minutes) and then observe as a classmate using your questionnaire interviews five people. Base your questionnaire on a current topic. Prepare the results of your project in a report to your instructor.

PART 4I: Exercise

Your authors maintain that "improper sampling is a source of error in many studies," and that "only random samples are appropriate for making generalizations from a sample to a universe." While random sampling is best for scientifically valid results, there are other commonly used sampling techniques.

Two of these are area samples and quota samples. Area samples are used when it is not economically feasible to obtain a full list of the universe. One way would be to list all the areas of a city and then select a number of these areas at random.

In a quota sample, the researcher knows ahead of time what proportions of the universe share some characteristic. He or she chooses the sample based upon the same proportion. For example, if a pizza shop owner knows that 20 percent of his customers attend X high school; 15 percent, Y high school; and 30 percent, Z high school, the sample would be set up using the same proportions.

Apply these distinctions to the following exercise.

Golden West Inc., is the oldest and largest furniture store chain in the Sacramento, California, area. The marketing manager has been taking an executive course in marketing at the local university where he has been exposed to the concept of store image. His curiosity has been aroused, and he would like to measure Golden West's image. He is confused, however, about what sampling techniques he should use.

The marketing manager has hired you to explain to him how to use the following sampling techniques for the study he proposes. For each of the sample types, discuss the procedures involved in selecting the sample as well as the limitations of the techniques.

1.   Simple random sample. See the appendix of any statistics textbook for a table of random numbers for selecting a sample of 500 people.

2.   Area sample. Select 10 census tracts at random and then select 500 people from within these tracts.

3.   Quota sample. Use sex and median household income as the criteria for selecting the sample.

PART 4J: A Real World Case: Relationships, Not Hardware

No matter which way you turn in the business world today, you'll find the apostles of the Information Revolution aggressively championing information technology as the key to global competitiveness. Information, they insist, is a "strategic asset." Successful organizations need CIOs--chief information officers--to manage it. These missionaries' Holy Grail is the seamless integration of hardware, software, and telecommunications technology into networks where people can get whatever information they need whenever they need it.

This sounds too good to be true--and it is. The so-called Information Revolution is just so much marketing hype, and information technology has become a dangerously misleading misnomer.

In the real world, technology isn't just a medium of information but a medium for relationships. Information matters, but it's the relationships--the formal and informal networks of people--that really govern how the organization runs and how value is created. That's why so many companies have gotten such consistently lousy returns on their information technology investments.

While it becomes easier to retrieve a piece of information from the corporate database, it often becomes a chore to talk with the people who collected it. Departments spend more and more time making sure they have enough data to generate the required Lotus 1-2-3 spreadsheet forecasts. The quantity of data flowing through the computer networks dramatically increases. The result is that, in most organizations, technology is bestowing better quality information and a declining quality of personal interaction.

The Information Revolution crowd has been looking through the wrong end of the telescope. For example, it loves to point to the American Airlines customer reservations system as a model of successful design. That's undoubtedly true; American's Sabre does a tremendous job of tracking and coordinating hundreds of thousands of pieces of data every day. It's a superb information management system.

And yet, let's look at the real impact of this technology. What Sabre did was allow American to create a whole new set of relationships with its customers. Travel agents and regular customers could link up with the airline in previously unimagined ways. A businessperson-on-the-go could craft an entire itinerary from a payphone anywhere in the U.S. By creating this new "relationships infrastructure," American could track demand patterns and alter its schedules accordingly.

So where was the real value of the technology? In the information it could process? Or in the new relationships it created with customers? The same holds true with the way technology has spawned new relationships in financial service networks. Increasingly, the value resides in the communities of shared interest, not in the reams of data these technologies create.

Information is a derivative of the relationship, not the other way around. American Express understands this, and uses its vast arsenal of technologies to craft all sorts of communal ties with its cardholders. Visa and MasterCard aren't there yet--preferring to define their technologies as transaction-information systems.

Indeed, if you carefully listen to most data-processing managers or CIOs talk, what you'll most likely hear is how well their high-tech networks handle data. It's a bit like listening to talented architects brag about their houses; they're so enthusiastic about the designs, they forget that families will have to live in them. Or urban planners so obsessed with eliminating traffic congestion that they neglect the quality of neighborhood life.

That shouldn't be so. If you look at how successful organizations have deployed technology, you'll discover that the management of information is consistently secondary to the management of relationships. Shift the focus from American Express to Federal Express. The value of the courier company's considerable technology investment won't be found in the fact that the customer can track down any package within 30 minutes. That's a gimmick, because customers aren't supposed to worry about their packages.

On the contrary, Federal Express's elaborate telecommunications networks are geared toward making the customer feel comfortable and relaxed. All the customer needs is a telephone and a packing slip--and sometimes, not even that. In other words, the networks are designed to support a certain kind of relationship with the customer. As far as the customer is concerned, Federal Express is far more concerned with managing its relationship than with managing the information.

That is a distinctly minority approach. Most companies have bit the "information as strategic asset" hook, line, and sinker. But think of how value is really created in most organizations. Casual meetings, quick phone calls, political alliances, friendships and quirky collaborations--in other words, human interactions--are the real dynamics that drive the organization. And yet, one rarely sees "information technology" supporting these efforts. While electronic mail has begun to trickle into some companies, the data processing department usually considers it a difficult and peripheral nuisance to manage.

The unpleasant reality is that most organizational technologists are more interested in getting the right computers to talk to each other than the right people to do so. They view networking computers as akin to phone networks--so long as people can talk to each other, who cares what they say? But just because people have ready access to timely information doesn't mean they care to use it--much in the same way people don't always make or take the phone calls they should.

Instead of asking, "What is the information that matters and how do we most effectively manage it?", companies must start asking, "What are the relationships that matter and how can the technology most effectively support them?" That requires a totally different systems emphasis. Most technologists would rather focus on information management because it is so much easier than working with people. It's time for organizations to recognize this, and where the real potential and value of these technologies lie.

_____

Source: Michael Schrage, "In Information Technology, the Key Is Good Relationships," *Wall Street Journal*, March 19, 1990, p. A18. © Michael Schrage 1990. Reprinted by permission.

_____

___1. According to the article, before embarking on an MkIS, one must ask:
   A. "How much will this system cost?"
   B. "How fast will this system work?"
   C. "What are the relationships that matter in this organization?"
   D. "What is the information that matters in this organization?"
   E. "How do we most effectively manage these systems?"

___2. The article emphasizes which factor of a successful MkIS?
   A. The nature of the data it works on.
   B. The quality of the data it works on.
   C. The accuracy of the models applied to the data.
   D. The realism of the analytical techniques applied to the data.
   E. The working relationships between the operators of the MkIS and the managers who use the output.

PART 4K: Answers to Questions

PART 4D: Completion

1. information/markets/environmental forces/ plans/changes
2. Marketing research
3. research project/syndicated services
4. ongoing/organized/generate/analyze/ disseminate/store/retrieve/marketing decisions
5. decision-making
6. data/usable information/work together
7. around the world
8. better decisions/expensive/unanticipated problems
9. decision-support system
10. speed/flexibility
11. data base
12. scanner
13. Single-source/demographics/ advertising/product purchases
14. industries/market trends/market share analysis
15. objective/situation/informal/formal/data/ report/follow-up study
16. company/environment/library/company officials
17. supposition
18. inside/outside/competitors/consumers
19. informal investigation
20. information/secondary data/primary/data/ sample/data/analyze/report/follow-up
21. project at hand
22. libraries/government/professional/ business/business/advertising/research
23. primary data
24. survey/observation/experimentation
25. people
26. person/telephone/mail
27. flexibility
28. central location/mall intercept
29. Focus groups
30. telephone survey
31. Mail surveys
32. observation method/actions
33. experimental method
34. test marketing/marketing effort
35. faster/expensive
36. simulated test market
37. wording/response/questionnaire/pretesting
38. universe
39. sample
40. primary data
41. conclusions/recommendations
42. follow up
43. Competitive intelligence
44. Employees
45. company's own personnel/outside organization
46. payoffs/inexact/research techniques/better decisions/communicate/continuing

PART 4E: True-False Questions

1. T 2. T 3. T 4. F 5. F 6. T
7. F 8. F 9. F 10. F 11. T 12. T
13. T 14. F 15. T

PART 4F: Multiple Choice Questions

1. C 2. A 3. C 4. A 5. C 6. C
7. A 8. D 9. D 10. D 11. E 12. D
13. B 14. E 15. E

PART 4G: Matching Questions

a. 13 b. 6 c. 16 d. 18 e. 21 f. 17
g. 20 h. 4 i. 7 j. 5 k. 1

PART TWO

TARGET MARKETS

```
┌─────────────────────────┐
│                         │
│                         │
└─────────────────────────┘
┌─────────────────────────┐
│                         │
│      CHAPTER 5          │
│                         │
└─────────────────────────┘
┌─────────────────────────┐
│                         │
│  MARKET SEGMENTATION    │
│  AND TARGET-MARKET      │
│      STRATEGIES         │
│                         │
│                         │
│                         │
│                         │
│                         │
│                         │
└─────────────────────────┘
```

PART 5A: Chapter Goals

After studying this chapter, you should be able to explain:

- The related concepts of market segmentation and target markets
- The process of market segmentation, including its benefits and conditions for use
- The difference between ultimate consumer markets and business user markets
- Bases for segmenting consumer markets
- Bases for segmenting business markets
- Three target-marketing strategies: aggregation, single-strategy concentration, and multiple-segment targeting

PART 5B: Key Terms and Concepts

1. Market [122]
2. Target market [122]
3. Market segmentation [123]
4. Ultimate consumers [125]
5. Business users [125]
6. Bases for consumer market segmentation [125]
7. Regional distribution of population [127]
8. Urban-suburban-rural distribution [128]
9. Metropolitan Statistical Area [128]
10. Primary Metropolitan Statistical Area [128]
11. Consolidated Metropolitan Statistical Area [128]
12. PRIZM [129]
13. Population distribution by age group [129]
14. Market segmentation by gender [131]
15. Family life cycle stages [131]
16. Singles [132]
17. Mingles [133]
18. Income distribution [133]
19. Disposable personal income [134]
20. Discretionary purchasing power [134]
21. Expenditure patterns [134]
22. Psychological segmentation [136]
23. Psychographic segmentation [138]
24. LOV [139]
25. VALS and VALS2 [139]
26. Behavioral segmentation [140]
27. Bases for segmenting business markets [142]
28. Market aggregation strategy [145]
29. Product differentiation [146]
30. Single-segment strategy [147]
31. Multiple-segment strategy [147]

PART 5C: Summary

A marketing program begins with a selection of a target market for whatever it is the firm is selling [122]. A market for our purposes may be defined as people with needs to satisfy, the money to spend, and the willingness to spend it [122]. This definition views a market from the firm's point of view, and implies that an exchange relationship and communication exist between buyers and sellers. Thus, in considering market demand for any given product, three factors are involved: (1) people with needs and/or wants, (2) their purchasing power, and (3) their buying behavior [122].

It is impossible to develop a specific product for each consumer. It is also difficult to develop a product that will satisfy all consumers equally well--a strategy known as market aggregation [145]. Market segmentation is a compromise. This is the process of dividing the total market into several smaller groups, such that the members of each group are similar with respect to the factors that influence demand [123]. A marketing mix is then developed for each segment that the seller selects as a target market. This strategy is consumer-oriented and is consistent with the marketing concept [123].

Market segmentation enables a company to make more efficient use of its marketing resources. There are disadvantages to this strategy. For example, it requires higher production and marketing costs than if a product differentiation strategy were used. The conditions for effective segmentation are that: (1) the bases for segmentation be measurable with available data, (2) the segments themselves be accessible through existing marketing institutions, and (3) the segments be large enough to be potentially profitable [124].

The total U.S. market can be divided into two broad segments: ultimate consumers and business users [125]. The consumer market is further broken down by geographic bases, demographic bases, psychological bases, and product-related bases [125]. Firms selling to the business market may use some of these same means of segmenting their market or they may use one of the following bases: type of customer, size of customer, and type of buying situation [142]. Normally, sellers use a combination of two or more segmentation bases.

There are three segmentation strategies a marketer can use: market aggregation, single-segment segmentation, and multiple-segment segmentation [143]. A satisfactory marketing program begins by identifying and analyzing the market for a product. Market aggregation uses one marketing mix to reach a single, mass, undifferentiated market [145]. In a single-segmentation strategy, a company still uses only a single marketing mix but it is focused on only one segment of the total market [147]. The third alternative involves selecting two or more segments and then developing a separate marketing mix to reach each one [147].

PART 5D: Completion

1. A market is defined as people or organizations with: (1) _____ to satisfy, (2) _____ to spend, and (3) the _____ to spend it.

2. A(n) _____ is a group of customers for whom the seller specifically designs a particular _____ .

3. There are two alternative target-market strategies: (1) a mass, aggregate strategy sometimes

69

called the "_____" approach, and a segmentation strategy, often called the "_____" approach.

4. _____ is the process of dividing the total market for a product or service into several _____ , such that the members of each group are _____ with respect to the factors that influence demand.

5. Market segmentation is _____ and thus it is consistent with the _____ .

6. By tailoring marketing programs to individual _____ , management can do a better _____ and make for efficient use of its marketing _____ .

7. Because of their size and limited resources, _____ firms have long employed market segmentation strategies. Now even very large companies are abandoning _____ strategies.

8. The three conditions for effective market segmentation are: (1) the basis for segmenting must be _____ and the data must be _____ , (2) the market segment itself should be _____ through existing _____ , and (3) each segment should be large enough to be _____ .

9. The ideal method for segmenting a market for a customer orientation perspective is on the basis of customers' _____ .

10. The first step is to divide a potential market into two broad categories: _____ and _____ .

11. Ultimate consumers buy products for their own _____ or _____ use and are satisfying _____ wants.

12. Business users are _____ , _____ , or _____ organizations that buy products to ____ in their own organizations, to _____ , or to _____ .

13. The most commonly used bases for segmenting the consumer market are: (1) _____ , (2) _____ , (3) _____ , and (4) _____ behavior.

14. In using these characteristics, three points to consider are: (1) buying behavior is rarely traceable to only _____ , (2) the characteristics are _____ , and (3) there are _____ for the number and range of categories used for most characteristics.

15. The _____ distribution of population is important to marketing because people within a given region broadly tend to share the same _____ , _____ , and _____ preferences.

70

16. There has been a decline in _____ population for many years, and this trend is expected to continue.

17. A Metropolitan Statistical Area (MSA) is defined as a geographical area with a(n) _____ of at least 50,000 people, and with a(n) _____ of at least 100,000 people.

18. Primary Metropolitan Statistical Areas (PMSA's) are identical to MSAs but have a population of at least _____.

19. A Consolidated Metropolitan Statistical Area (CMSA) is a(n) _____ center that consists of two or more closely related PMSAs.

20. As middle-income families have moved to the suburbs, the core areas of cities have changed as follows: (1) _____ have followed consumers from the cities to the suburbs, (2) since _____ locate close to their markets, they too have moved to the suburbs, and (3) a retailing void is developing in the inner cities.

21. The most widely used basis for segmenting markets is some _____ factor such as age, sex, stage in family life cycle, income distribution, education, occupation, or ethnic origin.

22. By the year 2000, population will grow more _____ and also be _____.

23. The youth market carries a three-way marketing impact: (1) children can _____ parental purchases, (2) billions of dollars are spent on this group by _____ and _____ , and (3) the children themselves make purchases of _____ for their own personal use.

24. The early middle-aged population segment will be an especially _____ and _____ market in the 1990s.

25. The fifties and early sixties group is _____ and financially _____.

26. The over-65 group is growing in _____ and as a(n) _____ of total population.

27. About _____ percent of women in their twenties and about _____ percent of women with children under 6 are working outside the home.

28. The nine-way, family-life-cycle model includes: (1) _____ (young single people); (2) _____ with no children; (3) _____ (young married couples with children); (4) _____ with dependent children; (5) _____ and alone; (6)

_____ couples, without children; (7) _____ (older married couples still with dependent children); (8) _____ (older married couples with independent children); and (6) _____ people still working or retired.

29. The marketer is interested in consumers' _____ , which is the amount available for personal consumption expenditures and saving.

30. Personal consumption expenditures include the following: (1) _____ for food, clothing, household utilities, and local transportation, and (2) _____ for rent or mortgage payments, and installment debt payments.

31. _____ is the amount of disposable personal income over and above fixed commitments and above that required for essential household needs.

32. _____ is a better or more sensitive indicator of the consumer's ability to spend for _____ .

33. The _____ market is large and growing at a rapid rate.

34. The African American and Hispanic markets are not more homogeneous than the white market: they contain subsegments based on _____, _____ , _____ _____ , and _____ stage.

35. While demographics correlate with _____ , they do not explain it.   Thus, marketers have looked at psychological factors such as _____, _____ , and _____ characteristics to produce better segmentation descriptions.

36. Although _____ characteristics should be good basis for segmenting markets, their _____ and _____ in the general population are impossible to <u>measure</u> .

37. _____ reflects how a person spends his time and what his beliefs are on various <u>social</u> , _____ , and _____ issues.

38. Psychographics studies the _____ and _____ aspects of a market.

39. Two means of segmenting on the basis of behavior are: (1) _____ desired, and (2) _____ .

40. Research has shown that _____ of the users may account for 80-90 percent of the total purchases made. This is called the "_____" of the market.

41. Many of the techniques for segmenting _____ markets are also used to segment _____ markets.

72

42. The text discusses three means of business market segmentation: (1) by _____ of customer, (2) by _____ of customer, and (3) by type of _____.

43. The federal government has developed a system of classifying manufactured products called the _____ (SIC) code.

44. Business customer size can be measured by factors such as _____, number of _____, number of _____, and number of _____.

45. The type of buying situation can vary from _____ buy to _____ rebuy, with _____ rebuy in between.

46. The three broad target market strategies are: (1) market _____, (2) _____ concentration, and (3) _____ segmentation.

47. The four guidelines that determine which segments should be the target markets are: (1) the target market should be _____ with the organization's _____ and _____, (2) it should be matched with the firm's _____, (3) _____ target markets should be sought, and (4) markets that have _____ and _____ competitors should be targeted.

48. As mentioned before, in a strategy of _____, the firm treats its total market as a single mass, aggregate market whose parts are considered to be alike in all major aspects.

49. This strategy is accompanied by a strategy of _____ in a company's marketing program.

50. _____ is the strategy in which a company tries to distinguish its product from competitive brands offered to the same aggregate market.

51. The seller implements this strategy either by: (1) changing some _____ feature of the product (the package or color of the product), or (2) using a(n) _____ that features a differentiating benefit.

52. A strategy of single-segment concentration involves selecting as the target market _____ segment from within the total market.

53. This strategy enables a firm to penetrate _____ in depth, and to acquire a reputation as a(n) _____ or a(n) _____ in this limited market.

54. In the strategy of _____, two or more groups of potential customers are identified as target-market segments and a separate _____ is developed to reach each segment.

55. In a multiple-segmentation strategy, a seller frequently will develop a(n) _____ of the same basic product for each market segment.

PART 5E: True-False Questions

If the statement is true, circle "T"; if false, circle "F."

T F 1. Disposable personal income is a smaller number than personal income.

T F 2. Ethnic groups are homogeneous as to income, occupation, and life-cycle stages.

T F 3. Market segmentation is a philosophy inconsistent with the marketing concept.

T F 4. The most commonly used basis for segmenting the consumer market is psychographic.

T F 5. The "heavy half" of all users may account for 80-90 percent of the total purchases made for a particular product.

T F 6. Market segmentation is the process of dividing the total market for a good or service into several segments, such that the members of each group are similar with respect to the factors that influence demand.

T F 7. Market aggregation is the opposite of market segmentation.

T F 8. Central cities are either growing very slowly or actually losing population.

T F 9. "Market segmentation" is to "rifle," as "market aggregation" is to "shotgun."

T F 10. In a strategy of market aggregation, the firm treats its total market as a single mass, aggregate market whose parts are considered to be alike in all major aspects.

T F 11. Market aggregation is a marketing concept-oriented strategy.

T F 12. In the strategy of multiple segmentation, two or more groups of potential customers are identified as target-market segments and a separate marketing mix is developed to reach each segment.

T F 13. The concept of market segmentation (ultimate consumers and industrial users) is quite useful as an aid in studying marketing, but the concept does not have much practical value in shaping a company's marketing program.

T F 14. A market may be defined as "people with needs to satisfy, with money to spend, and the willingness to spend it."

T F 15. CMSAs have larger populations than PMSAs.

PART 5F: Multiple Choice Questions

In the space provided write the letter of the answer that best fits the statement.

____ 1. All of the following are guidelines in selecting target markets EXCEPT:
   A. They should be compatible with the organization's goals and image.
   B. The marketing opportunity must match the company's resources.
   C. Marketing costs should be recaptured in at least five years.
   D. The markets will generate a sufficient sales volume at a low enough cost to result in a profit.
   E. Markets should be sought wherein the number of competitors are minimal.

____ 2. Psychographic research uses the following tool:
   A. LOV   C. VALS2   E. None of the above.
   B. VALS   D. All of the above.

____ 3. A condition for effective market segmentation is:
   A. The basis for segmenting must be measurable.
   B. The data must be accessible.
   C. The market segment should be accessible through existing marketing institutions.
   D. Each segment should be large enough to be profitable.
   E. All of the above.

____ 4. Probably the most commonly used basis for segmenting the consumer market is:
   A. Geographic.   C. Psychographic.   E. Cultural.
   B. Demographic.   D. Product-related.

____ 5. A market segmentation strategy has been likened to a(n)_____ approach.
   A. Cannon   C. Shotgun   E. Atomic bomb
   B. Rifle   D. Machine gun

____ 6. All of the following are disadvantages of using a multiple-segment strategy EXCEPT:
   A. It is expensive in both production and marketing.
   B. It results in greater sales volume.
   C. It increases inventory costs.
   D. It increases advertising expenses.
   E. It increases general advertising expenses.

____ 7. The largest populations occur in:
   A. MSAs.   B. PMSAs.   C. CMSAs.

75

_____ 8. The "heavy half" means that:
  A. Half of all firms will target a single market segment.
  B. Half of all customers will buy from half of all firms.
  C. Half of all customers will buy from a single firm.
  D. Half of the users may account for 80-90 percent of the total purchases made.
  E. Half of all firms will target multiple market segments.

_____ 9. The process of dividing the total market for a product into several groups, such that the members of each group are similar with respect to the factors that influence demand, is known as:
  A. Product differentiation.
  B. Monopolistic or imperfect competition.
  C. Market segmentation.
  D. Determining a demand schedule.
  E. Product planning.

_____ 10. An example of a business product is:
  A. Golf clubs purchased by a department store for sale to golfers.
  B. Dress purchased by a student.
  C. Guitars purchased for use by a rock-and-roll group.
  D. Grass seed sold to a suburban homeowner.
  E. None of the above.

_____ 11. Significant changes in disposable personal income will most likely influence the market demand for:
  A. Groceries.   C. Children's staple clothing.   E. Toothpaste.
  B. Automobiles.   D. Gasoline.

_____ 12. In a given year, which of the following is the smallest?
  A. Discretionary income.   C. "Take-home" pay.
  B. Personal income.   D. Disposable income.

_____ 13. In business markets, reordering paper towels for the company cafeteria would be called:
  A. A new buy.   C. A modified rebuy.   E. None of the above
  B. A straight rebuy   D. A combination new buy-modified rebuy.

_____ 14. Significant changes in discretionary income will most likely influence the market demand for:
  A. New houses.   C. Toothpaste.   E. Medical care.
  B. Vacations.   D. Automobiles.

___15. A company using a strategy of market aggregation would most likely be successful if it were marketing:

A. Ski boots.   C. Sugar.   E. Personal computers.
B. Designer blouses.   D. Luggage.

PART 5G: Matching Questions

In the space provided write the number of the word or expression from column 1 that best fits the description in column 2.

1	2
1. Behavioral segmentation	__ a. People with needs to satisfy, the money to spend, and the willingness to spend it.
2. Business users	
3. CMSA	__ b. Segmenting on the basis of personality, lifestyle, and behavioral characteristics.
4. Expenditure patterns	__ c. Unmarried couples of the opposite sex living together.
5. Family life cycle	
6. "Heavy half"	__ d. Identifying two or more groups of potential customers as target market segments and developing a separate marketing mix to reach each segment.
7. Market aggregation	
8. Markets	__ e. Treating a market as a single segment.
9. Market segmentation	__ f. The process of dividing a total market for a product into smaller groups, such that the members of each group are similar with respect to the factors that influence demand.
10. Mingles	
11. MSA	
12. Multiple segmentation	__ g. People who buy products for their personal use.
13. PMSA	__ h. A giant urban center that consists of two or more adjacent PMSAs.
14. PRIZM	__ i. Zip code clustering.
15. Product differentiation	__ j. When 50 percent of users account for 80-90 percent of total purchases.

77

16. Psychographic segmentation

17. Psychological segmentation

18. Singles

19. Single-segment strategy

20. Target market

21. Ultimate consumers

PART 5H: Problems and Applications

1. A while ago, Coca-Cola came out with "New Coke" and discontinued the manufacture of their old formula product. Due to consumer outrage, some months later they brought back original-formula Coke and called it "Coke Classic." What marketing strategies are they now using for these two products: market aggregation, product differentiation, single segmentation, or multiple segmentation strategies? Is this different from what they did in the past?

2. Refer to Question 1. Some people have argued that this episode amounts to a giant blunder on Coke's part. Do you agree?

3. "Blacks buy because they are black." To what extent is this statement true? Is it possible to segment markets on the basis of race? Why?

4. What are the demographic variables? What are their advantages and disadvantages for market segmentation?

5. Compare and contrast demographic segmentation with segmentation by distribution of disposable personal income.

6. What are the implications of an increasing and richer senior-citizen market for the demand for travel?

7. Identify several market segments for lawn mowers and state the variables that you could use to estimate the industry potential by county.

8. Consult the latest copy of The Conference Board, *A Guide to Consumer Markets*. Study the automobile market statistics.
    A. How would you segment the automobile market?
    B. Develop an example.

9. Obtain statistics on demographic changes in the United States in the next 10 years. Show how these will affect the demand for homes, automobiles, birthday cards, snow skis, and outdoor barbecue grills.

10. Using current data, make a list of the top-10 MSAs in the United States.

Rank	MSA	Population 19___ Millions
1		
2		
3		
4		
5		
6		
7		
8		
9		
10		

See the latest issue of "Survey of Buying Power," *Sales & Marketing Management*.

PART 5I (a): Exercise

In trying to develop a theory of buying behavior, marketers tried to go beyond such obvious factors as age, sex, race, etc., and in the early 1950s began to explore the concept of the family life cycle. The theory held that people bought because of the stage of life in which they and their nuclear families found themselves.

The nine-stage family life cycle offered in the text includes:

1. Bachelor stage: young, single people. 2. Young married couples without children. 3. Full Nest I: young married couples with children. 4. Single parents with dependent children. 5. Divorced without dependent children. 6. Middle-aged married without children. 7. Full Nest II: older married couples with dependent children. 8. Empty nest: older married couples with no children living with them. 9. Older single people, still working or retired.

1. Listed below are 20 products. Beside each item, write the appropriate family life cycle's number. In some cases, you may want to write more than one number.

79

a.	Mercedes Benz sportscar	_____	k.	Michael Jackson videotape	_____
b.	Regular Crest toothpaste	_____	l.	Imported coffee beans	_____
c.	Texaco gasoline	_____	m.	Premium wine	_____
d.	Life insurance	_____	n.	Symphony tickets	_____
e.	Health insurance	_____	o	Toro lawn mower	_____
f.	Auto insurance	_____	p.	Water bed	_____
g.	Greyhound bus tour	_____	q.	Condominium	_____
h.	Mr. Coffee coffee maker	_____	r.	Motor home	_____
i.	Tuition	_____	s.	Silverware	_____
j.	Madonna record	_____	t.	Tax preparation service	_____

2. Give your reasoning for each answer.

3. How valid is this method of categorization today?

PART 5I (b): **Exercise**

The most commonly used bases for segmenting consumer markets include the following categories: geographic, demographic, psychographic, and behavioral benefits desired and product usage rates. Assume that the geographic basis is a given: namely, it is where you now live. Using the data in text Table 5-1, list your best guess of the other segmentation bases for the brands shown in Column 1. In Column 2, choose the producer's probable target-market strategy--market aggregation, product differentiation, single-segment concentration, or multiple-segment strategy and briefly explain why you feel that way. To get you started, the information for WD-40 oil has been completed.

Brand	Segmentation Basis	Target-Market Strategy
1. WD-40 oil	Demographic: ages 20 through 65; generally males although women also buy it; family life cycle, education, occupation, religion, ethnic background, and income: irrelevant.	Product differentiation.
	Psychographic: social class: anything but upper class; personality: ambitious and self-confident; life-style: do-it-yourselfer.	
	Behavior toward product: convenience, versatility, high quality.	
2. Water Ski magazine	Demographic:	
	Psychographic:	

80

Behavior toward product:

3. Princess
   Line tours

Demographic:

Psychographic:

Behavior toward product:

4. Ajax
   cleanser

Demographic:

Psychographic:

Behavior toward product:

5. Levi "501"
   blue jeans

Demographic:

Psychographic:

Behavior toward product:

6. Marlboro
   cigarettes

Demographic:

Psychographic:

Behavior toward product:

7. Virginia
   Slims
   cigarettes

Demographic:

Psychographic:

Behavior toward product:

PART 5J: A Real World Case: Refocusing a Marketing Strategy

Dismayed by sagging mass-market sales, the Eastman Kodak Co. has unveiled 20 products designed to appeal to a specific photographers--everyone from small children to professionals shooting underwater.

In a sharp strategy shift, Kodak designed the products to appeal to specific age groups and photography professionals, rather than using a mass-market approach--a tactic that has produced only modest growth for the company in recent years. After sales increases of 15.2 percent in 1987 and 28 percent in 1988, Kodak's sales rose 8 percent in 1989, 2.8 percent in 1990, 2.7 percent in 1991 and 4 percent last year [1992].

The new products include a camera kit and project books for children, several pocket-sized cameras that are intended for older people, a single-use portrait camera, higher-quality film for professional photographers and an underwater slide film that is designed to produce truer colors.

Some analysts said a strategic shift was necessary for Kodak to expand the market, noting that the largest group of picture-takers, those 25 to 40 years of age, already have photography products.

B. Alex Henderson, an analyst with Prudential Securities, said that Kodak could bolster its sales by appealing to groups not yet exposed to photography or those intimidated by its increasing sophistication.

"The market has been stable for a long time," Henderson said.

Company officials said the collection was necessitated by competitive pressures from film manufacturers like Agfa, Fuji, and 3M, and the need to invigorate a market that might be softening.

"We are expanding usefulness and versatility," said Michael P Morlet, a Kodak vice president. "There is also a need for all of us in the industry to define the market. It is not fading away, but the way to change in the mindset is to introduce new products," Morley said.

As an example of new marketing opportunities, he cited a recent promotion by Kodak and the Holland America Line for four photographic cruises to Alaska. He said the cruises sold out faster than anything Holland had ever promoted.

Among the offerings designed to appeal to children, Kodak introduced story albums, which children fill with photographs they have taken to illustrate a story.

_____

_____

____1. Kodak is switching to a marketing strategy called:
    A. Market aggregation.　　B. Market segmentation.　　C. Product differentation.

____2. The article deals with segmenting the market based largely on a _____ basis.
    A. Geographic　　　C. Psychological　　E. Cultural
    B. Demographic　　　D. Product-related

____3. This market can be effectively segmented because:
    A. The basis for segmenting is measurable.
    B. The data is accessible.
    C. The market segment itself is accessible through existing marketing institutions.
    D. Each segment seems large enough to be profitable.
    E. All of the above.

PART 5K: Answers to Questions

PART 5D: Completion
1. needs/money/willingness
2. target market/marketing mix
3. shotgun/rifle
4. Market segmentation/smaller group similar
5. customer-oriented/marketing concept
6. market segments/marketing job/resources
7. small/mass marketing
8. measurable/obtainable/accessible/ marketing institutions/profitable
9. desired benefits
10. ultimate consumers/business users
11. personal/household/nonbusiness
12. business/industrial/institutional/use/ resell/make other products
13. geographic/demographic/psychological/ buying
14. one characteristic/interrelated/no rules
15. regional/values/attitudes/style
16. farm
17. urban population center/total population
18. one million
19. giant urban
20. retailers/service organizations/void
21. demographic
22. slowly/older
23. influence/parents/grandparents/goods and services
24. large/lucrative
25. large/well off
26. absolute numbers/percentage
27. 75/50
28. bachelor stage/young married couples/full nest I/single parents/divorced/middle-aged married/full nest II/empty nest/older single
29. disposable personal income
30. essential expenditures/fixed expenditures
31. Discretionary purchasing power
32. Discretionary purchasing power/ unessentials
33. Hispanic
34. income/occupation/geographic location/ life cycle
35. behavior/personality/lifestyles/ behavioral
36. personality/presence/strength/measure
37. Lifestyle/social/economic/political
38. psychological/behavioral
39. benefits/usage rate
40. half/heavy half
41. consumer/business
42. type/size/buying situation
43. Standard Industrial Classification
44. sales volume/employees/production facilities/sales offices
45. new/straight/modified
46. aggregatioin/single-segment/multiple-segment
47. compatible/goals/image/resources/ profitable/few/small
48. market aggregation
49. product differentiation
50. Product differentiation
51. appearance/promotional appeal
52. one
53. one small market/specialist/expert
54. multiple segmentation/marketing mix
55. different version

PART 5E: True-False Questions
1. T 2. F 3. F 4. F 5. T 6. T
7. T 8. F 9. T 10. T 11. F 12. T
13. F 14. T 15. T

PART 5F: Multiple Choice Questions
1. C 2. D 3. E 4. B 5. B 6. B
7. C 8. D 9. C 10. C 11. B 12. A
13. D 14. B 15. C

PART 5G: Matching Questions
a. 8 b. 17 c. 10 d. 12 e. 7 f. 9
g. 21 h. 3 i. 14 j. 6

CHAPTER 6

CONSUMER BUYING BEHAVIOR

PART 6A: Chapter Goals

After studying this chapter, you should be able to explain:

- The process consumers go through in making purchase decisions
- How commercial and social information sources influence buying decisions
- The influence of culture, subcultures, social class membership, and reference groups on buying behavior
- How buying decisions extend beyond the individual to the family and the household
- The roles of motivation, perception, learning, personality, and attitudes in shaping consumer behavior
- The importance of situational factors in buying

PART 6B: Key Terms and Concepts

1. Buying-decision process	[155]	21. Perception	[168]
2. Need recognition	[155]	22. Selective attention	[169]
3. High involvement	[156]	23. Selective distortion	[169]
4. Low involvement	[156]	24. Selective retention	[169]
5. Impulse buying	[156]	25. Learning	[169]
6. Patronage-buying motives	[158]	26. Stimulus-response theory	[169]
7. Satisfaction	[158]	27. Drives	[170]
8. Postpurchase behavior	[159]	28. Cues	[170]
9. Cognitive dissonance	[159]	29. Responses	[170]
10. Commercial information	[160]	30. Positive reinforcement	[170]
11. Social information	[160]	31. Negative reinforcement	[170]
12. Culture	[161]	32. Punishment	[170]
13. Subculture	[161]	33. Personality	[171]
14. Social class	[162]	34. Id	[172]
15. Reference groups	[164]	35. Ego	[172]
16. Family	[165]	36. Superego	[172]
17. Household	[165]	37. Self-concept	[172]
18. Motive	[167]	38. Actual self	[172]
19. Maslow's need hierarchy	[167]	39. Ideal self	[172]
20. Ethnographic research	[167]	40. Attitude	[173]

PART 6C: Summary

We previously defined markets as people with needs, with money to spend, and the willingness to spend it. It is this last element--consumer buying behavior--which is dealt with in this chapter. A model is presented which contains five parts: the buying-decision process, information, social and group influences, psychological forces, and situational factors [154].

There is a logical, six-stage process which consumers often go through in the course of making a buying decision: recognition of unsatisfied needs; the choice of an involvement level; identification and evaluation of alternatives; the actual purchase decision; and postpurchase behavior [155]. In the final stage, postpurchase behavior may involve some cognitive dissonance on the part of the buyer [159]. Understanding the decision-making process will enable the firm to make the consumer's decision making easier by suggesting solutions to his consumption problem.

Information drives the buying-decision process. There are two informational sources--the commercial environment (advertising, personal selling) [160] and the social environment (word-of-mouth, personal observation) [160]. Without this information, decisions cannot be made.

Buying behavior begins with aroused needs or motives. The motives create inner tensions that lead to behavior designed to satisfy the needs and thus reduce the tensions. This goal-oriented behavior is shaped by our perceptions [168]. Perceptions in turn are shaped by cultural, social-group, and psychological forces that make up our frame of reference [160-173].

Marketers must be aware of culture and its effect on buying behavior. Culture has the broadest and most general influence on buying behavior [161]. It refers to characteristics that individuals in the group have in common, such as language, religion, values, attitudes, and other behavior patterns. Culture is dynamic and changes over time.

Another sociocultural determinant of consumers' perceptions and buying behavior is the social class to which they belong [162]. Buyer behavior and consumption patterns do vary by social class. The reference group to which consumers belong, or aspire, also influences their behavior [164]. For example, styles, brands, and types of clothing or furniture are visible and quite susceptible to social influence.

Buyers' perceptions are shaped by forces that constitute their psychological field or frame of reference. Theories have been advanced as to how buyers learn. Two well developed theories are the stimulus-response [169] and the psychoanalytic [171], which includes the concepts of the "id," the "ego," and the "superego."

Situational influences deal with when, where, how, and why consumers buy, and the consumer's personal condition at the time of purchase [176]. Situational influences are often so strong that they can override all the other forces in the buying-decision process. In the final analysis, we still have not developed a cohesive, comprehensive theory of buyer behavior.

PART 6D: Completion

1. The reason marketing to consumers is becoming more complicated is that consumers are _____ and constantly _____ .

2. The decision-making process of the consumer as a problem to be solved consists of six steps: (1) recognition of a(n) _____; (2) choice of a(n) _____ level; (3) identification of _____; (4) _____ of alternatives; (5) purchase _____; and (6) _____ behavior.

3. Once consumers have recognized their unsatisfied needs, they must resolve _____ which may arise as they become aware of conflicting motives and conflicting uses of their scarce resources.

4. Early in the decision-making process, the consumer must _____or _____ decide how much effort to expend in satisfying a need.

5. High involvement needs require a large amount of _____ to be invested, _____ information search, a(n) _____ evaluation of information, clear and distinct _____ _____, and a(n) _____ likelihood of brand loyalty developing.

6. Low involvement needs on the other hand require a(n) _____ amount of time to be invested, _____ information search, a habit of _____ information or accepting it without _____, _____ and _____ brand judgments, and a(n) _____likelihood of brand loyalty developing.

7. The level of involvement must be viewed from the perspective of the _____, not the _____.

8. _____ (purchasing with little or no planning) is an important form of low-involvement decision making.

9. The search for alternative solutions to consumption problems is influenced by the following factors: (1) how much _____ the consumer already has from past experience and other sources; (2) how _____the consumer is in using that information; and (3) what the _____ and _____ costs are.

10. The criteria consumers use in evaluating alternatives are _____, their _____ toward various brands, and _____ from their family and friends.

11. Some of the most important patronage-buying motives are: (1) convenience of _____; (2) rapidity of _____; (3) ease of locating _____; (4) _____; (5) _____; (6) _____of merchandise; (7) _____ offered; (8) attractive

_____; (9) caliber of sales _____; and (10) _____ of other shoppers.

12. When using the product, consumers compare their _____ with their _____ to arrive at a perceived level of satisfaction--if experience meets or exceeds expectations, the result is _____.

13. _____ is when a buyer experiences postpurchase anxieties.

14. Dissonance typically increases: (1) as the _____ of the purchase increases, (2) the greater the similarity between items _____ and items _____, and (3) as the _____ of the decision increases.

15. Consumer will try to reduce dissonance. This may be reflected in their attempt to _____ information that is likely to increase their dissonance.

16. The buying-decision process is influenced by two information sources, the _____ environment, which consists of all marketing organizations and individuals who try to communicate with consumers, and the _____ environment, which is made up of family and friends who directly or indirectly provide information about products.

17. The most familiar form of commercial information is _____.

18. A normal kind of social information is _____ communication.

19. The way we think, believe, and act is determined by _____ and _____.

20. Culture may be defined as the complex of _____ and _____ created by a society and handed down from generation to generation as _____ and _____ of human behavior in a given society.

21. Cultural influences do _____ over time as old patterns gradually give way to the new.

22. Marketers can identify significant _____ market opportunities based upon such factors as race, nationality, religion, and urban-rural identification.

23. Social classes do exist in the United States; people's buying behavior is more strongly influenced by the _____ to which they belong, or to which they aspire.

24. Coleman and Rainwater's work on social-class structure placed people according to _____, _____, and _____ of residential neighborhood.

25. The social structure can be divided into five classes: (1) the _____ class: 2 percent; (2) the

_____ class: 12 percent; (3) the _____ class: 32 percent; (4) the _____ class: 38 percent; and (5) the _____ class: 16 percent.

26. Three basic conclusions about social class research that have great significance for marketing are: (1) a social class structure _____, (2) there are substantial differences among classes with respect to their buying _____, and (3) because of this diversity, social classes respond differently to a seller's _____.

27. A reference group may be defined as a group of people who influence a person's _____, _____, and _____.

28. A(n) _____ is a group of two or more people related by blood, marriage, or adoption living together in a household.

29. A(n) _____ consists of a single person, a family, or any group of unrelated persons who occupy a housing unit.

30. Who does the family buying is a question that should be treated as four separate questions because each one may affect different segments of the firm's marketing program and require different strategies. The four questions are: (1) who _____ the buying decision ? (2) who _____ the buying decision ? (3) who makes the _____ purchase ? and (4) who _____ the product?

31. All _____ starts with a recognized need.

32. A need must be _____ or _____ before it becomes a motive.

33. A(n) _____ is a need sufficiently stimulated that an individual is moved to seek satisfaction.

34. Motives can be grouped into two broad categories: needs aroused from _____ states of tension, and needs aroused from _____ states of tension.

35. Maslow identified five levels in his need hierarchy: (1) _____ needs, (2) _____ needs, (3) the need to _____ and _____, (4) the need for _____, and (5) _____ needs.

36. _____ research in marketing involves closely watching how consumers interact with a product and then deducing how it fits into their lives.

37. _____ is defined as the process whereby we receive stimuli (information) through our five senses, organize them, and then assign meaning to them.

38. In perceiving selectively, we sometimes pay attention by exception (_____),

we may alter information that is inconsistent with our beliefs and attitudes (_____ _____), and we may retain only part of what we have selectively perceived (_____).

39. _____ is defined as changes in behavior resulting from observation and previous experiences.

40. _____ theories hold that learning occurs as a person responds to some stimulus and is rewarded with need satisfaction if the response is correct, or is penalized for incorrect responses.

41. The five concepts that are fundamental to the learning process are _____, _____, _____, _____, and _____.

42. Learning emerges from _____.

43. A continually repeated rewarded response leads to _____.

44. _____ has been defined as an individual's pattern of traits which are a determinant of behavioral responses.

45. _____ theories contend that there are three parts to our mind: the id, the ego, and the superego.

46. The id houses the basic _____ drives, many of which are _____.

47. The superego is our _____, setting moral standards and directing the instinctive drives into _____ channels.

48. The ego is the conscious, _____ control center that maintains a balance between the uninhibited instincts of the __ and the socially oriented, constraining _____.

49. It is by way of psychoanalytic theory that marketers realized they must provide buyers with __ _____ for their purchasing; yet, they can also appeal subconsciously to dreams, hopes, and fears.

50. Studies of actual purchases show that people generally prefer brands and products that are compatible with their own _____.

51. _____ may be defined as a learned predisposition to respond to an object or class of objects in a consistently favorable or unfavorable way.

52. All attitudes share the following characteristics: (1) they are _____, (2) they have a(n)

_____, (3) they have _____ and _____, and (4) they tend to be _____ and generalizable.

53. _____ play a large part in determining how we behave.

54. In studying situational influences, marketers want to know _____ consumers buy, _____ they buy, _____ they buy, _____they buy, and the _____ under which they buy.

55. Marketing executives should be able to answer the following questions about when consumers buy goods and services: (1) how is it influenced by the _____, _____, _____, or _____? (2) what effect do _____ and _____ events have on the buying decision? and (3) how much time does the consumer have to _____ the purchase and _____ the product?

PART 6E: True-False Questions

If the statement is true, circle "T"; if false, circle "F."

T F 1. A high involvement purchase situation would require clear and distinct brand judgments.

T F 2. Repeated reinforcement leads to habits and brand loyalty.

T F 3. Cognitive dissonance is most likely to be found in the evaluation of the alternatives stage of the decision-making process.

T F 4. Altering information that is inconsistent with our beliefs and attitudes is known as selective distortion.

T F 5. Social class placement depends on income--the higher the income, the higher the social class.

T F 6. If we have a thorough knowledge of consumer buying habits, it is not so important to know a lot about consumer buying motives.

T F 7. The purchase decision ends with the decision-making process in buying.

T F 8. A consumer may not even be aware of the real motives for his or her buying a product.

T F 9. Once the consumer purchase-decision process is started, a potential buyer can withdraw at any stage before the actual purchase.

T F 10. The buyer must always move through the full purchase-decision process.

T F 11. The purchase-decision process starts when an unsatisfied need (motive) creates tension in a person.

T F 12. There is actually a very close relationship between consumers' attitudes and their buying decisions.

T F 13. It is extremely difficult to change customers' attitudes.

T F 14. A need must be aroused or stimulated before it becomes a motive.

T F 15. Temporary forces associated with the immediate purchase environment that affect behavior are known as situational influences.

PART 6F: Multiple Choice Questions

In the space provided write the letter of the answer that best fits the statement.

___ 1. Changing the size and quantities in which a product is packaged is a response to the factor of:
   A. When people buy.   D. Who makes the buying decision.
   B. Who does the buying.   E. Where the buying decision is made.
   C. How people buy.

___ 2. A reference group influence on buying behavior is most closely related to:
   A. Desire for conformity.   D. Desire for convenience.
   B. Growth of impulse buying.   E. Increased use of credit.
   C. Increase in leisure time.

___ 3. In psychoanalytic theory, "referee" or "umpire" comes closest to describing the function of the:
   A. Id. B. Ego. C. Superego. D. Personality. E. Subconscious.

___ 4. Which of the following is most likely a managerial response to the buying-habit factor of who makes the buying decision?
   A. Sponsor a television program for children.
   B. Prepackage meats and fresh produce.
   C. Supermarkets add a line of staple clothing.
   D. Open suburban branches.
   E. Offer seasonal discounts to retailers.

___ 5. Signals from the environment that determine the pattern of responses are called:
   A. Drives. B. Cues. C. Responses. D. Personality. E. Reinforcement.

_____ 6. Altering information that is inconsistent with our beliefs and attitudes is known as:
   A. Selective attention.
   B. Selective distortion.
   C. Selective retention.
   D. Self-image.
   E. None of the above.

_____ 7. Psychoanalytic theory of behavior holds that:
   A. People act in a rational manner.
   B. As people grow up, they acquire (learn) certain biological desires.
   C. A person's real motive for buying a given product is always obvious.
   D. The id and the superego are strong conflicting opposites, and the ego tries to balance the two.
   E. People are only motivated by frustrations and subconscious hopes and fears.

_____ 8. All of the following are patronage-buying motives EXCEPT:
   A. Price.
   B. Location convenience.
   C. Assortment of merchandise.
   D. Advertising.
   E. Services offered.

_____ 9. The Visa and MasterCard people are primarily concerned in:
   A. Who makes the buying decision.
   B. When consumers buy.
   C. Who actually uses the product.
   D. Where consumers buy.
   E. How consumers buy.

_____10. According to Coleman and Rainwater, the largest social class is the _____ class.
   A. Upper   B. Upper-middle   C. Lower-middle   D. Lower-lower   E. Upper-lower

_____11. The following are all high-involvement situations in decision making EXCEPT:
   A. Large amount of time invested.
   B. Little or no information search.
   C. Clear and distinct brand judgments.
   D. Strong likelihood of brand loyalty developing.
   E. Critical evaluation of information regarding product.

_____12. According to Maslow, the highest level of his need hierarchy is:
   A. Food.   B. Safety.   C. Social.   D. Self-respect.   E. Self-actualization.

_____13. The first stage in the decision-making model is:
   A. Choice of an involvement level.
   B. Identification of alternatives.
   C. Evaluation of alternatives.
   D. Need recognition.
   E. Decision.

_____14. All of the following are included in the commercial environment EXCEPT:
   A. Family.   B. Advertisers.   C. Retailers.   D. Manufacturers.   E. Sales people.

____15. Cognitive dissonance is associated with which stage of the decision making model?

    A. Choice of an involvement level.   D. Need recognition.

    B. Identification of alternatives.   E. None of the above.

    C. Evaluation of alternatives.

PART 6G: Matching Questions

In the space provided write the number of the word or expression from column 1 that best fits the description in column 2.

1	2
1. Attitude	____a. The meaning we attach, on the basis of our past experience, to stimuli as received through our five senses.
2. Buying-decision process	
3. Cognitive dissonance	____b. The complex of symbols and artifacts created by a society and handed down from generation to generation as determinants and regulators of human behavior.
4. Cues	
5. Culture	
6. Drives	____c. A group of people who influence a person's attitudes, opinions, and values.
7. Ego	____d. Changes in behavior resulting from previous experience.
8. Family	
9. Hierarchy of needs	____e. A theory that holds that learning occurs as a person responds to some stimulus and is rewarded with need satisfaction for a correct response.
10. Household	
11. Id	____f. Results for rewarded responses.
12. Impulse buying	____g. An individual's pattern of traits which are a determinant of his or her behavioral responses.
13. Learning	____h. According to psychoanalytic theory, the residence of basic instinctive drives.
14. Motive	
15. Patronage-buying motives	____i. A person's enduring cognitive evaluations, emotional feelings, or action tendencies toward some object or idea.

16. Perception

      j. Factors that influence where a consumer may shop.

17. Personality

      k. A state of anxiety brought on by the difficulty of choosing from among many alternatives.

18. Reference groups

19. Reinforcement

      l. The theory of Maslow.

20. Responses

      m. A group of two or more people related by blood, marriage, or adoption living together.

21. Satisfaction

22. Self-concept

23. Social class

24. Stimulus-response theory

25. Subculture

26. Superego

PART 6H: Problems and Applications

1.   A research report is speculating on the influence of the upper classes on the buying decisions of the lower classes for the following products: clothing, food, automobiles, and home-care goods. What conclusion would you expect for each of these goods? Report your results in a memo to your instructor.

2.   Should the family rather than the individual be the unit of analysis for marketing? What are the advantages and disadvantages of using the family as a unit of analysis? Include in your discussion who actually does the buying (see text).

3.   Do your religious beliefs influence your consuming habits? If so, how?

4.   Record your expenditures for a month, then analyze them and ask yourself: What percent was spent to impress others? What percent was spent to conform? What conclusions can you make about your buying behavior?

5.   To what extent are you really free to choose the food you eat? The clothing you wear?

6.   What is a decision-making model? What role does a model play in making the understanding of buyer behavior easier?

7.   Students, when asked to rank scholastically their college or university, consistently maintain that theirs is tougher and ranks higher than other schools they have heard of.   As consumers of higher education, why should students do this? What aspect of perception could help explain this tendency?

8.   Explain the meaning of the statement: "The pricing of funeral services represents a curious combination of costs, customs, and psychology."

9.   Ask 10 students to what extent their consuming practices are intended to impress other people. Tabulate your results and present them in class with your conclusions about buyer behavior.

10.   Develop an example of how the stimulus-response model could be used to learn the material in this chapter.

11.   "There is no society whose members deal rationally with automobiles." Do you think this is true? Explain.

PART 6I: Exercise

 According to the text, a motive or drive is a stimulated need that an individual seeks to satisfy. In trying to understand why we behave as we do, Abraham Maslow formulated his "holistic-dynamic" need-hierarchy. This useful theory arrayed our needs from the highest-level needs to lowest-level needs as follows:

Self-actualization
Esteem
Belonging and love
Safety
Physiological

Advertisers have known about Maslow for a long time. In your opinion, at which of the Maslow needs (there may be more than one) are the following advertising appeals aimed?

1.   "When you care enough to send the very best." (Hallmark Cards)

2.   "A diamond is forever." (DeBeers)

3.   "Oh-oh-oh what a feeling!" (Toyota)

4.   "Just do it!" (Nike)

5.   "You've come a long way, baby." (Virginia Slims)

6. "They melt in your mouth, not in your hands." (M&M candies)

7. "Reach out and touch someone." (AT&T)

8. "The breakfast of champions." (Wheaties)

9. "Quality is job 1." (Ford)

10. "We're looking for a few good men." (U.S. Marines)

11. "The good hands people." (Allstate Insurance)

12. "Be all that you can be." (U.S. Army)

13. "Own a piece of the rock." (Prudential Insurance)

14. "The un-cola drink." (7UP)

15. "Let your fingers do the walking." (Yellow Pages of telephone directories)

PART 6J: A Real World Case: The Push for Younger Beer Drinkers

Enough talking, already.

After three years of an advertising campaign that literally lectured viewers about the uniqueness of its flagship brand, Anheuser-Busch Cos. this week is introducing new ads for Budweiser that don't utter a single word.

It is also pulling the plug on it buzz phrase of the past three years, "Nothing beats a Bud," in favor of a new slogan, "Proud to Be Your Bud," sans voiceover, and delivered via song lyrics and on-screen print, one word at a time. That marks the fastest deep-sixing of a slogan in the company's history.

Although the St. Louis-based brewer says the aim of the new ads is to "recognize" and celebrate Bud drinkers, the objective is less altruistic: to jazz up Bud's maturing image that prefers to guzzle light beers. Budweiser may still be the dominant brand, but it is continuing to slip. Last year, Budweiser shipments declined for the second straight year, dropping 3% to 45.8 million barrels, according to Beer Marketer's Insights, a West Nyack, N.Y.-based newsletter. The brand shipped 49.8 million barrels in 1990.

Budweiser is also trying to keep its No. 1 position as brands in virtually every category are under attack from discount competitors. "Budweiser is a premium-priced brand beer in a market that is increasingly looking for popular prices," says Hellen Barry, vice president of marketing at Beverage Marketing Corp. "When the recession hit, people wanted to satisfy their taste for beer more cheaply. Well, they tasted just as good as the premium brands."

Budweiser is loath to admit to worrying about brand erosion and says the new ads aren't related to any such fears. "Beer is a much different product," says August A. Busch IV, vice president of Bud brands. "There is an art to brewing a fine beer. We don't believe Budweiser is suffering brand erosion."

Nevertheless, the new Bud ads are a 180-degree turn from the just-ditched effort, titled "Beer Talk," a series of 10 commercials. In some ads, all of which took place in a tavern, a group of older men lectured younger men about Budweiser. Each verbose spot ended, "To be continued."

The new 30-second ads, also from D'Arcy Masius Benton & Bowles, feature rock music and rapid editing of odd scenes to show spirit and camaraderie. One spot shows construction workers ascending in an elevator, when one hardhat opens his lunchbox and shows the guys (yes, only guys) baby pictures.

In the same spot, a proud father hugs his sons graduating from a police academy. That might raise a few eyebrows among antidrinking activists, given the image of beer-guzzling by construction workers on the job and cops on the beat. But the spots are careful to show Budweiser only in appropriate, after-work settings.

"Budweiser is saluting the American beer drinker," Mr. Busch said in a conference call with reporters yesterday.

The beer-chuggers saluted in another ad include a rain-drenched rescuer who just plucked a neighbor's heifer from a raging river, a bare-chested man jogging along a beach with his pet pooch, and three meat-loving guys rejecting an encyclopedic wine list to order a cold one.

Each spot shows the trademark Clydesdale horses, but not in their usual pose of sluggishly pulling a Bud cart. Instead, these animals are fast-moving, handsome ponies running at breakneck speed along a beach.

Budweiser declines to disclose the amount it is spending for the MTV-style ads, but says it will be a "well-funded and highly concentrated effort." The ads will be seen in prime time, late night and sports programming. According to Leading National Advertisers, which tracks advertising spending, Budweiser spent $107.6 million last year to push its suds, up 28% from $84.2 million in 1991.

The now-down-the-drain Beer Talk ads, says Mr. Busch, were "product driven," with the object to educate consumers about peculiar Bud factoids, such as how it is aged. "We were pleased with the campaign," says Mr. Busch, adding it is time "to go back to a campaign that focuses on the consumer."

Those appearing in the ads are virtually free of gray hair, unlike the previous Beer Talk campaign. Budweiser clearly wants to appeal to younger customers and says it isn't difficult to steer its message away from the underaged set. "We don't use people under 25 years old in our commercials," says Mr. Busch. Budweiser spots, he says are also devoid of "dancing girls" that populated beer spots in the 1980s.

Indeed, in one new Bud ad there is a woman in a bathing suit; but she is training to a competitive long-distance race.

D'Arcy, which first began working with Anheuser-Busch in 1915 when it was simply D'Arcy Advertising, bellied up to Budweiser with 25 to 30 different campaigns and slogans before hitting upon the winner, which Mr. Busch says he liked instantly.

How does he think it will stack up against other Bud campaigns, including, "This Bud's for You," which lasted over a dozen years, and "When You Said Budweiser, You Said It All," which droned on for a decade?

"We'd like to think," says Mr. Busch, "that this will last at least 10 years."

_____

Source: Kevin Goldman, "Bud Tries to Jazz Up Its Image to Attract Younger Beer Drinkers," *Wall Street Journal*, April 27, 1993, p. B8. Reprinted by permission of the *Wall Street Journal*, © 1993 Dow Jones & Company, Inc. All Rights Reserved Worldwide.

_____

____ 1. The Budweiser campaign represents a low-involvement level because:
A. The consumer lacks information about the alternative for satisfying the need.
B. A small amount of money is involved.
C. The product has considerable social importance.
D. The product is seen as having a potential for providing significant benefits.
E. None of the above.

____ 2. Budweiser has chosen an appeal based on _____ influences.
A. Social class   C. Subcultural   E. Reference group
B. Age and sex   D. Cultural

____ 3. The statement "we'd like to think that this [campaign] will last at least 10 years" implies buying behavior based on:
A. Stimulus-response theory.   D. Psychoanalytic theory.
B. Learning theory.   E. Self-concept theories.
C. Personality.

PART 6K: Answers to Questions

PART 6D: Completion
1. complicated/changing
2. need/involvement/alternatives/ evaluation/decision/postpurchase
3. conflicts
4. consciously/unconsiously
5. time/active/critical/brand judgments/strong
6. small/little or no/ignoring/evaluation/ vague/general/weak
7. consumer/product
8. Impulse buying
9. information/confident/time/money
10. past experience/feelings/opinions
11. location/service/merchandise/ crowding/prices/assortment/services/store appearance/personnel/mix
12. expectations/experience/satisfaction
13. Cognitive dissonance
14. dollar value/selected/rejected/importance
15. avoid
16. commercial/social
17. advertising
18. word-of-mouth
19. social forces/groups
20. symbols/artifacts/determinants/regulators
21. change
22. subcultural
23. class
24. education/occupation/type
25. upper/upper-middle/lower-middle/ upper-lower/lower-lower
26. exists/behavior/marketing program
27. attitudes/values/behavior
28. family
29. household
30. influences/makes/actual/uses
31. behavior
32. aroused/stimulated
33. motive
34. physiological/psychological
35. physiological/safety/belong/ love/esteem/self-actualization
36. Ethnographic
37. Perception
38. selective perception/selective distortion/ selective retention
39. Learning
40. Stimulus-response
41. drives/cues/responses/reinforcement/ punishment
42. reinforcement
43. habit
44. Personality
45. Psychoanalytic
46. instinctive/antisocial
47. conscience/acceptable
48. rational/id/superego
49. socially acceptable rationalizations
50. self-concept
51. Attitudes
52. learned/object/direction/intensity/stable
53. Situational influences
54. when/where/how/why/conditions
55. season/week/day/hour/past/ present/make/consume

PART 6E: True-False Questions
1. T 2. T 3. F 4. T 5. F 6. F
7. F 8. T 9. T 10. F 11. T 12. T
13. T 14. T 15. T

PART 6F: Multiple Choice Questions
1. C 2. A 3. B 4. A 5. B 6. B
7. D 8. D 9. E 10. E 11. B 12. E
13. D 14. A 15. E

PART 6G: Matching Questions
a. 16 b. 5 c. 18 d. 13 e. 24 f. 19
g. 14 h. 11 i. 1 j. 15 k. 3 l. 9
m. 8

CHAPTER 7

THE BUSINESS MARKET

PART 7A: Chapter Goals

After studying this chapter, you should be able to explain:

- The nature and importance of the business market
- The characteristics of business market demand
- The demographic makeup of the business market
- The buying motives, buying processes, and buying patterns in business markets

PART 7B: Key Terms and Concepts

1. Business market	[182]	17. Activity indicators of buying power [192]
2. Business products	[182]	18. Buying motives [194]
3. Business marketing	[182]	19. Buying-decision process [195]
4. Farm market	[183]	20. Buy classes [195]
5. Agribusiness	[184]	a. New-task buying [195]
6. Contract farming	[184]	b. Straight rebuy [195]
7. Reseller market	[184]	c. Modified rebuy [195]
8. Government market	[185]	21. Multiple buying influences (buying center) [196]
9. Services market	[185]	a. Users [196]
10. Nonbusiness market	[185]	b. Influencers [196]
11. International market	[186]	c. Deciders [196]
12. Derived demand	[186]	d. Gatekeepers [197]
13. Inelastic demand	[187]	e. Buyers [197]
14. Standard Industrial Classification (SIC) system	[189]	22. Direct purchase [197]
15. Vertical business markets	[192]	23. Reciprocity [198]
16. Horizontal business markets	[192]	24. Leasing goods [199]

PART 7C: Summary

The business market is made up of all organizations that buy goods and services to make other goods and services, to resell to other business users or consumers, or to conduct the organization's operations. This means that hospitals, farms, government (federal, state, and local), an advertising agency, a bank, and a retailer are part of the business market [182]. A useful classification system developed by the federal government, called the Standard Industrial Classification

(SIC) system, enables a company to identify small segments of the business market [189].

Different elements of the marketing mix--distribution, price, product, promotion--will take on special importance to the user. The business marketer must match his marketing mix with the demands of the business user. This means the executive must be aware of and adjust his marketing program in light of at least four general characteristics of business market demand. These are:

1. Demand is derived.
2. Demand is inelastic.
3. Demand is widely fluctuating.
4. The market is more knowledgeable [186-189].

The factors affecting business market demand are the number of potential business users and their purchasing power, buying motives, and buying habits [193]. Business buying motives generally are rational; however, the purchasing agent's self-interest must also be considered [194]. The concept of a buying center reflects the multiple buying influences often involved in business purchasing decisions. In a typical buying center we must discover if people are playing the roles of users, influencers, deciders, gatekeepers, or buyers [196].

The business buying goal is to get the optimum combination of price, quality, and service in the products that are bought. The business buying process involves a five-step process: need recognition, identifying alternatives, evaluating alternatives, the purchase decision, and post-purchase behavior [195]. Finally, overt patterns of buyer behavior in the business market differ significantly from overt patterns of consumer behavior. For example, frequency of purchases and negotiation periods would be among the list of different buyer behavior patterns. Orders are larger and direct purchases involving no middlemen are common. Reciprocity arrangements and leasing are also common in business marketing [198, 199].

PART 7D: Completion

1. _____ are organizations that buy goods and services for one of the following three purposes: (1) to make other _____, (2) to resell to other _____ or to _____, and (3) to conduct the _____ _____.

2. Business marketing is the marketing of goods and services to _____.

3. About _____ percent of all manufactured products are sold to business users.

4. In total, there are approximately _____ business users in the United States.

5. Traditionally, business markets were referred to as _____ markets, but in this textbook they will be referred to as _____ markets.

6. The proportion of farmers in the total population and the number of farmers has been _____ while the number of large corporate farms is _____.

7. The basic activity of resellers involves buying products and services from _____ _____ and reselling these items in essentially the same form to the _____ _____.

8. A unique feature of government buying is the competitive _____ system.

9. The services market includes all _____ carriers, public _____, _____, _____, _____, and _____ firms.

10. The nonbusiness business market segment includes such institutions as _____, _____and _____, _____, _____ and other _____ organizations, _____ , _____ , and _____ .

11. By identifying niches where they have a(n) _____ or _____ advantage, U. S. firms have found markets for many things.

12. The four general demand characteristics for business goods are: (1) demand is _____, (2) demand is _____, (3) demand is _____, and (4) the market is _____.

13. _____ is the demand for business goods that is derived from the demand for _____ of which the business items play a part in manufacturing.

14. The demand for many business products is inelastic--that is, the demand for the product will respond _____ to changes in price.

15. A basic reason for the general inelasticity of demand for business goods is that the _____ of a single part or material is ordinarily an inconsequential portion of the _____ of the finished product.

16. From a marketing point of view, there are the following three factors to consider regarding the inelasticity of business market demand: (1) the price changes must occur throughout an entire _____ unlike the demand of a(n) _____; (2) _____-over the long run, the demand for a given business product is more _____ ; and (3) the relative importance of a specific business product in the _____ of a finished good. We may generalize to this extent: the more significant the _____ of a business product as a percentage of the total price of the finished good, the greater the _____ of demand for this business item.

17. An exception to the rule that demand is widely fluctuating is the demand for agricultural _____ meant for processing.

18. Since business buyers are knowledgeable, greater emphasis is placed on _____.

19. The factors affecting the market for business products are: (1) the _____ of potential business users, (2) their _____, (3) buying _____, and (4) buying _____.

20. The _____ system (SIC) enables a company to identify relatively small segments of its business market.

21. The SIC system divides _____ in the U.S. into ___ groups.

22. _____ by manufacturers is highly concentrated in relatively few firms.

23. There is a substantial _____ in many of the major industries and among business users as a whole.

24. If the product is usable by virtually all firms in only one or two industries, it has a(n) _____ market.

25. If the product is usable by many industries, its market is said to be broad or _____.

26. The purchasing power of business users can be measured either by the _____ of business users or by their _____.

27. Firms selling to manufacturers might use as market indicators the number of _____, the number of _____, or the _____ added by the manufacturer.

28. Purchasing has become an important part of overall strategy for three reasons: (1) companies are making _____ and buying _____, (2) companies are under intense _____ and _____ pressures, and (3) more firms are developing long-term "_____" relationships.

29. Business buyers have two goals: to improve their own _____ in the firm, and to _____ their firm's position.

30. The systems approach divides the process into five stages: _____ recognition, identifying _____, evaluation of _____, the _____, and _____ behavior.

31. Three "buy classes" are: (1) _____ buying, (2) _____, and (3) _____.

32. Multiple buying influences occur in a buying center, which is defined as all the _____ or _____ who are involved in the process of making a decision to _____.

33. Some of the roles that may be played in a buying center are: _____, _____, _____, _____, and _____.

34. Nine overt patterns of buyer behavior in the business market which differ significantly from the overt patterns of consumer purchasing power are: (1) _____ purchasing, (2) nature of the _____, (3) _____ of purchase, (4) _____ of order, (5) length of _____ period, (6) _____ arrangements, (7) demand for _____, (8) dependability of _____, and (9) _____ instead of buying.

35. Four leasing benefits from the lessee's point of view are: (1) leasing allows the user to keep his or her investment capital _____, (2) new firms can enter a new business with less _____, (3) leased products are usually serviced by the _____, and (4) leasing is particularly attractive to users who need equipment seasonally or _____.

PART 7E: True-False Questions

If the statement is true, circle "T"; if false, circle "F."

T F 1. The demand for business goods is derived from the demand for consumer goods.

T F 2. The Standard Industrial Classification (SIC) system divides all the manufacturing in the United States into 10 basic categories.

T F 3. A basic feature of the demand in business markets is its elasticity.

T F 4. The market demand for most classes of business goods fluctuates considerably more than the demand for consumer goods.

T F 5. Business sellers place more emphasis on personal sales people than do sellers of consumer products.

T F 6. If a product is used by many different industries, its market is said to be horizontal.

T F 7. Business buyers are always rational buyers.

T F 8. Farmers ordinarily are not considered a part of the business market.

T F 9. Virtually all mineral and all forest and sea products in their natural state are business goods.

107

T F 10. The classification of products as convenience, shopping, and specialty goods has no applicability to business products.

T F 11. In the business market the negotiation period is usually longer and the average order size is larger than in the consumer market.

T F 12. Consumer products are not handled by business users.

T F 13. The acceleration principle states that when the actions of all the individual firms in an industry are combined, the effect is widely fluctuating demand.

T F 14. In economic terms, resellers create all forms of utility: time, place, image, possession, and form.

T F 15. "Gatekeepers" are people who control the flow of purchasing information within the organization and between the buying firm and potential vendors.

PART 7F: Multiple Choice Questions

In the space provided write the letter of the answer that best fits the statement.

____1. Which of the following products probably has a vertical market rather than a horizontal one?
  A. Floor wax.   D. Paper products.
  B. Typewriters.   E. Lumber.
  C. Navigational equipment.

____2. The business market is best defined as:
  A. All people or firms who buy products and services either to use in their business or to use in making other goods.
  B. All manufacturers.
  C. Sales of all manufactured supplies, equipment, materials, and parts.
  D. Ultimate users of a product or service.
  E. All manufacturers, wholesalers, and retailers.

____3. All of the following are buying patterns of business users EXCEPT:
  A. Infrequent purchases.   D. Longer negotiation period.
  B. Larger orders.   E. Specified quality requirements.
  C. Indirect purchases.

____4. Resellers create all of the following economic utilities EXCEPT:
  A. Form.   B. Time.   C. Place.   D. Possession.   E. Image.

108

5. Compared with consumer buying patterns, we usually find in the business market that:
   A. The negotiation period is shorter.
   B. Fewer middlemen are used.
   C. Products are purchased more frequently.
   D. The average order size is smaller.
   E. Fewer people are involved in the buying decision.

6. In the area of leasing business products, a usual benefit to the lessees is that:
   A. Lessees can rent equipment seasonally.
   B. Rented products are serviced by the lessor.
   C. They keep their investment capital free for other uses.
   D. It is easier for them to enter a business.
   E. All of the above are benefits to a lessee.

7. All of the following are general demand characteristics that help to distinguish the business market from the consumer market EXCEPT:
   A. Demand is derived.   D. Demand is relatively constant.
   B. Demand is inelastic.   E. The market is well informed.
   C. Demand is widely fluctuating.

8. Business buying motives tend to be:
   A. Practical and unemotional.
   B. To achieve the optimum combination of price, quality, and service.
   C. Influenced by buyers' attitudes, perceptions, and values.
   D. Influenced by buyers' self-interest.
   E. All of the above.

9. In a buying center, the person who sets the specifications and aspects of buying decisions because of his or her (1) technical expertise, (2) financial position, or (3) political power in an organization is the:
   A. User. B. Influencer. C. Decider. D. Gatekeeper. E. Buyer.

10. Business goods are different from consumer goods because of:
    A. Cost.
    B. Their ultimate use.
    C. The urgency of the purchase decision.
    D. The technical requirements of the purchase.
    E. The expense of making a wrong decision.

11. An example of a concentrated industry is:
    A. Concrete and gravel.   D. Women's dresses.
    B. Commercial printing.   E. Fresh meat.
    C. Light bulbs.

__12. All of the following are stages in the total buying process EXCEPT:
- A. Problem recognition.
- B. Evaluating alternatives.
- C. Negotiating with buyers.
- D. Purchase decision.
- E. Postpurchase behavior.

__13. In a buying center, the person who makes the actual buying decision regarding the product and the supplier is the:
- A. User. B. Influencer. C. Decider. D. Gatekeeper. E. Buyer.

__14. All of the following are considered part of the services market for business EXCEPT:
- A. Mining companies.
- B. Transportation firms.
- C. Public utilities.
- D. Insurance companies.
- E. Real estate firms.

__15. All of the following are examples of a horizontal business market EXCEPT:
- A. Grease.
- B. Typing paper.
- C. Window cleaners.
- D. Mechanical tomato harvesters.
- E. Lubricating oil.

PART 7G: Matching Questions

In the space provided write the number of the word or expression from column 1 that best fits the description in column 2.

1	2
1. Business market	___ a. Business or institutional organizations that buy products either to use in making other products or to use in their own business.
2. Business users	
3. Buy classes	___ b. Demand derived from the demand for consumer products in which that business product is used.
4. Buyers	
5. Buying-decision process	___ c. Demand that responds very little to changes in price.
6. Contract farming	___ d. Products that are usable by virtually all firms in only one or two industries.
7. Deciders	
8. Derived demand	___ e. Routine purchases.
9. Direct purchase	___ f. The business of "trade relations" departments.

110

10. Farm market

11. Gatekeepers

12. Government market

13. Horizontal business markets

14. Inelastic demand

15. Influencers

16. Leasing goods

17. Modified rebuys

18. New-task buying

19. Nonbusiness market

20. Reciprocity

21. Reseller market

22. Services market

23. SIC system

24. Straight rebuys

25. Users

26. Vertical business markets

___ g. A firm that agrees to furnish a farmer with supplies and equipment to grow a crop.

___ h. Selling to universities.

___ i. A federal industrial classification system.

___ j. A market consisting of a product that is usable by many industries.

___ k. People who control the flow of purchasing information within the organization and between the buying firm and potential vendors.

___ l. People who make the actual buying decision regarding the product and the supplier.

___ m. Deciding to rent equipment rather than buy it.

PART 7H: Problems and Applications

1. How can a business marketer make use of the SIC system?

2. Suppose you know that each gas station uses at least one battery charger, and that the useful life of a battery charger is 10 years. How would you use the SIC system to determine the market potential?

3.   Assume you are a firm selling work gloves and you would like to estimate the buying power of business users in Texas. Decide how you would do this and report your results in a memo to your instructor.

4.   It has been said that there is nothing that a large university is not likely to buy. Interview your college or university purchasing officer and in a memo to your instructor describe how the university purchases one of the following items:

A. stop signs	D. starter pistols	G. floor wax
B. meat slicers	E. cadavers	H. piano tuning
C. violins	F. tensiometers	I. basketball nets

5.   Find out the SIC code and description for wholesaling bakeries. Where would you find how many there are in the United States? In each state?

6.   Business buyers are people too. Sometimes it is not just a matter of cold, hard facts that causes them to buy, but psychological factors as well. After reviewing Chapter 7, write a report to your instructor discussing the psychological factors that may cause professional buyers to behave as they do.

7.   Office supplies (staplers, fax paper, file folders, etc.), personal computers, and small hand tools (pliers, screwdrivers, crescent wrenches, etc.) are items bought by both business users and households. Describe the purchase process for these items for each of the two groups. In what ways is the buying decision the same? In what ways is it different?

8.   Could households benefit from using the rational approach favored by business buyers? For what sort of products might this approach be used to advantage?

PART 7I: Exercise

In this chapter, your authors introduced the Standard Industrial Classification (SIC) system. There follows a list of manufacturers' SIC numbers. First, translate the number into its appropriate manufacturing category. To do this, consult Executive Office of the President, Office of Management and Budget, *Standard Industrial Classification Manual, 1987* (Springfield, VA: National Technical Information Service, 1987). Then match the manufacturing category with the appropriate city. In each case, it is one of the city's leading industries.

For example, 2011 is the SIC number for meat packing plants. This matches with Dakota City, Nebraska, site of one of Iowa Beef's largest meat processing plants.

SIC Number	Manufacturing Category	City	SIC Number
2011	Meat packing plants	Akron, Ohio	
2041		Baltimore, Maryland	
2082		Bayonne, New Jersey	
2084		Brigham Canyon, Utah	
2092		Canton, Ohio	
2111		Coos Bay, Oregon	
2421		Dakota City, Nebraska	2011
2721		Detroit, Michigan	
2771		Elkhart, Indiana	
2819		Gary, Indiana	
2911		Golden, Colorado	
3011		Kansas City, Missouri	
3312		Midland, Michigan	
3331		Minneapolis, Minnesota	
3531		Napa Valley, California	
3635		Peoria, Illinois	
3674		New York, New York	
3711		Seattle, Washington	
3721		"Silicon Valley," California	
3931		Winston-Salem, N. Carolina	

PART 7J: A Real World Case: Purchasing: The Fundamentals

Recently I heard from a reader, and for a writer that's always a gratifying experience. In this case it was particularly gratifying because the writer was calling about an article I had written more than seven years ago. It was entitled, "Back to Basics." The reader called to say that the message of the article is as appropriate today as it was then. His only suggestion was that its title should read, "Forward to Fundamentals."

With that in mind, let's reiterate the "basics," but express them as "fundamentals."

1. Purchasing is a prime value-contributing function, accountable for spending the largest single element of operating costs and sales income. By reason of its effect on inventories, plant and equipment investment, and company cash flow, purchasing has a significant impact on corporate profitability. Admittedly, it provides service and support to other value-creating functions. But that must not obscure its role as a profit (and loss) contributor.

2. Like other value contributing functions, purchasing must be managed so that it can achieve identified corporate objectives. The time is long past when purchasing performance could be measured by narrow engineering, manufacturing, or plant criteria.

- <u>Markets and competition have become global</u>, so that decisions on sourcing must reflect not only considerations of local supply and demand, but must also consider domestic and international strategies.

- <u>Markets have become highly volatile</u>. Sharp gyrations in currencies, copper, petroleum, and other commodities are increasing the risks of commitment. Those risks affect not only currency and commodity valuations, but also commodity availability. Effective purchasing demands that commitments be made within the guidelines of corporate risk criteria.

- <u>Technology is exploding</u>. What was state-of-the-art two years ago may be obsolete today. Obsolescence affects not only what we produce and how we produce it, but also how we sell it. Purchasing performance must be geared not only to improving product and plant productivity, but also to speeding up the process of innovation and new product introduction.

3. When purchasing is managed as a value-contributing function, it serves as a catalyst, synergizing its actions with those of other functions and outside suppliers.

- It becomes involved in new product planning and development, influencing marketing and engineering decisions as they relate to material specifications, source selection, future availability, and cost.

- It plays an active role on matters of make-or-buy; on questions of expanding product lines through internal manufacture or through vendor buy-outs.

- It interfaces with marketing, manufacturing, and finance to establish desired levels of inventory, turnover rates, delivery quantities and frequencies--and meshes these with supplier capabilities for optimal results.

- It integrates supplier resources and technology with internal resources on a continuing basis, thereby enhancing our technical and strategic position.

4. Managing purchasing as a value-contributing function demands the effective managing of resources--manpower, time, money, and information. This means that we must plan and allocate these resources according to their value-creating, profit-contributing potential.

Unfortunately, we too often allocate resources more to facilitate the service and support aspect of purchasing. We staff up to process requisitions, expedite purchasing orders, respond and react to questions and complaints from engineers, planners, production, and maintenance people.

If purchasing is to be a value-contributing function, it must recognize the actions and activities that create value. They improve vendor quality, delivery, and price performance. They avoid cost, reduce cost, increase our income, or improve our cash flow. They enhance our marketing, engineering, or production capabilities and are consistent with our business and financial

114

objectives. And once we recognize those actions and activities, we must allocate resources accordingly.

5. When purchasing acts in a value-contributing capacity, it is dedicated to a continuing process of self-improvement and innovation. Both the reality and perception of value change. What was adequate at one point in time, may be woefully inadequate later. Purchasing must constantly develop the technical, analytical, and negotiating skills of its people. It must expand and refine its information sources and systems. It must set clearer and more measurable criteria for evaluating suppliers and for assessing its own performance. And it must be firmly committed to the proposition that it can and does impact the bottom line.

———————

Source: Louis J. DeRose, "Forward to Fundamentals," *Purchasing World*, July 1988, p. 39. Reprinted with permission of Purchasing World, 1988.

———————

___1. The author is advocating the application of his "fundamentals" to:
   A. New-task buying.   D. All of the above.
   B. Straight rebuying.   E. None of the above.
   C. Modified rebuying.

___2. The major points of the article are directed toward:
   A. Users. B. Influencers. C. Deciders. D. Gatekeepers. E. Buyers.

PART 7K: **Answers to Questions**

PART 7D: Completion
1. Business users/goods and services/business users/consumers/organization's operations
2. business users
3. 50
4. 15 million
5. industrial/business
6. decreasing/increasing
7. supplier organizations/resellers' customers
8. bidding
9. transportation/utilities/financial/ insurance/legal/real estate
10. churches/colleges/universities/museums/ hospitals/health/political parties/labor unions/charitable
11. quality/performance
12. derived/inelastic/widely fluctuating/well informed
13. Derived demand/consumer goods
14. very little
15. cost/total cost
16. industry/single firm/time/elastic/cost/cost/ elasticity
17. products
18. personal selling
19. number/purchasing power/motives/habits
20. Standard Industrial Classification/SIC
21. all types of businesses/10
22. Value added
23. regional concentration
24. vertical
25. horizontal
26. expenditures/sales volume
27. employees/plants/dollar value
28. less/more/quality/time/partnering
29. position/further
30. need/alternatives/alternatives/purchase decision/postpurchase
31. new task/straight rebuys/modified rebuys
32. individuals/groups/purchase
33. users/influencers/deciders/ gatekeepers/buyers
34. direct/relationship/frequency/size/ negotiation/reciprocity/servicing/ supply/leasing
35. for other purposes/capital outlay/lessors/ sporadically

PART 7E: True-False Questions
1. T 2. T 3. F 4. T 5. T 6. T
7. F 8. F 9. T 10. T 11. T 12. F
13. T 14. F 15. T

PART 7F: Multiple Choice Questions
1. C 2. A 3. C 4. A 5. B 6. E
7. D 8. E 9. B 10. B 11. C 12. C
13. C 14. A 15. D

PART 7G: Matching Questions
a. 2 b. 8 c. 14 d. 26 e. 24 f. 20
g. 6 h. 19 i. 23 j. 13 k. 11 l. 7
m. 16

116

PART THREE

PRODUCT

117

CHAPTER 8

PRODUCT PLANNING AND DEVELOPMENT

PART 8A: Chapter Goals

After studying this chapter, you should be able to explain:

- The meaning of the word *product* in its fullest sense
- What a "new" product is
- The classification of consumer and business products
- The relevance of these product classifications to marketing strategy
- The importance of product innovation
- The steps in the product-development process
- The criteria for adding a product to a company's line
- Adoption and diffusion processes for new products
- Organizational structures for product planning and development

119

PART 8B: **Key Terms and Concepts**

1. Product	[210]	15. New-product development process	[223]
2. Consumer products	[212]	16. Business analysis	[223]
3. Business products	[212]	17. Market tests	[223]
4. Convenience goods	[213]	18. Test marketing	[223]
5. Shopping goods	[214]	19. Adoption process	[227]
6. Specialty goods	[214]	20. Diffusion	[227]
7. Unsought goods	[215]	21. Stages in the adoption process	[227]
8. Raw materials	[216]	22. Innovation adopter categories	[227]
9. Fabricating materials and parts	[217]	23. Innovation characteristics affecting adoption rates	[229]
10. Installations	[218]	24. Product-planning committee	[230]
11. Accessory equipment	[218]	25. New-product department	[230]
12. Operating supplies	[219]	26. Venture team	[231]
13. New product	[221]	27. Product manager	[231]
14. New-product strategy	[222]		

PART 8C: Summary

In order for a company to be successful today, it must have a well-defined program of new-product development. This program tends to be the cornerstone of a company's entire marketing program. For, if a company is successful in the development of new products, it has a good chance of being successful in its other marketing activities.

There is no agreement on a definition of a product. Narrow product definitions examine the physical characteristics, while broad definitions look not only at the physical aspects, but to the broader consumer aspects as well [210]. In marketing circles, greater weight is placed on product analysis from a consumer point of view than a company or production point of view. Products can be classified into two broad categories--consumer goods and business products [212]. Then each of these groups is further subdivided, because a different marketing program is required for each sub-group.

With the increasing spectrum of goods and services available to a consumer and the increasing levels of the consumer's standard of living, product development becomes a more critical element in the marketing mix [219]. Most products today do not constitute necessities for consumers, but they add to their comfort or well-being.

There are six steps in the development process for new products: idea generation, screening and evaluation of ideas, business analysis, product development, test marketing, and commercialization [222]. The early steps are especially important. If the firm can drop a product early on, a lot of time, effort, and expense can be avoided. The manufacturer and middleman must examine various criteria in their "go, no-go" decision meetings. Important among these is to ask if the product will fit from a marketing, production, and financial point of view. The key criterion is this: "Is there adequate market demand for the product?" Management should understand the adoption and diffusion processes for a new product. Adopters of a new product can be divided into five categories, depending on how quickly they adopt a given innovation [227]. In addition, there usually is a group of nonadopters.

Research has shown that the organization itself stands as a barrier to new product development [230]. It is important that top management be deeply committed to product innovation and give it their creative support. The firms that are reasonably successful in product innovation use one of four organizational structures for new-product development: product-planning committees, new-product departments, a product-manager system, or a venture team [230].

Product planning and development in the future will take on additional importance and create an opportunity for the discerning marketing firm as it goes about the business of providing new products. The consumer, with his greater discretionary purchasing power, does not just buy a product, but instead purchases a solution to a consumption problem. The product, in the final analysis, is just a tool consumers use to add to their comfort or well-being.

PART 8D: Completion

1. A product is defined in a narrow sense as a set of _____ assembled in a(n) _____ form.

2. The broad definition of a product introduces the concept that consumers are buying _____ that satisfy their _____.

3. Products are not necessarily physical or tangible but may be a(n) _____, a(n) _____, a(n) _____, or a(n) _____.

121

4. Any change in a feature of a product, no matter how minor, creates another _____.

5. The authors define a product as a(n) _____ of tangible and intangible attributes, including _____, _____, _____, _____, and _____, plus the _____ and _____ of the seller.

6. Products can initially be classified into two categories: _____ products and _____ products.

7. Based on consumer _____, consumer products are further classified as follows: _____ goods, _____ goods, _____ goods, and _____ goods.

8. There are several significant classifications of convenience goods: (1) customers have adequate knowledge of the particular product _____ going out to buy it; (2) it is bought with a minimum of _____ on their part; and (3) consumer are willing to accept any of several _____.

9. _____ are tangible products for which customers usually wish to compare quality, price, and style in several stores before buying. The search will continue as long as the customer believes the _____ from additional search are greater than the additional cost that might be incurred.

10. In terms of the consumer aspects of specialty goods, buyers: (1) have a strong _____ preference, and (2) are willing to expend considerable _____ in buying them.

11. _____ include new products that the consumer is not yet aware of and products that right now the consumer does not want.

12. The business goods classification used here is based on the broad _____ of the product.

13. _____ are business goods that will become a part of another tangible product and that have received no processing at all other than that necessary for physical handling.

14. Because there is little brand or other product differentiation for raw materials, competition is built around _____ and assurances that the producer can _____ the product specified.

15. Fabricating materials are business goods that become a part of the _____ product.

16. Fabricating materials will undergo further _____.

17. Fabricating parts will be assembled with no further change in _____.

18. Normally, buying decisions for fabricating materials and parts are based on the _____ and _____ provided by the seller.

19. Installations are _____ business products. An example would be large generators in a dam. The differentiating characteristic of installations is that they set the _____ of operations in a firm.

20. _____ is used in the operations of a business firm. Accessory equipment does not become an actual part of the _____. Examples are office equipment and motor vehicles.

21. Operating supplies are the _____ of the business sector; they are short-lived, low-priced items usually bought with fairly little _____. Examples would be pencils and floor wax.

22. Products go through a(n) _____, just as people do.

23. The product life cycle concept is important to marketing for two reasons: (1) it reminds us that products become _____, and (2) as the product ages, _____ decline.

24. Increased _____ has made product planning more important.

25. The cure for "product indigestion" is to develop really _____.

26. Although about ____ percent of new products fail, there is still a torrent of new product _____.

27. _____ products are truly unique.

28. Products may not be innovative but significantly different from _____ ones.

29. _____ products are new to a particular company but not new to the market.

30. The purpose of an effective overall _____ is the identity of the _____ the new product will play in the company's corporate and marketing goals.

31. The development of new products in well-managed firms goes through _____ steps or stages.

32. Management must find some means for the generation of _____ ideas.

33. After a company generates the product ideas, it must _____ them.

34. In the _____ phase, the new-product idea is expanded into a concrete _____.

123

35. When a product idea is first converted into an actual product, the step is called _____ _____.

36. In the _____ phase of product development, in-use tests are undertaken to assure that the product has a chance to be successful.

37. The final step in new-product development is called _____.

38. In evaluating new products, manufacturers often use the following seven criteria in their decision-making process: (1) there should be adequate _____; (2) the product should satisfy key _____ criteria; (3) the product should be compatible with _____ standards; (4) the product should fit into the firm's present _____ structure; (5) the product should be in keeping with the company's _____ and _____; (6) the product should fit into the firm's present _____ capability; and (7) there should be no _____ problems.

39. In considering the adoption of new products, middlemen should: (1) consider their relations with the _____, (2) have compatible distribution _____ and _____, and (3) should satisfy key _____ criteria.

40. The _____ is the process by which the innovation spreads through a social system over time.

41. _____ are venturesome consumers who are the first to adopt an innovation.

42. It is important that a firm be able to identify and then communicate with the _____ category of consumers because this market segment contains the greatest share of _____.

43. The _____, a deliberate group, represents about 34 percent of the market.

44. The next category of adopter also represents 34 percent of the market. These persons tend to be _____ and usually adopt innovation only as a response to social pressure from their peers. They are called the _____.

45. The last group of people in the adoption process are called _____. They are _____ and constitute about 16 percent of the population.

46. There are five basic characteristics of innovations that affect their adoption rate: (1) relative _____, (2) _____, (3) _____, (4) _____, and (5) _____.

47. A new-product development program needs _____ attention if it is to have a

chance of being successful. And it must be _____.

48. _____committees will be made up of representatives from the marketing, production, finance, engineering, and research departments.

49. A new-product department is _____, with the department head reporting directly to the president.

50. A venture team is composed of representatives from _____, _____, _____, and _____.

51. The biggest problem in the product-manager system is that a company will give the person in charge great _____ but little _____.

PART 8E: True-False Questions

If the statement is true, circle "T"; if false, circle "F."

T F 1. Convenience goods have very short channels of distribution.

T F 2. An example of a fabricating part is a button for sweaters.

T F 3. In a narrow sense, products are purely physical things.

T F 4. The product-manager organizational structure does not lend itself to use in a very large company.

T F 5. The biggest problem facing the product-manager form of product development is that a company often saddles these managers with great responsibility, but provides them with little authority.

T F 6. There is organizationally no "best way" to plan for new products.

T F 7. A product is new if the intended market perceives it that way.

T F 8. Forklift trucks and office desks are examples of operating supplies.

T F 9. The classification of products as convenience, shopping, specialty, and unsought goods has no applicability to industrial products.

T F 10. "Product indigestion" is a result of too many "me-too" products.

125

T F 11. Test marketing comes early in the new-product development process.

T F 12. The single most important criterion in deciding whether to add a new product to a firm's existing product assortment is: "Is this convenient to make?"

T F 13. A six-pack of Coors beer bought in a supermarket for cash at noon is a different product from the same six-pack of Coors bought at midnight at a convenience store on a credit card.

T F 14. Laggards make up the largest group of innovation adopters.

T F 15. A Ford automobile should always be considered a shopping good.

PART 8F: Multiple Choice Questions

In the space provided write the letter of the answer that best fits the statement.

____ 1. Which of the following is the best organization structure for new-product planning and development?
   A. Product planning committee.   D. Product-manager system.
   B. New-product department.   E. Any of the above.
   C. Venture team.

____ 2. An example of a really innovative product would be:
   A. A new lemon-lime soft drink.   D. All of the above.
   B. A new freeze-dried coffee.   E. None of the above.
   C. A new digital watch.

____ 3. All of the following departments are generally represented on a new-product planning committee EXCEPT:
   A. Marketing.   C. Accounting.   E. Engineering.
   B. Production.   D. Finance.

____ 4. Generally, which of the following is the responsibility of the new-product manager?
   A. Developing market plans.   D. Developing a field sales force.
   B. Determination of advertising. E. All of the above.
   C. Preparation of budgets.

____ 5. The adopter category with the largest number of opinion leaders is the:
   A. Innovators.   C. Late majority.   E. Early majority.
   B. Early adopters. D Laggards.

126

____ 6. A product is a:
   A. Symbol.
   B. Set of tangible physical and chemical attributes.
   C. Need-satisfier.
   D. All of the above.
   E. None of the above.

____ 7. The degree to which a new product idea may be sampled on some limited basis is called:
   A. Relative advantage.
   D. Trialability.
   B. Compatibility.
   E. Observability.
   C. Complexity.

____ 8. The adopter category with the smallest number of people is the:
   A. Innovators.
   D. Late majority.
   B. Early adopters.
   E. Laggards.
   C. Early majority.

____ 9. The steps in the new-product development process are:
   A. Test marketing.
   D. Product development.
   B. Business analysis.
   E. Idea generation and evaluation.
   C. Commercialization.
   A. ABCDE   B. BACED   C. EBDAC   D. EDBAC   E. EBADC

___10. All of the following are producers' criteria for new products EXCEPT:
   A. Adequate market demand.
   D. Fits the company image.
   B. No legal objections.
   E. Fits from the financial standpoint.
   C. Meets labor union needs.

___11. Promotional activity is most important for which of the following classes of business goods?
   A. Raw materials.
   D. Accessory equipment.
   B. Fabricating parts.
   E. Operating supplies.
   C. Installations.

___12. In what area are customer brand preferences usually strongest?
   A. Shopping goods.
   D. Fashion merchandise.
   B. Impulse goods.
   E. Business goods.
   C. Specialty goods.

___13. The cure for "product indigestion" is:
   A. Innovation.
   D. Higher prices.
   B. Imitation.
   E. Meeting competition.
   C. Collusion.

___14. Product innovations are important because:
  A. As products age, their profits decline.
  B. Competition makes products obsolete.
  C. Consumers are becoming more selective.
  D. Natural resources are becoming more scarce.
  E. All of the above.

___15. In organizing for new-product development, setting up a small, multidisciplinary group with representatives from engineering, production, finance, and marketing research is called a:
  A. Product-planning committee.   D. Venture team.
  B. New-product department.   E. Multidisciplinary committee.
  C. Product manager organization.

PART 8G: Matching Questions

In the space provided write the number of the word or expression from column 1 that best fits the description in column 2.

	1		2

1. Accessory equipment

        ___ a. A set of tangible and intangible attributes including packaging, color, price, quality, and brand, plus the services and reputation of the seller.

2. Adoption process

3. Business products

        ___ b. An individual's decision-making act.

4. Consumer products

        ___ c. An example is floor wax.

5. Convenience goods

        ___ d. A means of developing new products while avoiding organizational "red tape."

6. Diffusion of innovation

        ___ e. A class of industrial products used to aid the production operations of a business user.

7. Fabricating materials

8. Installations

        ___ f. Business goods that become part of another physical product and that have received no processing at all.

9. New-product department

10. Operating supplies

        ___ g. New products that the consumer is not yet aware of.

11. Product

12. Product development

13. Product manager

14. Product-planning committee

15. Raw materials

16. Shopping goods

17. Specialty goods

18. Test marketing

19. Unsought goods

20. Venture team

____ h. Manufactured business goods--the long-lived, expensive, major equipment of a business user.

____ i. The process by which innovation is communicated within social systems over time.

____ j. Goods possessing a strong brand preference for which a group of buyers are willing to make a special buying effort.

PART 8H: Problems and Applications

1. Go to a local retail store and talk with a department head to determine how he evaluates new products for his store to carry.

2. The manufacturer of completely salt-free, low-calorie frozen dinners is attempting to determine who the innovators for his product might be. Identify for him the most likely innovators. What appeals would you use in promoting the product?

3. As noted in the text, there have been few really new products developed in the last five years, and most products are simply changes of existing or past products. Make a list of consumer products that you consider new and original and that have been introduced to the market within the last two or three years.

4. Interview 10 students (college or high school) and ask them if they have any problems with the writing instruments they now use. Also ask them if they have any suggestions for improvement of the writing instrument they now use. Record the answers. Write a memo to your instructor summarizing your results. Also include a section on implications for product planning and development for writing instruments.

5. Design a model for screening new-product ideas for a firm in one of the following fields:
   A. Materials handling   B. Automobile parts   C. Razor blades   D. Sporting goods

6. Explain why a department store is an industrial user. What types of products and services are involved?

PART 8I (a): Exercise

Marketers, especially in fashion-related businesses, have been interested in how consumers come to adopt new products. Research has made evident five adopter categories: innovators, early adopters, early majority, late majority, and laggards.

Below are ten psychographic characterizations, five male and five female. Place the name of each character beside the adopter category to which he or she belongs.

Adopter Category

Innovators

Early adopters

Early majority

Late majority

Laggards

1. Angelo is a high school dropout. He has worked in a factory for nine years. He married at 19 and has two children. He is unhappy and cynical. He fantasizes by going to the movies (occasionally an X-rated one) and reading girlie magazines. His world is characterized by one word: "frustration."

2. Boyd is a successful professional. He is divorced, the father of a 10-year-old. His speech is confident, perhaps owing to his award-winning work on the college debating team. He is fashion-conscious, dressing the way he pleases. He uses his three credit cards to buy most things. His clients tease him about being a "clothes horse."

3. Christopher is a devoted family man. The proud father of three youngsters, his greatest pleasure is taking them fishing or playing ball with them. A confirmed "do-it-yourselfer," he feels his home is the best possible psychological and financial investment he can make. He is brand-conscious but tries to get the best value for his money. A high school graduate, he is a journeyman machinist.

4. Doyle is a self-made businessman. He had to go to work at 14 when his father died. He finished high school at 28 by taking night school classes. He likes leisure suits and wash-and-wear shirts (short sleeves) because "they are practical." He watches TV and spends a lot of time talking back to it. He argues easily, especially when someone such as his daughter tells him "opportunity is dead in America."

5. Edward is a retired widower. He putters about his too-large home. He fantasizes about

the past, wishing with all his heart that he could relive parts of it. His earlier caution toward strangers has given way to outright suspicion. This includes anything "new-fangled." Eisenhower was the last president he really trusted. He pays cash for everything.

6.   Francie is a contented housewife. A high school graduate, she married her "steady" and promptly had three children. Although the honeymoon is definitely over, she still loves her husband and is proud of him for being a good provider. She watches "soap operas" and the talk shows when the children are taking their naps. Her spare time is given over to her family and church. She has been happy all her life.

7.   Gayle has a master's degree, is married to a professional man, has one child, and lives in the suburbs where she is active in community affairs. She is a club woman and hates "soap operas." Indeed, time is so precious she hardly has time to accomplish all she sets out to do.

8.   Hannah is on Social Security with her husband. Her days melt one into the other, broken only by Sundays, when she goes to church alone. Her children and grandchildren seldom visit but they telephone occasionally. She has worked in the polling booth for 17 years and is proud of her work for the country. Television and an occasional book are her only entertainment.

9.   Inez discovered women's liberation when her husband of 9 years deserted her and their two sons. She is angry and it shows in the way she votes, talks to people at the store, and even treats the dog. She has started taking night classes in women's studies at the local community college. She reads voraciously and watches TV news and public affairs programs.

10.   Jean is cool and elegant. Although 36, she looks 25. And small wonder since she is so self-assured, so weight-conscious, and such a cosmopolitan dresser. She and her wealthy husband are moderate Republicans. Some of the other wives at the country club don't quite know what to make of her. Said one: "If you ask me, she leads a double life."

PART 8I (b): **Exercise**

1. Classify the following goods indicating whether they are convenience, shopping, specialty, or unsought goods. Assume you are your present age and have your present income.

Item	Convenience	Shopping	Specialty	Unsought
1. Automobile, sedan 2. Blender 3. Bread 4. Camera, 35mm 5. Carpeting				

Item	Convenience	Shopping	Specialty	Unsought
6. Chain saw				
7. Coffee beans				
8. Drugs, prescription				
9. Electric shaver				
10. Fur coat, ladies				
11. Heating pad				
12. Hot dogs				
13. Gourmet ice cream				
14. Milk, homogenized				
15. Mobile home				
16. Ring, engagement				
17. Saddle, western				
18. Shoes, jogging, men's				
19. TV, color				
20. Water bed				

2. Now assume your income is the same as it is at present but you are twice as old as you are now. Did any classifications change? Why?

3. Now assume your income has quadrupled but you are the same age as you are now. Did any classifications change? Why?

PART 8I (c): Exercise

1. The class will be divided into groups of about five or six students each.

2. Each group will have about 30 minutes to:

    a. Generate an idea for an entirely new and unique good or service in which:

        (1) Product features are identified.
        (2) Product distinctiveness is explained.
        (3) Market demand is estimated along with the product's potential profitability.

    b. Write a one-sentence statement that sets out the marketing concept for your company's new product.

    c. Develop a distinctive logo, name, and/or slogan for your product.

3.   Each group will be given a few minutes to present their new product idea to the class.

PART 7J: A Real World Case: Clearly Ahead

Last month a rather telling graphic depiction of the soft drink industry's current packaging mix appeared on the front page of *USA Today*. On a container basis, metal cans now account for 75 percent of domestic soft drink sales, followed by glass bottles at 14 percent and PET [polyethylene terephthalate] bottles at 11 percent. Traditionally, we've been accustomed to measuring package size on a volumetric basis, and the same numbers can be viewed from a slightly different perspective.

According to A.C. Nielsen, 1989 package share grew for both can and family-sized PET, while glass bottles experienced another year of share point erosion. More specifically, total foodstore can share jumped 3 share points to 39.4 percent of the mix. Two-liter share increased 0.2 points to 38.1 and 16-ounce and half-liter NR [no-return] bottles dropped 0.8 points from 8.6 in 1988 to 7.8 in 1989. And, while some glassmakers have hailed 20-ounce as the new single-serve packaging standard, combined sales of pint-sized and 20-ounce non-refillables slid 0.4 points from 8.7 to 8.4.

The trends we are witnessing may be rather obvious, but we should all take exception with those who would have us believe with the advent of large can multipacks, we are entering an era of the most significant packaging transition to occur since the late '50s. How can anyone overlook the overnight transition from 64-ounce glass to 2-liter plastic in 1978? What about the phenomenal growth of pre-labeled single service glass during the late '70s and early '80s? And, what about the disappearance of refillable soft drink bottles? Personally, I have a tough time rationalizing statements suggesting the soft drink industry may be moving to a single-package market in the not-too-distant future.

Sure, large can multipacks have been a tremendous driving force for volume growth during the past five years, but let's not be too quick to cast our final judgment. Six-packs still dominate the multipack mix, and some sources point to a sales advantage in excess of 4:1 vis-a-vis larger multiples. Let's also not forget traditional supermarkets and foodstores are only part of the current sales mix targeted by soft drink marketers.

Most industry veterans will agree availability and in-home inventory drive consumption. It's a smart business decision to make soft drinks available anywhere people congregate. It also behooves the smart marketer to increase the average customer transaction size by encouraging trade-ups to larger packages. This is hardly a new phenomenon. It is why the industry went from 32- to 48- to 64-ounce glass bottles before moving to 2-liter plastic. It's why Pepsi originally challenged Coke's 6.5-ounce bottle with "12 full ounces." We could go on with 16 and 20-ounce,and\3- and 4-liter, but the point should be clear--trading up is nothing new.

At the same time we should be aware of a few other factors that play a major role in shaping consumer purchasing behavior. Why are large 16-ounce glass multipacks limping along while large can multipacks are booming? What happened to two-, three- and four-bottle 2-liter multipacks? Some would have us believe price is the only consideration in the normal buying decision. If that were the case, we would all probably by drinking a lot more RC, and six-packs of cans would have to sell $1.05 to compete with 99-cent 2-liter bottles. Why would anyone pay 75 cents for a single can or 49 cents for a 12-ounce cup filled with ice and a little soda?

Isn't value a more important determinant of what sells in terms of soft drinks? And doesn't value connote a lot more than the "P" word? Maybe it means a convenient package that fits in the refrigerator when others don't. It could mean spending a buck for a drink at the corner gas station when the nearest grocery store is two miles and 14 traffic lights up the road. Value or perceived value is a relative measure that means different things to different people. A good value in one market may represent a downright lousy deal in another. And who decides what factors contribute to or represent value? You guessed it--consumers.

I'll agree pricing has a very big influence on this purchasing equation, but it is not the only contributing factor, as some would have us believe. I'd like one of these "P" word-prophets to explain the demise of 89-cent eight-packs of 16-ounce refillables.

There is an old adage in the retail trade that sums it up quite succinctly. "We promote what we sell and we sell what we promote." Maybe that helps explain what consumer preference is really all about. After all, not everyone walks beyond the end aisle with a fistful of coupons in one hand and a calculator in the other.

_____

Source: Bruce Oman, "A Clear Choice?" *Beverage World*, June 1990, p. 78. Used by permission Beverage World Magazine and Mr. Bruce Oman.

_____

___1. The article is arguing that as consumer goods the soft drink industry would consider soft drinks to be:
   A. Convenience goods.   D. Unsought goods.
   B. Shopping goods.   E. Any of the above.
   C. Specialty goods

___2. As business goods, soft drink packaging would be considered:
   A. Raw materials.   D. Accessory equipment.
   B. Fabricating materials   E. Operating supplies.
   C. Installations.

_____3. The author is emphasizing which of the following criteria for a new type of soft drink package?
  A. There should be adequate market demand.
  B. The product should fit from a financial standpoint.
  C. The product should be compatible with current environmental standards.
  D. The product should fit into the firm's present marketing structure.
  E. The product should fit in with existing production facilities.

PART 8K: Answers to Questions

PART 8D: Completion
1. attributes/identifiable
2. benefits/needs
3. service/place/person/idea
4. product
5. set/packaging/color/price/quality/ brand/services/reputation
6. consumer/business
7. buying behavior/convenience/shopping/ specialty/unsought
8. before/effort/brands
9. Shopping goods/benefits
10. brand/time and effort
11. Unsought goods
12. uses
13. Raw materials
14. price/deliver
15. finished
16. processing
17. form
18. price/service
19. manufactured/scale
20. Accessory equipment/finished product
21. "convenience goods"/effort
22. life cycle
23. obsolete/profits
24. consumer selectivity
25. new products
26. 80/introductions
27. Innovative
28. existing
29. Imitative
30. new-product strategy/role
31. six
32. new-product
33. screen
34. business analysis/business proposal
35. prototype development
36. market-test
37. commercialization
38. market demand/financial/environmental/ marketing/image/objectives/production/ legal
39. producer/policies/practices/financial
40. diffusion of innovation
41. Innovators
42. early-adopter/opinion leaders
43. early majority
44. skeptical/late majority
45. laggards/tradition-bound
46. advantage/compatibility/complexity/ trialability/observability
47. top management/soundly organized
48. Product-planning
49. small
50. engineering/production/finance/marketing research
51. responsibility/authority

PART 8E: True-False Questions
1. F 2. T 3. T 4. F 5. T 6. T
7. T 8. F 9. T 10. T 11. F 12. F
13. T 14. F 15. F

PART 8F: Multiple Choice Questions
1. E 2. E 3. C 4. E 5. B 6. D
7. D 8. A 9. C 10. C 11. C 12. C
13. A 14. E 15. D

PART 8G: Matching Questions
a. 11 b. 2 c. 10 d. 20 e. 1 f. 15
g. 19 h. 8 i. 6 j. 17

```
┌─────────────────────────┐
│                         │
│                         │
└─────────────────────────┘
┌─────────────────────────┐
│                         │
│      CHAPTER 9          │
│                         │
└─────────────────────────┘
┌─────────────────────────┐
│                         │
│     PRODUCT-MIX          │
│     STRATEGIES           │
│                         │
│                         │
│                         │
│                         │
│                         │
│                         │
└─────────────────────────┘
```

PART 9A: Chapter Goals

After studying this chapter, you should be able to explain:

- The difference between product mix and product line
- The major product mix-strategies:
- Positioning
- Expansion
- Trading up and trading down
- Managing a product throughout its life cycle
- Planned obsolescence
- Style and fashion
- The fashion-adoption process

- Alteration
- Contraction

137

PART 9B: Key Terms and Concepts

1. Product mix	[238]	15. Maturity stage [248]
2. Product mix breadth and depth	[238]	16. Decline stage [248]
3. Product line	[238]	17. Fad [249]
4. Positioning	[239]	18. Product abandonment [253]
5. Expansion of product mix	[242]	19. Planned obsolescence [254]
6. Line extension	[242]	20. Technological (functional) obsolescence [254]
7. Mix extension	[243]	21. Style (psychological or fashion obsolescence) [254]
8. Trading up	[244]	22. Style [254]
9. Trading down	[244]	23. Fashion [254]
10. Product alteration	[245]	24. Fashion adoption process [254]
11. Contraction of product mix	[245]	25. Fashion cycle [254]
12. Product life cycle	[246]	26. Trickle-down theory [255]
13. Introduction stage	[247]	27. Trickle-across theory [255]
14. Growth stage	[248]	28. Trickle-up theory [255]

PART 9C: Summary

Product mix strategies are the means by which the product element of the marketing mix is utilized in the development of the overall marketing program. There are a number of basic and fundamental product mix strategies. These could include positioning the product [239]; expanding the product mix by increasing the number of lines or the depth within a line [242]; trading up or trading down [244]; altering the design, package, or other product features of existing products [245]; and contracting the product mix [245].

The concept of the product life cycle is important to an understanding of the marketing implications at each stage (introduction, growth, maturity, decline, and abandonment) of the product's development [246]. The managing of a product as it moves through its product life cycle is an ongoing challenge to management--especially in the sales decline stage [253].

Some product strategies are highly controversial, such as the concept of planned obsolescence [253], built around the ideas of style, fashion, and the fashion cycle. Fashion, as a sociological and psychological phenomenon, is a reasonably predictable pattern of stylistic obsolescence [254]. Three patterns--the "trickle-down," "trickle-across," and "trickle-up"--are evident in the fashion adoption process [255]. Style obsolescence, in spite of its critics, is based upon consumer psychology and is accepted by many consumers.

PART 9D: Completion

1. The term _____ refers to the full list of all products offered for sale by the firm.

2. A(n) _____ is a group of products intended for essentially similar uses and possessing reasonably similar physical characteristics.

3. The ability to _____ a product in the market is a major determinant of a company's revenues and profits.

4. A product's _____ is the _____ the product projects relative to _____products and to other products marketed by the same company.

5. Positioning strategies include positioning in relation to: (1) a(n) _____, (2) a(n) _____ or _____, (3) _____ and _____, and (4) a(n) _____.

6. Another product mix strategy is to _____ the number of _____ and/or the _____within a line.

7. When a company adds a similar item to an existing line with the same brand name, this is termed _____.

8. Adding a new product line to the firm's present assortment is known as _____.

9. When a firm adds a higher-priced prestige product to its line to attract a higher-income market, this activity is called _____.

10. The seller also hopes the _____ of its new product will help the sale of its existing _____ products.

11. When a firm adds a lower-priced item to a line of prestige products in the hope of expanding its market opportunities, this is called _____.

12. Both trading up and trading down are _____ strategies because the new products may _____ buyers.

13. Rather than developing new products, firms often look toward _____ their existing products, a more _____ and less _____ strategy.

14. Alteration of the product may be achieved through redesigned _____.

15. _____ the product mix can take the form of either eliminating a(n) _____or _____ the assortment within a line.

16. A product life cycle consists of the _____over an extended period of time for all brands composing a(n) _____ category.

17. The product life cycle can be divided into four stages: _____, _____, _____, and _____.

18. In the introductory stage of the product life cycle, the firm's promotional program attempts to stimulate demand for the _____ product category rather than only the seller's _____.

19. During the growth stage, there is a tendency for the profits of the product to _____ near the end of the stage.

20. During the maturity phase of the product life cycle, the product profits to both producers and middlemen _____.

21. In the final stages of the product life cycle, the manufacturer is faced with the decision of whether or not to _____ the product.

22. The _____ of the life cycle varies among products.

23. A(n) _____ is a product or style that becomes popular overnight and then falls out of favor just as quickly.

24. A product may be in its _____ stage in one nation and in its _____ stage in another.

25. The _____ of the product life cycle curve for a product category can be controlled.

26. Some marketing executives prefer entering the market during the _____ stage rather than having to play catchup later.

27. However, there are compelling reasons for _____ entry.

140

28. During the growth stage of the life cycle, a company has to devise the right _____ for its brand in that _____ category.

29. A product's life may be extended during the maturity stage if it can be _____, by new _____, or by finding _____ for the product.

30. It is during the _____ stage that a company finds its greatest challenges in life cycle management.

31. Planned obsolescence has been classified into the following two major categories: (1) _____ or _____ obsolescence, which means obsolescence due to innovation; and (2) _____ obsolescence, which is intended to make people feel out of date if they continue to use existing products.

32. A(n) _____is a distinctive characteristic of a product.

33. A(n) _____ is any style which is popularly accepted by groups of people over a reasonably long period of time.

34. The concept of fashion is based upon deeply rooted _____ and _____ factors.

35. There are three basic theories of fashion adoption. In the _____ theory, fashion is adopted through a process of downward vertical flow through several socioeconomic classes.

36. The _____ theory states that the fashion adoption process takes place by horizontal flow _____ several socioeconomic classes.

37. In the _____ theory, the cycle is initiated by people in the lower sociological groups and then taken up by those in higher groups.

38. To be successful, managers must know the current stage of the _____ before they decide whether or not to carry a particular product.

PART 9E: True-False Questions

If the statement is true, circle "T"; if false, circle "F."

T F   1. In general, fads taper off slowly in their consumer acceptance.

T F   2. Consumers can make a fashion fail simply by not buying it.

T F 3. "Style" obsolescence and "psychological" obsolescence mean the same thing.

T F 4. Positioning deals with a product's image.

T F 5. When a chain of hamburger outlets adds a two-patty "whopper," they are engaged in trading up.

T F 6. The most risky and expensive stage of the product life cycle is the introductory stage.

T F 7. There is wide agreement that the best entry strategy is to delay entry until the market has been tested.

T F 8. In some industries, redesigning a product has a marked influence on a company's product mix.

T F 9. The theory that best explains the adoption process for most fashion is the trickle-across theory.

T F 10. A fad cannot have its own product life cycle.

T F 11. Consumers may actually dictate that a company follow a strategy of planned obsolescence.

T F 12. A style is a particular kind of fashion.

T F 13. The product mix has both breadth and depth.

T F 14. Trading up and trading down are both risky strategies.

T F 15. It is not possible for a product to be in one stage of the product life cycle for the international market while it is in another stage for the domestic market.

PART 9F: Multiple Choice Questions

In the space provided write the letter of the answer that best fits the statement.

____ 1. Generally, the riskiest and most expensive stage in the product life cycle is:
    A. Introduction. B. Maturity. C. Decline. D. Growth. E. Saturation.

____ 2. At which stage of the product life cycle do profits reach their highest level?
    A. Introduction.   D. Decline.
    B. Growth.   E. Abandonment.
    C. Maturity and saturation.

____3. When Bausch & Lomb, the optics manufacturers, announced that they were beginning to market a new alcohol-free mouth rinse (Clear Choice), this was an example of a product mix strategy called:
   A.   Trading up.   D.   Trading down.
   B.   Positioning the product.   E.   Planned obsolescence.
   C.   Expansion of product mix.

____4. Which of the following factors might influence changes in a firm's product mix?
   A.   The trend to avoiding cholesterol-laden food.
   B.   The trend to greater convenience in packaging.
   C.   An increased number of competitive products.
   D.   All of the above.
   E.   None of the above.

____ 5. Which of the following strategies did 7-UP use in their "Never had caffeine, never will" advertising campaign? Positioning:
   A.   In relation to a competitor.   D.   In relation to a target market.
   B.   By price.   E.   In relation to a product class.
   C.   By quality.

____6. An example of expanding the breadth of a company's product mix is:
   A.   3M added a system of office copiers to its line of Scotch Tapes.
   B.   A state university started a night school and adult education program.
   C.   General Motors' Pontiac discontinued the Fiero and added the Oldsmobile Reatta.
   D.   Campbell's added a line of low-salt soups.
   E.   Heinz added spicy ketchup to its lineup of ketchups.

____ 7. The word that comes closest to describing the concept of positioning in marketing is:
   A. "Image."   B. "Distribution."   C. "Promotion."   D. "Design."   E. "Target."

____8. Which of the following is an example of trading up?
   A.   RJR Industries merged with Nabisco.
   B.   Chevron added higher priced synthetic motor oil to its line.
   C.   A cigarette manufacturer added mentholated filter tips to its line.
   D.   A dress shop simplified the assortment of sizes and styles it carried.
   E.   Sears, Roebuck added H & R Block outlets to its stores.

____9. As a strategy, trading down is:
   A.   Dangerous because it may hurt the firm's reputation.
   B.   Dangerous since sales for the new item can come at the expense of older products.
   C.   Often confusing to consumers.
   D.   All of the above.
   E.   None of the above.

____10. Styles that begin in lower socioeconomic strata and are later accepted by other groups fall into the "trickle-_____ process."
    A. Down   B. Across   C. Up

____11. If Elizabeth Taylor were to begin wearing hats again and other women were to follow her lead, this would be an example of the "trickle-_____ process."
    A. Down   B. Across   C. Up

____12. The type of obsolescence thought to be socially and economically desirable is _____ obsolescence.
    A. Technological   B. Style   C. Psychological   D. Fashion

____13. An example of expanding the depth of a company's product mix is:
    A. Canon added office copiers to its line of cameras.
    B. Coca Cola added Cherry Coke to its line of soft drinks.
    C. Budweiser added snack foods to its line of beer.
    D. 3M added Post-it note pads to its line of Scotch Tapes.
    E. Sears Roebuck bought Dean Witter securities brokerage.

____14. When a firm adds a lower-priced item to its line of prestige products, it is called:
    A. Trading up.   D. Trading down.
    B. Positioning the product.   E. Planned obsolescence.
    C. Contracting the product mix.

____15. According to your authors, the greatest challenges in life cycle management are to be found in the _____ stage.
    A. Introduction   B. Growth   C. Maturity   D. Decline   E. Saturation

PART 9G: Matching Questions

In the space provided write the number of the word or expression from column 1 that best fits the description in column 2.

1	2
1. Fad	____a. Everything sold by a firm.
2. Fashion	____b. A distinctive manner of construction or presentation in any art, product, or endeavor.
3. Fashion adoption process	
4. Fashion cycle	____c. The image a product projects relative to competitive products marketed by the firm in question.

144

5. Line extension

6. Mix extension

7. Planned obsolescence

8. Positioning

9. Product life cycle

10. Product line

11. Product mix

12. Style

13. Style (fashion) obsolescence

14. Trading down

15. Trading up

16. Trickle-across

17. Trickle-down

18. Trickle-up

____ d. Adding a lower-priced item to a line of prestige products.

____ e. The strategy of making a product out-of-date.

____ f. A style that is popular for a long period of time.

____ g. A fashion cycle that moves within several social classes.

____ h. The wavelike movement of introduction, rise, popular culmination, and decline.

____ i. When a firm adds a similar item to an existing product line with the same brand name.

PART 9H: Problems and Applications

1. Expansion of product mix: a mail-order, auto parts business.

You and other members of your family have, for several years, operated an autodealership in the Portland, Oregon, shopping area dealing in domestic cars. Competition between domestic brands became particularly intense during the early 1990s. In addition, stiff competition has existed for several years from nearby foreign car dealerships. To find business elsewhere, you experimented with a number of new services, renting (short term) and leasing your present product mix. Because there are already a number of firms and individual auto consumers in these markets, it occurred to you instead to try to promote a small-scale, mail-order, auto parts business. After six months of operation, while you ran the auto dealership, mail-order sales amounted to $7,500. Your cost in flyers, mailing, and material was about $5,000. Your mailing list is up to 1,000 firms and individual consumers in the local area, selected on a random basis for you by a mail-order

145

listing company. Your present auto-dealer business, exclusive of mail order, grosses $3,300,000 per year.

Evaluate and make your recommendation in a memo to your instructor. Use, as a basis of your evaluation, the manufacturer's and middleman's criteria for addition of new-product line. Develop your own rating system.

2.   What is your position on planned obsolescence? Is it good or bad? Why?

3.   Central to the economic theories of the late Joseph Schumpeter of Harvard was the concept of "creative destruction." What did he mean by this and what does it have to do with technological obsolescence? Would he agree with your authors' views regarding technological obsolescence? Would a labor union leader or member answer the same way?

4.   Develop three strategies for extending the maturity stage of the product life cycle for hand-held calculators.

5.   Is there any possible reason why a company would insist on keeping a product well into the sales-decline stage even if it is losing money? Can you think of an example of such a product?

6.   Make a trip to your local supermarket and list all the laundry detergent products carried. Develop a tabulation sheet and record your findings by manufacturer. [Record: firm name, detergent type, package sizes, prices.]

     A.   What conclusion can you make about laundry detergents' product lines? And product mix?
     B.   What conclusions can you make about positioning the product?
     C.   What conclusion can you make concerning the strategy of product differentiation and market segmentation?
     D.   What observation can you make about breadth and depth dimensions of the detergent product mix?

PART 9I: Exercise

1.   After first drawing a typical product life cycle sales curve, mark on it where you would place each of the following products:

     a. Wringer washing machine   f. Refrigerator
     b. Black and white TV   g. Videocasette recorder (VCR)
     c. Color TV   h. Camcorder
     d. Personal computer   i. Automobile
     e. Backyard satellite dish   j. Mangle

Introduction	Growth	Maturity	Decline

2.   Defend your placement of each item.

3.   Rank, in order of importance, the elements of the marketing mix, by stage in the product life cycle, for any of the above durable goods.

Marketing Mix	Introduction	Growth	Maturity	Decline
Product				
Price				
Promotion				
Distribution				

4.   What conclusion can you make about the management of the marketing mix?

147

PART 9J: **A Real World Case: Potential Suicide**

Just three weeks after taking over as chief of Mercedes Benz, Helmut Werner is unleashing a makeover of the flagship of Daimler Benz, Germany's largest industrial company. In a dramatic break with decades of tradition, Werner proclaimed that the producer of luxury autos will make lower-priced vehicles.

They will include a subcompact "city car" that goes head-to-head with such autos as the soon-to-be-launched Renault Twingo, which will cost a mere $10,000 or so. Werner also wants to go into minivans and four-wheel-drive recreational vehicles. "If they can do it, it will cause a revolution at Mercedes," says Daniel T. Jones, an auto specialist at the Cardiff Business School in Wales.

Losing Ground Werner is responding to declining Mercedes sales and profits and a growing sense in the industry Mercedes vehicles are overpriced and too narrowly targeted. In recent years, Mercedes has lost ground to such high end Japanese introductions as Lexus and Infiniti. Also, it was passed in sales for the first time in 1992 by archrival BMW.

To pull off his revolution, Werner will have to do a sweeping overhaul of Mercedes' product development and manufacturing. He may be just the manager for the task. A 56-year-old finance specialist, Werner is credited with turning around Daimler's Freightliner truckmaking subsidiary and making it No. 1 in the U.S. market. Mercedes has already slashed 13,000 jobs from its 180,000 German payroll and eliminated several management levels, but Werner says that is not enough. "No one in the world is prepared to pay for German complacency on the cost front," he warns.

That's a thinly veiled signal to Germany's militant IG Metall labor union that something has be done about high labor costs. In another break from tradition, Mercedes is making cars outside of Germany. It is already assembling cars in South Korea and Mexico, and it has earmarked $570 million for a Spanish minivan plant. Now, says Werner, a full-car production facility in a foreign market is being considered.

But that's just the start. In a move that will rock Mercedes' engineer-dominated culture to its foundations, Werner wants to do away with the company's comfy cost-plus approach to pricing its cars. In the future, sticker prices will be set by a market-driven target price. Engineers and plant bosses will have to meet that price. The first test will be the new 190 model "Baby Benz," set to arrive this summer. Werner has decided to price it at under $25,000 in Germany. That's about the same as its predecessor, though it's loaded with $5,000 worth of extras.

Werner says costs in Germany can be cut about 30%. Industry mavens rate cost-paring as the makeover's litmus test. "The really key issue is building to a price," says Michael Smith, manager of DRI Europe's London-based auto consultancy. "It's quite clear Mercedes will have to do that to compete."

However, Werner's new-product strategy has left some auto analysts gasping--and worried. "This could be suicidal," warns one London stockbroker. "Who wants a Mercedes Corolla instead of a dream car?" But fierce competition and last year's 30% drop in Mercedes' pretax profit to an estimated $1.3 billion don't leave Werner much choice.

_____

Source: John Templeton, "Mercedes is Downsizing--And That Includes the Sticker," *Business Week*, February 8, 1993, p. 38. Reprinted from February 8, 1993 issue of *Business Week* by special permission, copyright © 1993 by McGraw-Hill, Inc.

_____

___1. Which of the following strategies is Mercedes about to use? Positioning:
- A. In relation to a competitor.
- B. By price.
- C. By quality.
- D. In relation to a target market.
- E. In relation to a product class.

___2. In what stage of the product life cycle is Mercedes likely to be found?
- A. Introduction.
- B. Growth.
- C. Maturity.
- D. Saturation.
- E. Decline.

___3. Mercedes is about to use a product mix strategy called:
- A. Expanding the product mix.
- B. Contracting the product mix.
- C. Planned obsolescence.
- D. Trading up.
- E. Trading down.

PART 9K: Answers to Questions

PART 9D: Completion

1. product mix
2. product line
3. position
4. position/image/competitive
5. competitor/product class/attribute/price/ quality/target market
6. expand/lines/depth
7. line extension
8. mix extension
9. trading up
10. prestige/lower-priced
11. trading down
12. perilous/confuse
13. improving/profitable/risky
14. packaging
15. Contracting/entire line/simplifying
16. aggregate demand/generic product
17. introduction/growth/maturity/decline
18. entire/brand
19. decline
20. decline
21. abandon
22. length
23. fad
24. maturity/introductory
25. shape

26. introductory
27. delaying
28. strategies/product
29. modified/promotion/new uses
30. sales-decline
31. technological/functional/style
32. style
33. fashion
34. sociological/psychological
35. trickle-down
36. trickle-across/within
37. trickle-up
38. fashion cycle

PART 9E: True-False Questions

1. F 2. T 3. T 4. T 5. T 6. T
7. F 8. T 9. T 10. F 11. T 12. F
13. T 14. T 15. F

PART 9F: Multiple Choice Questions

1. A 2. B 3. C 4. D 5. D 6. A
7. A 8. B 9. D 10. C 11. A 12. A
13. B 14. D 15. D

PART 9G: Matching Questions

a. 11 b. 12 c. 8 d. 14 e. 7 f. 2
g. 16 h. 4 i. 5

150

```
┌─────────────────────────────┐
│                             │
│                             │
└─────────────────────────────┘
```

CHAPTER 10

BRANDS, PACKAGING, AND OTHER PRODUCT FEATURES

PART 10A: Chapter Goals

After studying this chapter, you should be able to explain:

- The nature and importance of brands
- Characteristics of a good brand name
- Branding strategies of producers and middlemen
- Why and how a growing number of firms are building and using brand equity
- The nature and importance of packaging and labeling
- Major packaging strategies
- The marketing implications of other product features--design, quality, warranty, and postsale service--that can satisfy consumers' wants

151

PART 10B: Key Terms and Concepts

1. Brand	[262]	17. Label	[278]
2. Brand name	[262]	18. Brand label	[278]
3. Brand mark	[262]	19. Descriptive label	[278]
4. Trademark	[262]	20. Grade label	[278]
5. Producer's brand	[262]	21. Major labeling laws	[279]
6. Middleman's (store) brand	[262]	22. Nutrition labeling	[279]
7. Brand names becoming generic terms	[265]	23. Product design	[280]
		24. Product color	[280]
8. Branding of fabricating parts and materials	[266]	25. Product quality	[281]
9. Generic products	[269]	26. Total quality management	[281]
10. Multiple-brand strategy	[269]	27. Warranties	[282]
11. Brand equity	[270]	a. Express warranty	[282]
12. Trademark (brand) licensing	[272]	b. Implied warranty	[282]
13. Packaging	[273]	28. Product liability	[283]
14. Package	[273]	29. Warning label	[283]
15. Family packaging	[275]	30. Consumer Product Safety Act	[283]
16. Multiple packaging	[275]	31. Postsale service	[284]

PART 10C: Summary

A prerequisite to effective marketing is the ability to distinguish one's products from those of competitors. Some of the means used for this product differentiation are branding, packaging, warranties, product design, labeling, and product servicing. The adoption by the marketer of these strategies for product differentiation brings mixed blessings. Each of these distinctive product features enables the marketer to set his products apart from those of competitors and to build a consumer following [262]. On the other hand, distinctive product features add to the cost of marketing and increase the marketer's exposure to additional risks [263].

The most common and effective way for a marketer to distinguish his products from others is to brand them; that is, to identify his goods and services with his name [262]. Branding is an essential key to promotion, channel management, and pricing. The most effective brands are also trademarks, the ownership of which enjoys legal protection [262]. It is not unusual for a brand name to be one of a business's most valuable assets; indeed, many companies have bought other companies simply to obtain their brand names.

Branding has considerable value to both the consumer and the marketer. It provides the customer with a means by which he can continue to buy products which satisfy. In general, branded products are of a better quality, since the manufacturer or the seller has been willing to put his name on them [262].

To the seller, branding provides an opportunity for demand stimulation. Branding helps to stabilize prices and expand the product mix [263]. Branding often adds value to a product unto itself. This has been called brand equity. One of the paradoxes of successful branding is the chance that a brand name will become a generic name for a particular product [265].

There are a number of common brand policies and strategies utilized by both manufacturers and middlemen. Some of the strategies are the determination of the number of brands to carry or to manufacture, the branding of a line of products, the use of multiple brands to bring about market saturation, and trademark licensing, in which the owner of the brand allows another firm to quickly and cheaply penetrate a market [266].

In recent years, the field of packaging has received increased attention as a product-differentiating tool of marketing [273]. This increased emphasis is due to utilitarian as well as promotional reasons. Often it is the package that sells the product rather than the product itself.

Other image-building features which have significant marketing implications include labeling, product design, color, quality, product warranty, and product servicing [279-285].

PART 10D: Completion

1. A brand is a(n) _____ and/or _____ intended to identify the product of one seller or a group of sellers.

2. A(n) _____ consists of words, letters, and/or numbers that can be _____.

3. A(n) _____ is the part of the brand that appears in the form of a symbol, design, or distinctive coloring or lettering.

153

4. A(n) _____ is a brand that has been adopted by a seller and given legal protection.

5. Brands owned by middlemen are called _____ brands, while those owned by producers are called _____ brands. These manufacturers' brands have often been called _____ brands, while middlemen's brands are called _____ brands.

6. Brands make it easy for consumers to identify _____ or _____.

7. Branding helps the brand owner to _____ the product.

8. Branding also differentiates a product and tends to reduce _____ comparisons among similar types of products.

9. The two responsibilities that come with brand ownership are: (1) to _____ the brand, and (2) to maintain a consistent _____ of output.

10. Some products are not branded since they are difficult to _____ from others. The _____ nature of fresh fruit and vegetables tends to discourage branding.

11. It is hard to find a good brand name since we are running out of _____.

12. Good brands have certain characteristics. A good brand should _____ about the product.

13. It should be easy to _____, _____, and _____.

14. It should be _____.

15. It should be _____, thus allowing new products to be added to the product line.

16. It should be capable of _____ protection.

17. If a brand name becomes too successful and is used by the general public to refer to a class of products, such as aspirin, the brand is said to have become a(n) _____ name.

18. In order to prevent the generic use of a brand name, the seller can: (1) use the brand name in conjunction with the _____ name, (2) use the brand name with the _____ name, and (3) give notice to the public that the brand has been _____.

19. Manufacturers who market their entire output under their own brand name are typically _____, _____, and _____.

20. These manufacturers are most likely to have broad product lines, extensive distribution

channels, and _____ shares of the market.

21. Middlemen often carry only producers' brands, especially when the brands have high _____.

22. In an attempt to develop market preference for their parts and materials, some producers _____ them.

23. To be effective, (1) the product must also be a consumer good that is bought for _____ purposes, and (2) the item must be a key part of the _____.

24. Often middlemen carry their own brands in addition to those of producers. This gives middlemen more _____ over their target market, and allows them to undersell the producer's brand and still earn higher _____.

25. A retailer's brand can _____ its products.

26. In the past, the heaviest buyers of middlemen's brands were _____ or _____ shoppers seeking bargains; now consumers at _____ income levels buy these products.

27. The "_____"--producers' brands fighting middlemen's brands--shows every indication of becoming more intense.

28. Some supermarket chains introduced unbranded products and sold them under their _____ names.

29. There are three common strategies for branding a line of products within a product mix: (1) separate _____ for each product, (2) combining the firm's _____ with an individual _____, and (3) the _____ alone.

30. Using the company name for branding purposes (_____), makes it simpler and less expensive to introduce new, related products to a line.

31. A strategy often used to increase total sales in a market is the _____ strategy.

32. Sometimes owning a brand may be more valuable than owning real estate. This is called _____-- the value a brand adds to a product.

33. Building a brand's equity consists of developing a favorable, memorable, and consistent _____.

34. Under _____ or _____ licensing, the owner of a trademark grants permission (a

license) to other firms to use the owner's brand name and brand mark on the _____ products.

35. Packaging comprises a group of activities including designing and producing a(n) _____ or _____ for a product.

36. There are four major reasons for packaging: (1) to protect the product _____ it is bought, (2) to protect the product _____ it is bought, (3) to be part of a firm's _____ marketing program, and (4) to be part of a firm's _____ marketing program.

37. Companies may decide to develop a family resemblance when packaging related products. This is called _____.

38. There is a trend toward _____--placing several units of the same product in one container.

39. Packaging is not perfect. It has been criticized because it depletes _____, is too _____, may cause _____ problems, may be _____, and may contribute significantly to the _____ problem.

40. A label is the part of the product that gives _____ about the product and the seller.

41. Basically, there are three types of labels: (1) a(n) _____ label, (2) a(n) _____ label, and (3) a(n) _____ label.

42. There are three major features of the Federal Fair Packaging and Labeling Act: (1) _____ labeling requirements, (2) opportunities for industry to adopt packaging standards _____, and (3) establishment of _____ to set packaging _____ when it is deemed necessary.

43. Good product design can improve a product's operation, quality, and appearance while at the same time it can _____ manufacturing costs.

44. _____ often is the main factor in a consumer's acceptance or rejection of a product.

45. _____ of a product is the most difficult image-building feature to define.

46. Often, _____ are deeply involved.

47. In recent years, many firms have implemented _____ (_____) programs.

48. The courts have recently held that product warranties are both _____ and _____.

49. In order to accomplish needed installations and postsale services, manufacturers have adopted one of two service strategies: _____ service centers, or _____ service centers.

PART 10E: True-False Questions

If the statement is true, circle "T"; if false, circle "F.".

T F   1. Many producers not only produce under their own brands but produce similar products for others.

T F   2. One requirement for a good brand is that it be capable of registration and legal protection under the Lanham Act.

T F   3. The Nutrition Labeling and Education Act (1990) has been accepted without complaint by the food industry.

T F   4. The "battle of the brands," a significant marketing development during the past decade, seems to be coming to an end.

T F   5. In many cases, paying for the change in packaging is less expensive than keeping the old package and continuing to pay for advertising.

T F   6. The public's rising standards of health and sanitation place additional importance on packaging.

T F   7. The phenomenon of trademark licensing has fallen into disfavor in recent years.

T F   8. Branding is so important to a product's success, it is always advantageous to brand a product.

T F   9. It is now abundantly clear that the national manufacturers will win the "battle of the brands."

T F 10. All brands are trademarks.

T F 11. A private brand can be owned by a retailer but not a wholesaler.

T F 12. Branding assures the customer of the quality of the product.

T F 13. Without branding, there would be little incentive for a manufacturer to maintain uniform quality.

157

T F 14. In family branding, it is important that product quality be uniform among products.

T F 15. Brand equity is the value a brand adds to a product.

PART 10F: Multiple Choice Questions

In the space provided write the letter of the answer that best fits the statement.

____ 1. Branding offers all the following advantages to the consumer EXCEPT:
   A. Helps identify the seller or manufacturer.
   B. Helps in comparing competing products.
   C. Helps in repeat buying.
   D. Helps get a better quality product over the years.
   E. Helps sellers control their market.

____ 2. Which of the following products is not likely to be branded?
   A. Automobile replacement parts.
   B. Fine china.
   C. Fresh produce.
   D. Hand tools.
   E. Canned goods.

____ 3. Why do middlemen benefit from carrying their own brands as well as producers' brands?
   A. Producers' brands generally allow greater profits to middlemen.
   B. Both brands are often made by the same manufacturer.
   C. Producers' brands are usually of high quality; thus both brands can better satisfy the range of quality demanded by the consumer.
   D. Middlemen's brands usually sell for less than producers' brands.
   E. None of the above.

____ 4. Warranties are changing because of:
   A. Threats posed by potential product-liability claims.
   B. A general feeling in the country of "let the seller beware."
   C. The inadequacy of express warranties.
   D. Courts broadening the scope of warranty coverage by recognizing the concept of implied warranty.
   E. All of the above.

____ 5. All of the following statements regarding product quality are correct EXCEPT:
   A. There is no agreement on the definition of product quality.
   B. Individual expectations affect judgments of quality.
   C. All producers agree that excessive quality is desirable.
   D. Since the mid-1980s, industry has paid more and more attention to product quality.
   E. In recent years, TQM programs have been introduced in many organizations.

158

___ 6. Packaging has been criticized because it:
- A. Depletes our natural resources.
- B. Is excessively expensive.
- C. Can be deceptive.
- D. May cause health problems.
- E. All of the above.

___ 7. From the consumer's point of view, branding is important because it:
- A. Tends to lower the price of a product.
- B. Lets the consumer know what producer is standing behind the product.
- C. Assures the buyer that there is a reasonable consistency of quality.
- D. Assures the consumer of getting high-quality products.
- E. Reduces a consumer's repair bills on mechanical products.

___ 8. Linoleum, aspirin, cellophane, and nylon are all:
- A. Brands. B. Generic names. C. Copyrights. D. Brand marks. E. Trademarks.

___ 9. Manufacturers are likely to sell their products unbranded when:
- A. They do not want to shoulder the promotional burden.
- B. Some products cannot be differentiated from those of another firm.
- C. The physical nature of the product precludes branding each unit.
- D. They are reluctant to maintain consistent quality.
- E. All of the above conditions are reasons for not branding.

___10. Which of the following is a characteristic of a good brand?
- A. Suggests something about the product's characteristics.
- B. Easy to pronounce.
- C. Easy to spell and remember.
- D. Capable of being registered and legally protected.
- E. All of the above.

___11. The Nutrition Labeling and Education Act of 1990 was concerned with _____ labeling:
- A. Brand   B. Descriptive   C. Grade

___12. Placing several units in one container is called _____ packaging.
- A. Reuse   B. Family   C. Multiple   D. Identical   E. Any of the above.

___13. Management may use a packaging strategy in order to:
- A. Gain shelf space.
- B. Serve a safety purpose.
- C. Identify the product.
- D. Deter shoplifting.
- E. Any of the above.

___14. Public property is to copyright as brand is to:
- A. Label.   B. Generic brand.   C. Packaging.   D. Trademark.   E. Brand name.

____15. Brand equity provides the following benefit to the firm:
   A. A favorable, memorable, consistent image.
   B. Increased sales.
   C. Creates a barrier for competitors wishing to enter the market.
   D. Helps a product survive changes in consumer tastes.
   E. All of the above.

PART 10G: Matching Questions

In the space provided write the number of the word or expression from column 1 that best fits the description in column 2.

1	2

1. Battle of the brands

2. Brand

3. Brand mark

4. Brand name

5. Descriptive label

6. Express warranty

7. Family brand

8. Generic products

9. Grade label

10. Implied warranty

11. Label

12. Middleman's brand

13. Packaging

14. Producer's brand

15. Product warranty

____a. A name, term, symbol, and/or special design that is intended to identify the goods or services of a seller or to differentiate them from those of competitors.

____b. A brand that is given legal protection.

____c. Another name for a private brand.

____d. Another name for a national brand.

____e. Producers' vs. middlemen's brands.

____f. The part of a product that carries verbal information about the product or seller.

____g. Warranties stated in written or spoken words

____h. Identifies the quality with a letter, number, or word.

____i. Owner of a trademark grants permission (a license) to another firm to use its brand on the licensee's products.

160

16. Trademark

17. Trademark licensing

PART 10H: Problems and Applications

1.   What, if any, are the competitive advantages to a manufacturer's extending the scope and duration of his warranties?   Write a report for your instructor.

2.   Read two current articles dealing with legislation on labeling or packaging. Report on compliance with these laws. (Suggestion: See the "Legal Developments in Marketing" section in any issue of *Journal of Marketing*.)

3.   Go to stores selling tires and obtain a copy of their written warranties. Compare the warranties and prepare a memo. (Hint: Consult the latest edition of "Buying Guide Issue," *Consumer Reports*. Read: "Guarantees & Warranties.")

4.   List six examples not noted in the text of brands that suggest something about the product's characteristics: (Hint: Consult Adrian Room, *Dictionary of Trade Name Origins* (London: Routledge & Kegan Paul, 1982).

_____   _____

_____   _____

_____   _____

5.   Now list six examples of brand names that are easy to pronounce, spell, and remember.

_____   _____

_____   _____

_____   _____

6.   Campbell's Soup uses the following brand names for soups: Homestyle, Chunky, Creamy Natural, and Manhandler. Each label has a different design. Write a report to your instructor discussing the characteristics of the market segment for each of these brands. Does Campbell also use a product differentiation strategy? Why?

7.   Assume that all brand names have been eliminated by law and only generic names can be used. Write a memo to your instructor discussing the implications of this law:
    A. For consumer decision making.
    B. For implementation of a strategy of product differentiation by a producer.

8.   A manufacturer, Munchkin Bottling, persuaded PepsiCo and Dr Pepper-SevenUp to let them use their logos on their baby bottles. Is this the ultimate, cynical get-'em-while-they're-young marketing strategy? Write a report to your instructor on the licensing of products to

161

capture the youth market. See "The Right One, Baby," *Business Week*, May 10, 1993, p. 34.

9. Why did most American auto manufacturers cut back their warranties?

10. Theodore Levitt, one of marketing's leading thinkers, has been heard to state: "There is no such thing as a commodity. All goods and services are differentiable." Do you agree with this statement? Write a report in memo form to your instructor supporting or disagreeing with Levitt.

PART 10I: Exercise

Beside each of the manufacturers' names, write the number of the brand that manufacturer markets. This is not just a memory exercise, but one that should make you ask why the brands and manufacturers match up the way they do.

Brand		Manufacturer
1. Betty Crocker	____	A. American Brands
2. Brillo soap pads	____	B. American Home Products
3. Chef-Boy-ar-dee	____	C. BCI Holdings Corp.
4. Cracker Jacks	____	D. Borden, Inc.
5. Dynamo	____	E. Bristol-Myers Squibb Co.
6. Excedrin	____	F. Campbell's Soup
7. Gatorade	____	G. Clorox
8. Green Giant	____	H. Coca-Cola
9. Imperial Margarine	____	I. Colgate-Palmolive
10. Jell-O	____	J. CPC International
11. Karo Syrup	____	K. Dial Corporation
12. Kingsford Charcoal	____	L. General Mills
13. L'Oreal cosmetics	____	M. Gillette
14. Master Locks	____	N. Grand Metropolitan
15. Minute Maid	____	O. H. J. Heinz
16. Pampers	____	P. Kellogg
17. Planters Peanuts	____	Q. Nestle S.A.
18. Popsicle	____	R. Pepsico, Inc.
19. Pop-tarts	____	S. Philip Morris
20. Right Guard	____	T. Procter & Gamble
21. Ruffles	____	U. Quaker Oats
22. Schick	____	V. Ralston Purina
23. StarKist	____	W. RJR-Nabisco
24. Tropicana	____	X. Sara Lee
25. Twinkies	____	Y. Unilever
26. V-8 juice	____	Z. Warner-Lambert

PART 10J: **A Real World Case: Packaging's Pros and Cons**

As of presstime we haven't heard a peep about plans for another Earth Day celebration, which in years past was an April event. But America has an avowed environmentalist in the vice president's office and an enthusiastic new director at the Environmental Protection Agency. The Administration will not ignore the environment.

Elected officials are deliberating cuts in existing federal spending, but some will nevertheless continue to introduce new environmental cleanup programs.

Government agencies have taken action to restrict the use of environmental claims on product labels, but marketers won't give up hope of portraying their products as environmentally superior to their competitors'.

How do we know? How can we make these predictions? Answer: Results of PACKAGING's 9th annual Consumer Survey are in. Among the findings:

■Americans are every bit as troubled about the trash problem today as they were at this time last year. Asked whether their concerns about trash this year were greater than, the same as, or less than they were in 1992, only 3% of our respondents said they were less concerned. Roughly 499% said they were more concerned.

■More than 44% of our respondents said the recycling of used packages in general was "extremely" important to them. Almost that many said it was "somewhat" important.

■Consumers say the importance of package recyclability as a determining factor in their product-purchase decisions has not decreased. More than 44% said it was "extremely important," 43% said it was "somewhat important."

■Shoppers remain as skeptical of environmental claims as they were one year ago. Allowed to choose as many adjectives as they felt applicable, 31.5% of our respondents called environmental claims on labels "insufficient," 29.4% called them "confusing," and 24.5% called them "misleading."

New, improved claims Clearly, old statements such as "recyclable," "safe for the environment," and "made with 25% recycled plastic" have lost their ability--if indeed they ever had it--to sway consumers from one product to another. Whatever claims are allowed in the future and actually make a difference to shoppers will have to be different from those with which we're now familiar.

With somewhat less certainty we predict more legislative emphasis on source reduction in packaging and less on recycled content in packaging as a means of fighting the trash war:

■Nearly 83% of consumers say they believe some products use too much packaging. That figure

163

is virtually unchanged from last year.

■By more than two-to-one, consumers in our survey said "simpler packaging" could do more to solve the problem of packaging waste than "packaging made with recycled materials."

■Asked about how much of their trash they thought was made up of packaging waste this year compared with last, only 12.5% of our respondents said "more." Almost 57% said "the same" and a surprising 29.9% said "less." It's unclear whether our respondents considered items placed in the recycling bin to be trash. If not, that could help explain the perceived decrease in packaging waste. Another possibility is that consumers believed they were using less packaging--or, better yet, that they had noticed the effects of source reduction.

A bit much but still OK Are we ready to predict a sweeping change of course in consumer buying habits away from novel, convenient packages and toward mundane but efficient ones? No way.

■Only one third of our respondents said they were willing to reject products that appeared to be overpackaged as a means of reducing waste. Two-thirds said they still preferred to buy packages that were easy to "recycle."

Another reading of the last two bullet points reveals not confusion but perceptiveness. Packaging that contains recycled materials is not the same as packaging that is easy to recycle. Perhaps consumers responding to our survey full understand the difference. Perhaps they are saying they didn't expect "closed loop" recycling of the type that has been demanded by some environmental activists.

This could take a little pressure off packagers--specifically those in food. In the past some of them have felt compelled to seek FDA approval and spend huge sums of money on closed-loop technologies enabling use of recycled post-consumer packaging in manufacturing new food-contact materials.

However the results are interpreted, what's obvious is the consumer's unabated concern for the environment and the role packagers can play in helping to protect it. Despite all we've heard about the short attention span of the American public, this is an issue that continues to demand attention from elected officials and packagers alike.■

Source: Greg Erickson, "In the Mind of the Consumer; Part I: The Environment," *Packaging Magazine*, April 1993, pp. 50-51. Reprinted by permission of Cahners Publishing Co.

___ 1. According to the article, the major criticism of packaging is that:
   A. It depletes natural resources.
   B. It is too expensive.
   C. It may be a health hazard.
   D. Products use too much packaging.
   E. It may be deceptive.

___ 2. According to the survey described in the article, most consumers are demanding:
   A. Packages that are easy to recycle.
   B. "Closed loop" recycling technologies.
   C. Packages that contain recycled materials.
   D. More complicated and convenient packages.
   E. More expensive packaging.

165

PART 10K: **Answers to Questions**

PART 10D: Completion

1. name/mark
2. brand name/vocalized
3. brand mark
4. trademark
5. middlemen's/producers'/national/private
6. goods/services
7. promote
8. price
9. promote/quality
10. differentiate/perishable
11. possibilities
12. suggest something
13. pronounce/spell/remember
14. distinctive
15. adaptable
16. legal
17. generic
18. company/generic/copyrighted
19. large/well financed/well managed
20. large
21. consumer acceptance
22. brand
23. replacement/finished product
24. control/gross margins
25. differentiate
26. lower-income/upper-income/all
27. battle of the brands
28. generic
29. names/company name/product name/ company name
30. family branding
31. multiple-brand
32. brand equity
33. image
34. trademark/brand/licensee's
35. container/wrapper
36. before/after/trade/consumer
37. family packaging
38. multiple packaging
39. natural resources/expensive/health/ deceptive/solid-waste
40. information
41. brand/descriptive/grade
42. mandatory/voluntarily/administrative agencies/regulations
43. lower
44. Color
45. Quality
46. personal tastes
47. total quality management/TQM
48. expressed/implied
49. factory/middlemen

PART 10E: True-False Questions

1. T 2. T 3. F 4. F 5. T 6. T
7. F 8. F 9. F 10. F 11. F 12. T
13. T 14. T 15. T

PART 10F: Multiple Choice Questions

1. B 2. C 3. D 4. E 5. C 6. E
7. C 8. B 9. E 10. E 11. B 12. C
13. E 14. D 15. E

PART 10G: Matching Questions

a. 2 b. 16 c. 12 d. 14 e. 1 f. 11
g. 6 h. 9 i. 17

PART FOUR

PRICE

167

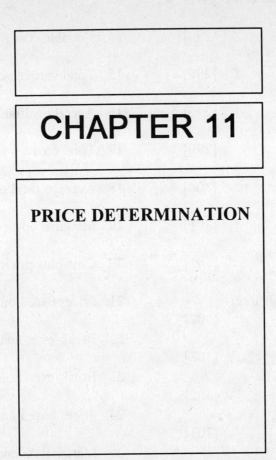

CHAPTER 11

PRICE DETERMINATION

PART 11A: Chapter Goals

After studying this chapter, you should be able to explain:

- The meaning of price
- What price means in our economy, to an individual firm, and in a consumer's mind
- The concept of value and how it relates to price
- Major pricing objectives
- Key factors influencing price
- The types of costs incurred in producing and marketing a product
- Approaches to determining prices, including cost-plus pricing, marginal analysis, and setting prices in relation only to other prices in the market
- Break-even analysis

169

PART 11B: Key Terms and Concepts

1. Price [296]

2. Utility [296]

3. Barter [296]

4. Pricing objectives [299]

    a. Achieve target return [300]

    b. Maximize profit [301]

    c. Increase sales [301]

    d. Maintain or increase market share [302]

    e. Stabilize prices [302]

    f. Meet competition [302]

5. Inverse demand [303]

6. Price elasticity of demand [304]

7. Average fixed cost curve [306]

8. Average variable cost curve [306]

9. Average total cost curve [307]

10. Marginal cost curve [307]

11. Fixed cost [307]

12. Total fixed cost [307]

13. Average fixed cost [307]

14. Variable cost [307]

15. Total variable cost [307]

16. Average variable cost [307]

17. Total cost [307]

18. Average total cost [307]

19. Marginal cost [307]

20. Cost-plus pricing [307]

21. Prices based on marginal costs [308]

22. Break-even analysis [310]

23. Break-even point [310]

24. Prices based on marginal analysis [312]

25. Marginal revenue [312]

26. Average revenue [312]

27. Pricing to meet competition [314]

28. Perfect competition [314]

29. Kinked demand [314]

30. Oligopoly [314]

31. Pricing below competition [315]

32. Pricing above competition [315]

PART 11C: Summary

Price acts as a basic allocator of the factors of production. Although difficult to define, price is the mechanism whereby value and utility are placed on a good or service so as to facilitate exchange between buyers and sellers. Price turns out to be value expressed in dollars and cents. It is a mechanism whereby an accommodation is reached between two individuals who are willing to pay two different prices for the same good or service [298].

Management must first identify its pricing goal before setting the base price on a product. Seller price objectives can be profit oriented (achieve target return on investment or sales and to maximize profits), sales oriented (increase sales or maintain or increase share of the market), or status-quo oriented (stabilize prices or meet competition) [299-303]. Often, socially accepted goals are announced and publicized, but in the final analysis, firms tend to follow a long-term profit-maximization goal.

It is important for the marketer to know the objectives in price determination. The key factors in determining price are to estimate the demand, estimate the market share, anticipate the competitive reaction, select the pricing strategy and consider the company's marketing policies, and finally, determine the costs of producing or buying the product [303-307].

Price determination is at the heart of price management. Price setting, in practice, will be accomplished by one of the following major methods:

1. Total cost plus a desired profit [307].
2. Marginal analysis [312].
3. Setting the price in relation to competitive market conditions [313].

Once the executives are agreed upon the pricing objectivesand they are clearly stated, the firm can move to the heart of price management--the actual determination of the basic price for their products and services.

Price management rests on a basic understanding of costs and their behavior [306]. The interrelationships among total fixed cost, total variable cost, total cost, average fixed cost, average variable cost, average total cost, and marginal cost show the relationship among all costs, fixed and variable. By including a desired profit in either the fixed costs or variable costs, the price setter can refer to his table or graphs and find the appropriate price, once the decision is made regarding the intended output. In the short run, management can set a price for the next unit sold equal to its marginal cost.

Break-even analysis provides one way to include market demand in the basis for price determination while still considering costs [310]. However, on balance, the break-even method of setting price is not without its limitations. It assumes that costs are static and requires an empirical determination of the company's cost curve. Also other market information, such as

171

demand, which actually exists at several different selling prices, is difficult to estimate.

Price setters can employ marginal cost analysis and set their prices where marginal cost equals marginal revenue [312]. This approach has limited use because it does not take into consideration important factors that exist in real-life market situations.

Price can be based on, and set in relation to, the competitive market price only [313]. A market-based method of pricing is used when a customary price level exists or if the market is an oligopoly. Variations to market-based pricing are to set a price above or below the competitive level [315]. In the final analysis, price determination is the result of a set of complex variables interacting between and among buyers and sellers and their environments.

PART 11D: Completion

1. _____ is the amount of money and/or other items with utility needed to acquire a product.

2. _____ is the attribute of an item that makes it capable of satisfying human wants.

3. Exchanging goods and/or services for other products is called _____.

4. Sellers price a combination of: (1) a specific _____ or _____, (2) several _____ _____, and (3) the _____ provided by the product.

5. A product's price influences the price paid for the _____ of production.

6. The price of a product is a major determinant of _____.

7. Differentiated _____, a favorite _____, high _____, _____, or some combination of these and other factors may be more important to consumers than _____ .

8. Most consumers believe the price-quality nexus--high price means _____, low price means _____.

9. Consumers are demanding more _____ for their money. Value is the ratio of _____ to _____ and any other incurred costs.

10. Management should first determine its pricing _____ before determining the price itself.

11. Pricing goals can be _____-oriented, _____-oriented, or _____-oriented.

12. The profit goals in pricing are: (1) to achieve a target return on _____ or on its

172

_____, and (2) to _____ profits.

13. The sales-oriented goals in pricing are: (1) to increase _____ volume, and (2) to maintain or increase _____.

14. The status-quo-oriented goals in pricing are: (1) to stabilize _____, and (2) to meet _____.

15. _____ is used by many retailers and wholesalers as a short-term pricing objective.

16. _____ is used by industry leaders in manufacturing.

17. In profit maximization, the goal should be to maximize profits long term on _____ rather than on each single _____ marketed.

18. The goal in increasing sales volume is to achieve _____ or to discourage _____ from entering a market.

19. Market share is pursued vigorously because most industries are not _____ much and they have excess _____.

20. A major reason for seeking price stability is to avoid _____.

21. In an industry where there is a price leader and where the product is highly standardized, most firms have a(n) _____ pricing policy.

22. _____ price or _____ price means the price of one unit of the product at its point of production or at the resale point.

23. Two steps in demand estimation are to determine the _____, and to estimate the _____ at different prices.

24. The _____ price for a product is the price at which customers consciously or unconsciously value it.

25. Inverse demand means the _____ the price, the _____ the unit sales.

26. By estimating sales at various prices, the seller is, in effect, determining the _____ for the product and thus determining its _____.

27. Competition can come from three sources: from _____, from

_____, and from _____ seeking the same consumer dollar.

28. Company pricing procedures must be considered with respect to the other marketing mix elements such as the _____ itself, the _____, and _____ _____.

29. _____ are elements that remain relatively constant regardless of the level of output.

30. _____ include, among other things, factory labor and materials.

31. _____ is the cost of producing and selling one more unit.

32. The ATC curve will slope _____ as long as marginal costs are less than average unit costs.

33. The MC and ATC curves intersect at the _____ point of the _____curve.

34. The three major price-setting methods that are price-based are: (1) _____ plus a(n) _____; (2) marginal analysis (a consideration of both market _____ and _____) and (3) competitive _____.

35. A price based on the _____ approach means that the selling price for a unit is equal to the unit's total cost plus an amount to cover the anticipated _____ per unit.

36. _____ pricing may be feasible if management wants to keep its labor force employed during a slack season.

37. Middlemen's customary markups are the markups they normally get to cover their expenses and still make a reasonable _____.

38. Most retail prices are really only price _____.

39. _____ may use different markups for different products in order to meet competition and other aspects of market demand.

40. Middlemen do not set their own base prices. They only add a(n) _____ to the price set by the _____.

41. Cost-plus pricing is a weak and unrealistic pricing method since it ignores _____ and _____.

42. A break-even analysis involves developing tables and/or charts that will help a firm determine

at what level of output _____ will equal _____, assuming a certain
_____.

43. The formula for the break-even point in units equals total _____ divided by unit contribution to _____.

44. Break-even analysis assumes that total fixed costs are _____.

45. Break-even analysis has a limited value as a pricing tool in firms where _____ and/or _____ fluctuate frequently.

46. Break-even analysis also ignores whether we can actually _____ the break-even amount.

47. _____ is the additional income received from the sale of the last unit.

48. _____ is the total revenue divided by the quantity of output.

49. Optimum _____ occurs at a point at which marginal _____ equals marginal _____.

50. Marginal analysis as a basis for setting price has enjoyed limited use because _____ is (are) needed for plotting curves exactly.

51. A firm is most likely to use the pricing-to-meet-competition method when the market is highly _____ and the product is _____ significantly from competitive models.

52. A sharp drop in revenue that occurs when the price is raised above the prevailing market level shows that the individual seller faces a(n) _____.

53. Occasionally, the market is dominated by only a few producers selling similar products. This type of market structure is called a(n) _____.

54. An example of pricing _____ the competitive level is discount-house pricing.

55. Above-market pricing can be imposed when the product is _____ and when the seller has _____ in his field.

PART 11E: True-False Questions

If the statement is true, circle "T"; if false, circle "F."

T F   1. Average variable cost will increase with each additional unit of output.

T F 2. The threat of potential competition is greatest when the field is easy to enter and profit prospects are positive.

T F 3. Cost-plus pricing is weak and unrealistic because it ignores competition and market demand.

T F 4. An individual seller in an oligopoly faces a kinked demand curve.

T F 5. Break-even analysis suffers from the same deficiency as cost-plus pricing in that it has no way in which to incorporate market demand.

T F 6. The terms "price" and "value" mean the same things.

T F 7. The answer to the pricing question is simple--sell at a lower price than your competitors.

T F 8. Oligopolies engage in price-cutting since their products are highly differentiated.

T F 9. The major pricing goal of large American corporations is to drive competitors out of business.

T F 10. Maximum profit occurs at the point where the marginal revenue curve intersects the marginal cost curve.

T F 11. Companies following the goal of stabilizing prices are very likely to start price wars.

T F 12. Sometimes an item is priced too low. A situation where higher prices lead to greater unit sales is called "perverse demand."

T F 13. Target return on sales or on investment is not a very widely used pricing goal.

T F 14. Discount houses operate on the principle of low markup and high volume.

T F 15. Marginal cost analysis considers both market demand and production costs.

PART 11F: Multiple Choice Questions

In the space provided write the letter of the answer that best fits the statement.

____ 1. A firm's fixed costs are $200,000, and average unit variable costs are $7.50. At a selling price of $10 a unit, the break-even point is _____ units.
   A. 20,000   B. 80,000   C. 8,000   D. 75,000   E. 200,000

____ 2. When Ford Motor Company sets a "15% return on investment" as its pricing goal, this objective is most likely to:
   A. Stabilize prices.
   B. Maintain a target share of the market.
   C. Meet competition.
   D. Achieve a target return.
   E. Increase market share.

____ 3. The goal of stabilizing prices is most likely to be used by:
   A. Wal-Mart
   B   A large discount house.
   C. Aluminum Corporation of America (Alcoa).
   D. Safeway Stores, Inc.
   E. A small manufacturer of a little-known brand of clothing.

____ 4. The strategy of pricing below the competitive level would most likely be used by all of the following EXCEPT:
   A. A discount appliance dealer.
   B. An oligopolist selling an undifferentiated product.
   C. A grocery chain in an urban market.
   D. A farmer selling bagged onions.
   E. A ski shop at the end of the season.

____ 5. Competition can come from:
   A. Directly similar products.
   B. Available substitutes.
   C. Unrelated products seeking the same consumer dollar.
   D. Any of the above.
   E. None of the above.

____ 6. The major goals of pricing are oriented toward:
   A. Profit.   D. The status quo.
   B. Sales.   E. Any of the above.
   C. Market share.

____ 7. Which of the following is a correct statement regarding costs and cost curves of individual firms?
   A. The average total cost curve is horizontal.
   B. On a break-even chart, the total fixed cost line is horizontal.
   C. Variable costs per unit are constant.
   D. The unit marginal cost curve (MC) intersects the unit average total cost curve (ATC) at the highest point on ATC.
   E. None of the above is correct.

____8. The strategy of pricing above the competitive level would most likely be used by all of the following EXCEPT:
  A. A manufacturer of prestige luggage such as Gucci.
  B. An oligopolist selling an undifferentiated product.
  C. A resort hotel on a private ocean beach.
  D. A restaurant specializing in French provincial cuisine.
  E. A private jet service to Hawaii.

____9. All of the following are major pricing goals of large American companies EXCEPT:
  A. Achieve target return on investment.
  B. Drive competitors out of business.
  C. Increase share of the market.
  D. Maximize profits in the long run.
  E. Achieve target return on sales.

____10. All of the following statements regarding price are true EXCEPT:
  A. It is a major determinant of the market demand for an item.
  B. Branding has no effect on price.
  C. It affects a firm's competitive position.
  D. It affects a firm's market share.
  E. It affects a firm's revenue and net profit.

____11. An oligopolist has all the following characteristics EXCEPT:
  A. Many sell essentially similar products.
  B. The demand curve facing an individual seller is a kinked one.
  C. He avoids pricing above the market level.
  D. He engages in nonprice competition.
  E. He consistently sells below the market level.

____12. The *least* aggressive pricing goal is to:
  A. Stabilize prices.   D. Increase market share.
  B. Maximize profits.   E. Achieve target return on investment.
  C. Maintain market share.

____13. The attribute an item has that makes it capable of satisfying human wants is called:
  A. Price.   C. Utility.   E. A factor of production.
  B. Value.   D. A tangible good.

____14. _____ pricing is used by industry leaders because they can set their price more independently of competition.
  A. Profit-maximization   D. Predatory
  B. Sales-oriented   E. Status-quo-oriented
  C. Target-return

178

____15. Companies that aggressively use the major marketing mix elements of product, promotion, and distribution are engaged in:
    A. Profit maximization.   D. Status-quo-oriented pricing.
    B. Nonprice competition.   E. Target-return-on-investment pricing.
    C. Predatory pricing.

PART 11G: Matching Questions

In the space provided write the number of the word or expression from column 1 that best fits the description in column 2.

1	2
1. AFC	____ a. Unit selling price is equal to total unit cost plus a profit factor.
2. ATC	____ b. The cost of producing one more unit.
3. AVC	____ c. $\dfrac{TFC + TVC}{Q}$
4. Base or list price	
5. Break-even analysis	____ d. $\dfrac{TC}{Q}$
6. Cost-plus pricing	____ e. $\dfrac{TVC}{Q}$
7. Expected price	____ f. Unit price times market demand in units.
8. Fixed cost	____ g. An attribute of a product that makes it capable of want satisfaction.
9. Inverse demand	____ h. Competition characterized by little product differentiation and avoidance of price competition.
10. Kinked demand	
11. Marginal cost pricing	____ i. The higher the price, the greater the units sold.
12. Marginal cost	____ j. The ratio of perceived benefits to price and any other incurred costs.
13. Marginal revenue	
14. Oligopoly	
15. Price	

16. TC

17. TFC

18. Total revenue

19. TVC

20. Utility

21. Variable cost

22. Value

PART 11H: Problems and Applications

1. Based upon your experience, indicate the prices or price ranges which you consider fair for the following items: a meal in a good restaurant, tuition to a top university, a new pair of tennis shoes, a one-bedroom apartment (unfurnished), and two pro-football tickets. Explain your reasoning in each case.

2. Assume a firm has a selling price of $90 a unit and that its out-of-pocket (variable) costs per unit are $25. If its total fixed costs are $9,500, how many units will have to be sold to break even?____. Remember, the break-even point in units = total fixed cost/unit contribution to overhead.

3. Compute the break-even point for a selling price of $30 in Question 3. It is equal to _____ units, which is_____ more units than would be needed at a selling price of $90.

4. For some products, cost is irrelevant. What products? Discuss.

5. Oligopolists, for their own good, will simply set their prices at the level of competition and let it stay there. Discuss. Illustrate graphically what their demand, average revenue, and marginal revenue curves are.

6. Discuss some of the forces limiting the importance of price in a company's marketing program.

7. What is a marketing order for an agricultural product? How do these orders affect the price of farm products?

8. Why is a firm's or an industry's pricing structure of great interest to the antitrust division

of the Justice Department of the United States?

9. The real meaning of price may be in noncost variables. Explain.

10. Some firms consciously price to prevent competition. Discuss.

11. Define price from the standpoint of the businessman, the economist, and the consumer. Is there any one best definition?

12. How important is the pricing variable in a firm's marketing mix? Will it change at different stages in the product life cycle? Explain.

13. Chain-store prices tend to be lower than prices in other stores. Why?

14. Is it true that you get what you pay for? Explain.

15. What pricing policy may be followed in a declining market of a recession?

16. As demonstrated in the text, prices can have different meanings; a definition hinges on the problem of determining exactly what it is that the person is buying. Talk to five fellow students about the writing instruments they use.
    A. Find out the number and kind they own.
    B. Ascertain how much, if anything, they paid for each.
    C. What can you conclude regarding price? Write a report to your instructor.

    Record your findings below.

Student	M/F	Kind Owned	Number	Price Paid	Major	Year in School
1						
2						
3						
4						
5						

17. What variables can determine the demand for each of the following goods and services?
    A. Fresh asparagus.
    B. Apple personal computer.
    C. Hewlett-Packard calculator.
    D. Car wash.
    E. Bread.
    F. Boeing 747 aircraft.
    G. A horror movie.
    H. A pizza.

Based on the list, which ones can be manipulated by the firm? What conclusions can you make?

PART 11I: Exercise

Table 11-1 contains a schedule of a firm's fixed and variable costs.

A.   Complete the table by computing total cost, average fixed cost, average variable cost, average total cost, and marginal cost.

B.   On the small graph (Figure 11-1), plot and label total fixed costs, total variable costs, and total costs.

C.   On the large graph (Figure 11-2), plot the average fixed cost, average variable cost, average total cost, and marginal cost. Label all four curves.

D.   Referring to Figure 11-2, at what point does the marginal cost (MC) curve intersect the average total cost (ATC) curve? Explain why the ATC curve is declining up to the intersection point and rising beyond it.

E.   Again referring to Table 11-1 and assuming that the firm is operating at an output level of four units, under marginal cost pricing, the firm will accept an order for one unit at $ _____ instead of at the full cost of $ _____ because it is trying to cover only its variable or out-of-pocket cost.

Table 11-1 Costs for Individual Firms

Quantity Output Q	Total Fixed Cost, TFC	Total Variable Cost, TVC	Total Cost, TC = TFC + TVC	Marginal Cost Per Unit, MC	Average Fixed Cost, AFC = TFC/Q	Average Variable Cost, AVC = TVC/Q	Average Costs Per Unit, ATC = TC/Q
0	$200	0	_____		_____	_____	_____
1	$200	50	_____	_____	_____	_____	_____
2	$200	90	_____	_____	_____	_____	_____
3	$200	120	_____	_____	_____	_____	_____
4	$200	160	_____	_____	_____	_____	_____
5	$200	220	_____	_____	_____	_____	_____
6	$200	300	_____	_____	_____	_____	_____
7	$200	400	_____	_____	_____	_____	_____
8	$200	520	_____	_____	_____	_____	_____
9	$200	670	_____	_____	_____	_____	_____
10	$200	900	_____	_____	_____	_____	_____

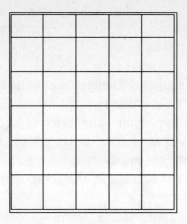

Fig. 11-1

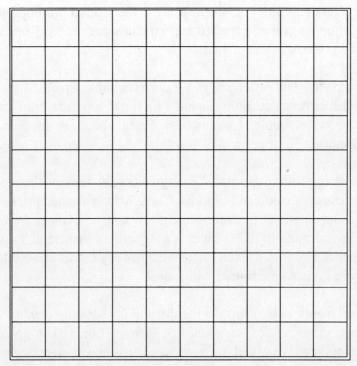

Fig. 11-2

PART 11J: A Real World Case: Sales are Sales ... Right?

It seems everything is on sale these days, and regulatory officials aren't buying it. The number of sales and markdowns at retail stores has exploded in recent years, leaving customers perplexed about pricing tactics and wondering whether they are really getting bargains. Responding to a rising tide of consumer complaints, regulators are closing in.

"The key issue is how do you go about judging whether a sale price has market validity," says Steven Cole, vice president of the Council of Better Business Bureaus. "Was [the regular price] a good faith price or a fictitious one set up just for the purpose of having a future sale?"   The

183

council has been meeting with a group of big retailers and attorneys general from six states to come up with new advertising standards.

One of the most closely watched regulatory changes is coming in Massachusetts. This May [1990], the state will put into effect a law that regulators consider among the toughest to govern retailers on matters such as price comparison claim, price and quality disclosure, and the availability of merchandise advertised as marked down. Also under the rule, sales advertised in retail catalogs, which are printed months in advance, must disclose that the so-called original price is really only a reference price and not necessarily the actual former price.

Sales have become more suspect simply because they're so commonplace. Once confined mostly to end-of-the-season clearances, markdowns now are a year-round promotional tactic. The trend snowballed as competition intensified between department stores and off-price retailers, which have been gaining market share in recent years.

Markdowns seem to be occurring faster and faster. Last month, Spiegel Inc. mailed out its spring catalog filled with seasonal fashions, including a floral sundress "you'll wear long after dark." The price: $68. Just a couple of weeks later, Spiegel sent out another catalog featuring the very same floral sundress. The price: $54--on sale.

Many industry watchers considered this past Christmas season perhaps the most promotional ever. That's partly because of troubled Campeau Corp., which slashed prices in its department stores to generate cash, prompting other stores to follow suit. "Campeau was the catalyst and had other stores insecure enough to follow, which exaggerated that trend," says Bruce Misset, an analyst at Oppenheimer & Co. As a result, many analysts say stores are hurting their profit margins because they've gone so overboard with sales.

While shoppers bagged plenty of bargains during the holiday season, they are wary. "I caught almost all my Christmas gifts on sale," says Martelle Shaw, a Long Island, N.Y., teacher who treated herself to a raccoon coat marked down 50%. But she was suspicious. "I don't really think all of these sales were for real."

There's also a feeling of frustration among consumers. "All the price cutting has made people anxious that they aren't getting the absolute best price," says Leo Shapiro, chairman of a retail consulting firm that interviewed 300 Chicago-area shoppers after Christmas. He says 82% of those shoppers believed they could probably have found even better deals "if they had just looked a little harder."For their part, regulators aren't so sure all advertised bargains are such good deals. Last December, the New York state attorney general filed suit against Sears, Roebuck & Co. charging that the company's "everyday low price" strategy has created a "false impression" that Sears' prices represent significant discounts from former prices. Sears, which adopted the policy to try to kick the habit of constant sales, has denied the charges.

A similar lawsuit was filed by New York City's Department of Consumer Affairs against

Newmark & Lewis Inc., a consumer electronics chain based in Hicksville, N.Y., that also adopted a so-called lower-pricing strategy last year. Newmark & Lewis has denied the charges that it engaged in deceptive advertising.

Last August, three St. Louis furniture stores agreed to pay $352,000 in restitution to consumers under settlements negotiated by the Missouri attorney general's office. The state alleged that the stores had boosted the manufacturer's suggested retail price when advertising their sale prices. Under the settlement, about 2,500 consumers were refunded, on average, about $150 each on furniture they had purchased earlier from the stores. Industry watchers are anxiously awaiting the outcome of a suit that Colorado filed against May Department Stores Inc.'s May D&F unit. Among the allegations in that case, which is slated to go to trial in May, the Colorado attorney general charged that May D&F misled consumers on offering sale prices for a limited time only, when such prices are offered "continuously throughout most calendar periods." The state also alleged that May used preprinted price tags with inflated regular prices, which "deceptively convey the impression of regular selling prices." A May spokesman declined comment.

Determining value has gotten tougher lately because stores are selling more private-label merchandise, often putting them on sale at 50% off or more. Even though a shirt with a store's own label looks like a great deal when marked down, the retailer still makes a healthy profit, says George Hechtman, a partner of McMillan & Doolittle, retail industry consultants. Unfortunately, private-label sales make comparison-shopping almost impossible. "With Liz Claiborne you know what it is worth by shopping at different stores," says Mr. Missett, the Oppenheimer analyst. "But with private-label merchandise you have no standard to judge by." The same kind of problems can occur with discount stores specializing in electronic goods like stereos and VCRs. Their advertising dares customers to find lower prices on comparable merchandise, when in fact in some cases the goods are specially made for the store, so identical items don't exist elsewhere.

Some stores say they are backing off on sales as a marketing strategy. Dayton Hudson says that last year it cut storewide sales promotions by a third. The Minneapolis-based chain says the move has allowed it to focus on selling its full-price merchandise. And Toys "R" Us Inc. says that because it constantly adjusts prices, it doesn't need to advertise sales to generate traffic.

But industry sources believe most retailers continue to play the markdown game because customers have come to expect discounts on everything. "Once you start doing this, you're on a treadmill," says Robert Buchanan, an analyst with Alex. Brown & Sons. "And I don't see how they're going to get off."

Source: Teri Agins, "As Retailers' Sales Crop Up Everywhere, Regulators Wonder If the Price Is Right," *Wall Street Journal*, February 13, 1990, p. B1. Reprinted by permission of the *Wall Street Journal*, © 1990 Dow Jones & Company, Inc. All Rights Reserved Worldwide.

185

___1. According to the article, all of the following pricing goals are probable EXCEPT:
   A. Increase profit.   C. Increase market share.   E. Meet competition.
   B. Increase sales   D. Stabilize prices.

___2. These marketers are conceivably using any of the following pricing strategies EXCEPT:
   A. Profit maximization.   D. Status-quo-oriented pricing.
   B. Nonprice competition.   E. Target-return-on-investment pricing.
   C. Predatory pricing.

PART 11K: Answers to Questions

PART 11D: Completion
1. Price
2 Utility
3. barter
4. good/service/supplementary services/ want-satisfying benefits
5. factors
6. market demand
7. product features/brand/quality/convenience/ price
8. high quality/low quality
9. value/perceived benefits/price
10. objective
11. profit/sales/status-quo
12. sales/investment/maximize
13. sales/market share
14. prices/competition
15. Target return on sales
16. Target return on investment
17. total output/product
18. rapid growth/potential competitors
19. growing/production capacity
20. price competition
21. follow-the-leader
22. Base/list
23. expected price/sales volume
24. expected
25. higher/greater
26. demand curve/price elasticity
27. directly similar products/available substitutes/unrelated products
28. product/distribution channels/promotional methods
29. Fixed costs
30. Variable costs
31. Marginal cost
32. downward
33. lowest/ATC
34. total cost/desired profit/demand/supply/ market conditions
35. cost-plus/profit
36. Marginal-cost
37. profit
38. offers
39. Retailers
40. percentage/producer
41. competition/market demand
42. total revenue/total cost/selling price
43. fixed cost/overhead
44. constant
45. demand/average unit costs
46. sell
47. Marginal revenue
48. Average revenue
49. volume of output/cost/revenue
50. accurate, reliable data
51. competitive/not differentiated
52. kinked demand
53. oligopoly
54. below
55. distinctive/acquired prestige

PART 11E: True-False Questions
1. F 2. T 3. T 4. T 5. T 6. F
7. F 8. F 9. F 10. T 11. F 12. F
13. F 14. T 15. T

PART 11F: Multiple Choice Questions
1. B 2. D 3. C 4. B 5. D 6. E
7. B 8. B 9. B 10. B 11. E 12. A
13. C 14. C 15. B

PART 11G: Matching Questions
a. 6 b. 12 c. 16 d. 2 e. 3 f. 18
g. 20 h. 14 i. 9 j. 22

APPENDIX B

FINANCIAL ACCOUNTING IN MARKETING

PART A: **Useful Formulae**

1. Net profit = Gross sales
   - Cost of goods sold
   - Gross margin
   - Expenses

   _____

2. Cost of goods sold = Value of stock on hand at beginning of period
   + Net cost of items purchased during period
   - Value of stock that remains unsold at end of period

   _____

3. Cost of goods manufactured = Value of goods partially completed at beginning of period
   + Cost of raw material, parts, labor, and factory overhead incurred during period
   - Value of goods still in process at end of period

   _____

4. Gross margin = Net sales
   - Cost of goods sold or manufactured

   _____

5. Markup percentage based on:

   a. Cost = $\dfrac{\text{Dollar markup}}{\text{Cost}}$

   b. Selling price = $\dfrac{\text{Dollar markup}}{\text{Selling price}}$

6. Computation of selling price =

	$	%
Selling price		
-Cost		
Markup	$	%

7. Percentage markup on:

    a. Selling price   =

$$\text{Selling price} = \frac{\text{Percentage markup on cost}}{100\% + \text{percentage markup on cost}}$$

    b. Cost   =

$$\text{Cost} = \frac{\text{Percentage markup on selling price}}{100\% - \text{percentage markup on selling price}}$$

8. Rate of stockturn   =

$$\text{Rate of stockturn} = \frac{\text{Cost of goods sold}}{\text{Average inventory at cost}}$$

9. Markdown percentage   =

$$\text{Markdown percentage} = \frac{\text{Dollar markdown}}{\text{Total net sales in dollars}}$$

10. Return on investment (ROI) =

$$\text{ROI} = \frac{\text{Net profit}}{\text{Sales}} \times \frac{\text{Sales}}{\text{Investment}}$$

PART B: Key Terms and Concepts

1. Price elasticity of demand	[320]	11. Cost of goods sold	[323]
2. Elastic demand	[320]	12. Expenses	[324]
3. Inelastic demand	[320]	13. Markup on cost	[324]
4. Balance sheet	[321]	14. Markup on selling price	[325]
5. Operating statement	[321]	15. Gross margin percentage	[328]
6. Net profit	[322]	16. Net profit percentage	[328]
7. Gross margin	[322]	17. Operating expense percentage	[328]
8. Gross sales	[323]	18. Stockturn rate	[328]
9. Sales returns and allowances	[323]	19. Markdown percentage	[328]
10. Net sales	[323]	20. Return on investment	[329]

PART C: Completion

1. Price _____ refers to the responsiveness of quantity demanded to price changes.

2. _____ demand occurs when: (1) reducing the unit price causes a(n) _____ in total revenue, or (2) raising the unit price causes a(n) _____ in total revenue.

3. The demand for necessities tends to be _____ .

4. The demand for products bought with discretionary income typically is more _____ .

5. A(n) _____ shows the assets, liabilities, and net worth of a firm at a given time, while a(n) _____ is a summary of the firm's income and expenses.

6. The main difference between the operating statement of a middleman and that of a manufacturer is in the _____ section.

7. The most important figure in the sales section of the operating statement is the _____ figure because it represents the net amount of _____ out of which the company pays for its products and expenses. This figure is also the one upon which many _____ are based.

8. It is usually recommended to value inventories at _____ or _____ value and use the _____ of the two figures.

9. _____ is one of the key figures in the entire marketing program because _____ are deducted from _____ to determine net profit.

10. Net profit is the difference between _____ and _____ .

11. Markup may be expressed as a percentage of either the _____ or the _____ price.

12. Markups are figured on the selling price at each _____ in a distribution channel.

13. The efficiency of marketing operations can often be measured by means of the _____ ratio.

14. A(n) _____ is a reduction from the original selling price.

15. The reason that markdowns do not appear on the profit-and-loss statement is that they occur _____ the item is _____.

16. A standard measure of managerial performance and the operating success of a company is its rate of return on _____ .

17. Determining the ROI involves the use of two separate elements: rate of _____ and the rate of _____ .

Answers to Questions

PART C: Completion

1. elasticity of demand
2. Elastic/increase/decrease
3. inelastic
4. elastic
5. balance sheet/operating statement
6. cost of goods sold
7. net sales/sales revenue/operating ratios
8. cost/market/lower
9. Gross margin/operating expenses/gross margin
10. gross margin/total expenses
11. cost/selling
12. level of business
13. stockturn
14. markdown
15. before/sold
16. investment
17. profit on sales/capital turnover

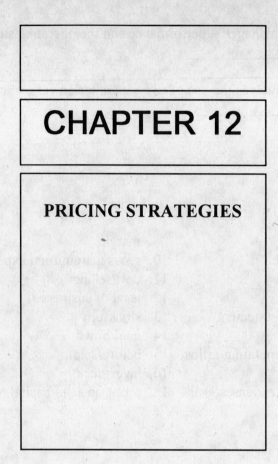

CHAPTER 12

PRICING STRATEGIES

PART 12A: Chapter Goals

After studying this chapter, you should be able to explain:

- Pricing strategies for entering a market, notably market skimming and market penetration
- Price discounts and allowances
- Geographic pricing strategies
- Special strategies, including one-price and flexible price approaches, unit pricing, price lining, resale price maintenance, leader pricing, and odd pricing
- Legal issues associated with pricing
- Price competition versus nonprice competition, including the concepts of value pricing and a price war

192

PART 12B: Key Terms and Concepts

1. Strategy [334]

2. Market-skimming pricing [334]

3. Market-penetration pricing [335]

4. Quantity discount [336]

    a. Noncumulative discount [336]

    b. Cumulative discount [337]

5. Trade (functional) discount [337]

6. Cash discount [337]

7. Seasonal discount [338]

8. Forward dating [338]

9. Promotional allowance [338]

10. Price discrimination [338]

11. Robinson-Patman Act provisions [339]

    a. Cost defense [339]

    b. Buyer's liability [339]

12. FOB factory (mill) pricing [340]

13. Uniform delivered pricing [341]

14. Zone delivered pricing [341]

15. Freight absorption pricing [341]

16. One-price policy [342]

17. Flexible-price (variable-price) strategy [342]

18. Single-price strategy [343]

19. Price lining [343]

20. Odd pricing [344]

21. Unit pricing [345]

22. Leader pricing [345]

    a. Leaders [345]

    b. Loss leaders [345]

23. Unfair-practices (unfair-sales) acts [345]

24. Resale price maintenance [346]

25. Suggested list price [346]

26. Price competition [347]

27. Value pricing [347]

28. Price war [350]

29. Nonprice competition [351]

PART 12C: Summary

One of the most important policy decisions is the pricing policy of the firm. The pricing policy can often be used as a promotional tool to expand the demand for the company's products.

The market for a company's products can be expanded by giving cumulative and quantity discounts [337] and trade (functional) discounts [337]. The demand for the entire line or for selected items can be stimulated by using some combination of cash discounts [337], seasonal discounts [338], forward dating [338], and promotional allowances [338]. Attention is also focused on the following concepts: one price versus flexible prices [342], unit pricing [345], price lining [343], resale price maintenance [346], leader pricing [345], odd pricing [345], and price competition versus nonprice competition [347]. Geographic considerations also play a role in pricing: such choices as FOB factory pricing [340], uniform delivered pricing [341], and freight absorption pricing [341] must be weighed. Special attention must be paid to the pricing of new products and one must consider whether to use market-skimming pricing [334] or market-penetration pricing [335] strategies when launching a new product.

The choice of a specific policy is influenced for the most part by the price strategy followed. Price policies and strategies are used by the marketer to stimulate demand, expand demand, maintain price stability, and effectively meet, prevent, and outperform the competition.

The law and current court rulings are flexible yardsticks by which the firm's pricing policy must be measured. The Robinson-Patman Act is one of the most important laws affecting marketing. Its main provisions--price discrimination, injury to competition, and buyer's liability--are receiving new meaning almost daily [339].

The nature of the competition, the type of product or service being offered, and customer perception of price play a dynamic role in the selection of price, policy, and strategy. The price manager, in a sense, is standing on quicksand. His movements can cause his death; however, strategic moves can enable him to pull himself free of peril. By manipulation of the policies and strategies discussed in this chapter, the price manager can, and should, anticipate competitive reactions, market trends, and selling opportunities. Such foresight should aid him in planning, analyzing, and controlling the price and terms of sales and in implementing his price policy and strategy.

PART 12D: Completion

1. In managing the price section of the firm's marketing mix, management first decides on its _____, then sets the _____ for a good or service, and finally designs the appropriate _____ compatible with the rest of the _____ .

2. A(n) _____ is a broad plan of action by which an organization intends to reach its goal.

3. _____ pricing involves setting a price that is _____ in the range of expected prices. This strategy is particularly suitable for _____.

4. Market-skimming keeps demand within the limits of a firm's _____ .

5. _____ pricing is a strategy in which a(n) _____ initial price is set in order to reach a mass market immediately.

6. Discounts and allowances result in a deduction from the _____ or _____ price.

7. Quantity discounts are deductions from a seller's _____ that are offered to encourage a customer to buy in _____ or to concentrate his purchases with _____.

8. They may be based on the size of the purchase either in _____ or in _____ .

9. The two types of quantity discounts currently in use are _____ and _____.

10. Noncumulative quantity discounts are based on the size of an individual order of _____ or _____ products, and are intended to encourage _____.

11. _____ discounts, those based on the _____ bought over a specified period, are advantageous to the seller because they tie customers more closely to him.

12. Trade discounts (_____) are a reduction from the _____ offered to buyers in payment for _____ they perform.

13. A(n) _____ is a reduction from prices granted to _____ for paying their bills within a specified time.

14. The cash discount is computed on the net amount after first deducting _____ and _____ discounts from the base price.

15. The three elements present in a cash discount are: (1) the _____ discount, (2) the _____ during which the discount may be taken, and (3) the time when the bill becomes _____.

16. _____ encourage buyers to place orders during the slack season.

17. Forward dating is a variation of seasonal and cash discounts in which the seller will seek orders in the _____ and the bill will be dated _____ at 2/10, N/30.

18. Promotional allowances are price reductions granted by sellers to buyers in payment for _____ performed by the buyer.

19. Whenever price differentials exist, there is price discrimination, which may be in violation of the _____ Act.

20. The main provisions of the Robinson-Patman Act outlaw _____ discrimination and _____ to competition.

195

21. Exceptions and defenses are that price differentials are allowable in response to changing conditions which affect the _____ of goods. Price differentials may be granted if they do not exceed differences in the cost of manufacture, sale, or delivery resulting from: (1) differences in the _____ or (2) _____ of sale of the product.

22. Under the Robinson-Patman Act, if a buyer forces a seller to grant an unlawful _____, he is as guilty as the seller who granted it.

23. Promotional _____ and _____ are legal only if they are offered to all competing customers on proportionally equal terms.

24. _____ discounts are potentially illegal under the Robinson-Patman Act.

25. _____ discounts are legal if all buyers within a given group were offered the same discount.

26. Under FOB point-of-production pricing, the _____ quotes the selling price at the factory and the _____ selects the mode of transportation and pays the cost of transportation.

27. In _____ pricing, the same delivered price is quoted to all buyers, regardless of their _____.

28. Under _____ pricing, the seller divides the market into a set number of geographic zones and a uniform price is set within each zone.

29. A(n) _____ policy is adopted to offset some of the competitive disadvantages of FOB factory pricing.

30. A one-price policy is a policy whereby the firm charges the _____ price to all similar types of _____ who buy identical _____ of the product.

31. A(n) _____ policy is one used when a firm will sell identical quantities to similar buyers at _____ prices.

32. With flexible pricing, buyer-seller _____ often determines the final price.

33. A(n) _____ strategy is an extreme variation of the one-price policy.

34. Under a policy of unit pricing, for each separate product and package size there is a shelf label which states the _____, and the price expressed in _____ and _____ per pound, ounce, pint, or other standard quantity measure.

35. _____ came about because package size proliferation made it virtually impossible to compare prices of similar products.

36. _____ consists of selecting a limited number of prices at which the business will sell related products.

37. _____ sets prices at uneven (odd) amounts rather than at even amounts.

38. The goal of _____ is to temporarily cut prices on a few items to attract customers.

39. The items whose prices are cut are called _____; if the leaders are priced below cost, they are called _____.

40. The intent of unfair-practice acts is to regulate _____.

41. Resale price maintenance was employed by _____ to govern prices at the retail level. Another technique they use is the suggested _____.

42. _____ is the result of a decision by management consistently to offer prices that are as low as possible and to offer a minimum of services.

43. _____ aims to improve the ratio of its benefits to its price--the product's value.

44. _____ begin when one firm cuts its price in order to increase sales volume and/or market share and competitors retaliate.

45. In nonprice competition, sellers maintain stable _____ and attempt to improve their _____ by emphasizing other aspects of their marketing program.

46. In price competition, sellers move up and down their _____ by changing prices.

47. In nonprice competition, sellers attempt to shift their demand curves to the _____ by means of _____, _____, or some other device.

PART 12E: True-False Questions

If the statement is true, circle "T"; if false, circle "F."

T F 1. Sometimes the demand for a product can be increased by raising its price.

T F 2. Product differentiation is a form of nonprice competition.

T F 3. A market-skimming strategy can be effectively used in the maturity stage of the product life cycle.

T F 4. In sales to business firms, a variable-price policy is more likely to be in violation of the Robinson-Patman Act than is a one-price policy.

T F 5. All other things being equal, an FOB factory price is a higher price than a freight absorption price.

T F 6. Market-penetration pricing by innovators may discourage other firms from entering the field.

T F 7. It makes sense for retailers to follow a one-price policy when trade-ins are involved.

T F 8. Generally, higher-income buyers are more likely to be aware of unit pricing than lower-income buyers.

T F 9. Cumulative quantity discounts encourage large individual orders but do not tend to tie a given customer to the seller.

T F 10. Trade discounts are a reduction from list prices and are offered for services rendered by the middleman getting the discount.

T F 11. Seasonal discounts encourage buyers to pay their bills quite soon after they receive the merchandise.

T F 12. An example of leader pricing is offering a turkey at cost just before Thanksgiving.

T F 13. Forward dating is a variation of both a trade discount and a cash discount.

T F 14. "Trade discounts" are the same things as "functional discounts."

T F 15. Actually, uniform delivered pricing is pricing FOB at the buyer's location.

PART 12F: Multiple Choice Questions

In the space provided write the letter of the answer that best fits the statement.

_____ 1. All of the following are geographic pricing strategies EXCEPT:
   A. FOB factory pricing.   C. Zone delivered pricing.   E. Unit pricing.
   B. Uniform delivered pricing. D. Freight absorption pricing.

_____ 2. Discounts that are based on the total volume bought over a period of time are called:
   A. Cumulative discounts.   C. Cash discounts.   E. Noncumulative discounts.
   B. Seasonal discounts.   D. Quantity discounts.

___ 3. As a major pricing policy, price lining does all of the following EXCEPT:
   A. Make it easier for management to plan their purchases.
   B. Simplify the customer's buying decision.
   C. Put a squeeze on price lines every time costs go up.
   D. Make it easier to price such things as dresses and shoes.
   E. Violate the Robinson-Patman Act.

___ 4. Regarding nonprice competition:
   A. It involves sellers shifting their demand curves so that they are increasing the number of units sold without a change in price.
   B. It is not compatible with promotion.
   C. It is not compatible with product differentiation.
   D. It means that sellers are manipulating demand by changing the price.
   E. None of the above.

___ 5. Cash discounts are used to encourage:
   A. Buyers to provide warehousing by buying in advance of the season.
   B. Buyers to pay their bills promptly.
   C. Middlemen to perform more services.
   D. Cooperative advertising on the part of retailers.
   E. A freight absorption pricing strategy on the part of wholesalers.

___ 6. An invoice dated March 11, 1993, has a trade discount of 40 percent, a quantity discount of 10 percent, and terms of trade of 2/10, N/30. If the list price is $1,831.80, the net price is _____ assuming the buyer pays by March 21, 1993.
   A. $952.54 B. $897.58 C. $969.39 D. $1,077.10 E. $1,055.56

___ 7. A manufacturer of tennis balls who wishes to maintain production during the winter season for more efficient use of plant and equipment would offer merchandise with terms of 1/10, net 30 days effective May 1. This is known as:
   A. A seasonal discount.   C. A trade discount.   E. A promotional allowance.
   B. Forward dating.   D. A functional discount.

___ 8. All of the following are characteristics of market-skimming pricing EXCEPT:
   A. Used in the late stages of the product life cycle.
   B. Can lead to healthy profit margins.
   C. Acts as a hedge against a possible mistake in setting the price.
   D. Covers research and development costs quickly.
   E. The product's distinctiveness lends itself to effective marketing.

___ 9. A wholesaler who receives a chain discount of 40-20-20 percent off a list price of $317.10 would pay:
   A. $253.68.   B. $121.77.   C. $126.84.   D. $236.18.   E. $201.19.

____ 10. In spite of the fact that purchases are made at many different wholesale costs, a certain retailer follows the practice of selling each type of fashion apparel at only three, four, or five well-established retail prices. This is called:
   A. Price lining.
   B. Odd pricing.
   C. Forward dating.
   D. Market-penetration pricing.
   E. Resale price maintenance.

____ 11. A firm with excess capacity whose fixed costs per unit of product are high and whose variable costs are low is a candidate for _____ pricing.
   A. Zone delivered
   B. Uniform delivered
   C. Freight absorption
   D. FOB point-of-production
   E. Market-skimming

____ 12. Every cash discount includes the:
   A. Percentage discount itself.
   B. Time period during which the discount can be taken.
   C. Time when the bill becomes overdue.
   D. All of the above.
   E. None of the above.

____ 13. Discounts granted to customers for paying their bills within a specified period of time are called:
   A. Cumulative discounts.
   B. Noncumulative discounts
   C. Quantity discounts.
   D. Cash discounts.
   E. Promotional allowances.

____ 14. Fair-trade laws had the effect of permitting:
   A. The federal government to determine prices.
   B. State governments to determine prices.
   C. Large stores to sell at prices lower than those of small stores.
   D. Manufacturers to set the retail price of their products.
   E. Chain-store operators to get a competitive edge over small independent stores.

____ 15. The Robinson-Patman Act is concerned primarily with the regulation of:
   A. Restraint of trade.
   B. Unfair competition.
   C. Price discrimination.
   D. Nonprice competition.
   E. Cartels.

PART 12G: Matching Questions

In the space provided write the number of the word or expression from column 1 that best fits the description in column 2.

1	2
1. Cash discount	____ a. A reduction offered from list prices in order to encourage large or repeat purchases.
2. Cumulative discount	____ b. The base or basic price for a product.
3. FOB factory price	____ c. Selecting a limited number of prices at which a store will sell its merchandise.
4. Forward dating	
5. Freight absorption pricing	____ d. A reduction offered from full prices in payment for marketing services performed.
6. Leader pricing	____ e. A deduction granted a buyer for paying a bill within a specified period.
7. Market-penetration pricing	
8. Market-skimming pricing	____ f. Prohibits price discrimination.
9. Noncumulative discount	____ g. Sometimes called "postage stamp pricing."
10. Nonprice competiton	____ h. An example of this pricing is "FOB destination."
11. Odd pricing	____ i. In reality, patronage discounts.
12. Price lining	____ j. Sometimes called "fair trade laws."
13. Promotional allowance	____ k. Price strategy selected for a temporary price cut in order to attract patrons.
14. Quantity discount	____ l. An example of this is a price of $19.95.
15. Resale price maintenance	
16. Robinson-Patman Act provisions	
17. Seasonal discount	
18. Suggested list price	

19. Trade discount

20. Unfair practices acts

21. Uniform delivered pricing

22. Unit pricing

23. Value pricing

24. Zone delivered pricing

PART 12H: Problems and Applications

1. Two customers, living in the same city, buy a new car from the same dealer. The cars are identical. One buyer pays $150 more than the other. Is this a violation of the Robinson-Patman Act? Explain.

2. The Miller Meat Co. has just moved into a new plant with a capacity four times that of their old plant. Mr. Miller is reviewing his price policy. In the past, his terms were FOB destination. However, the Miller Meat Co. would like to expand its present market. Explain to Mr. Miller several price policies you think he might consider. What are the advantages and   disadvantages of each?

3. Ms. Phipps has just bought five new desks for her office. The invoice shows a cost of $2,160.00 and is dated October 16, 1992. The terms are 2/10, N/30. How much should she pay the Zimmer Office Mfg. Co. if she pays the bill by October 26, 1992? $_____. How much will she be required to pay if she pays the bill on November 11, 1992? $ _____.

4. Assume Ms. Phipps's is on the East Coast and her supplier is on the West. Although the bill is dated October 16, the desks did not arrive until October 28. What should Ms. Phipps do? How could the supplier take care of this problem in the future?

5. If Ms. Phipps pays her bill promptly, the 2 percent earned for a 20-day period represents a saving at the rate of ___ percent a year.

6. Visit a Hoover vacuum dealer and find out what Hoover has to offer as a line of vacuum cleaners. Also obtain the list price for each item in the line. What can you conclude about pricing multiple products?

7. Interview four different types of local retailers and determine what terms of sale are customarily applied to their product or service. What accounts for the difference among retailers?

8. Visit an automobile dealer and a wholesale auto parts house and determine if they have a variable-price policy or a one-price policy for parts. Report your findings in memo form to your instructor.

9. What recent court cases have involved the Robinson-Patman Act? Briefly explain the situation in each case. The loose-leaf service on trade regulations offered by the Commerce Clearing House is one source of information; "The Legal Developments in Marketing" section in the *Journal of Marketing* is another.

10. Visit a grocery store in the community and record the prices for a quart of nonfat milk, a 16 oz. loaf of rye bread, a can of dog food, a dozen AA eggs, a six-pack of Coors Beer, and a six-pack of Pepsi Cola. What conclusions can you make about odd pricing? Report your findings and conclusions in a memo to your instructor.

11. The R. B. Snow Co., a manufacturer of fountain pens, is currently considering marketing a product in two price categories. It has completed some price research and found the demand curve to be relatively inelastic from $1.69 to $1.79 and relatively elastic from $1.59 to $1.69, as shown in the following figure.

The company would like to maintain a gross margin of 20 percent. If the cost of the pen is $0.671 and the wholesaler wants a 15 percent markup and the retailer wants a 40 percent markup, can the company make a 20 percent gross margin at a retail selling price of $1.59?

	Gross margin required above cost
A. Selling price to wholesaler	20%
B. Wholesale price to retailer	15%
C. Retail price to consumer	40%
D. Snow Co. computed gross margin on a retail price of $1.59	_____
E. Snow Co. gross margin at $1.79	_____

12. In price competition, sellers attempt to move up and down their demand curves by changing the price. In nonprice competition, sellers attempt to shift their demand curves to the right by means of product differentiation, promotional activities, or some other device. Write a memo explaining how a producer can attempt to accomplish nonprice competition by leasing or selling on consignment. This subject is discussed in the chapter entitled The Business Market.

PART 12I (a): Exercise

Philips-Gouday, Inc., is the third largest manufacturer of ceiling and wall insulation in the nation.
The insulation is made of fiber glass and comes in three forms: (1) thinner-sized rolls that are
stapled between wall studs and ceiling joists, (2) thicker-sized battens that are mostly laid between
ceiling joists, and (3) large bags of loose fiber glass used by "blown-in" insulation contractors. All
three forms are light but quite bulky. As a consequence, shipping costs are high, not because of
weight but because of the volume involved.

The company has five mills: Albany, New York; Atlanta; Chicago; Los Angeles; and Portland,
Oregon. It has two traditional customers: home improvement centers and insulation contractors.
A third type, potentially the largest, has recently emerged. This is the public utility that sells
insulation at cost to its metered customers, who pay off the cost of the insulation over a period of
time through their utility bills.

In keeping with the rest of the industry, the company has consistently maintained a single
geographic pricing policy. They sell their products "FOB mill," with each customer bearing the
full cost of freight and insurance from the moment the shipment leaves the factory to arrival at its
destination.

In view of the potential sales in the emerging third market, you, as traffic manager for P-G, have
decided to review the company's entire geographic pricing policy and make a recommendation to
your boss, the vice-president of marketing. You are not necessarily tied to a single policy. You
want to keep and even expand your market share of your traditional markets and you also want to
become the principal factor in the utility market.

In the space provided, evaluate each pricing policy. Select the most appropriate alternative(s) and
justify your choice(s).

FOB mill

Uniform delivered pricing

Zone delivered pricing

Freight absorption pricing

PART 12I (b): Exercise

As president of a consulting firm specializing in marketing, you must make recommendations to your clients regarding the pricing of eight as yet unnamed new products. You are trying to decide between recommending market-penetration and market-skimming pricing strategies. As you decide, you will estimate carefully the "expected" price--also being mindful not to set the price too low.

New Product	Recommended Price, Strategy, and Justification
1. Givency perfume	
2. "Light" beer	
3. Wine cooler	
4. Cake mix	
5. Electric car	
6. Gasohol	
7. Solar-powered hot tub	
8. Rollerblades	

PART 12J: A Real World Case: Discounting for Market Share

No matter how you look at it, the recession has been good to discount cigarette brands. And no one could be happier than the people working on the Doral brand at R. J. Reynolds.

This year Doral has jumped to fifth place in the SuperBrands ranking, tying Kool, which is Brown & Williamson's only Top 10 brand. That's a surge of four spots in just a year.

But discount brands continuye to be the only success story in the U.S. cigarette market, due mainly to high taxes and price hikes by manufacturers on full-price brands. But the discount sub-category has grown enormously, accounting for 23% of the market.

A discount brand is certainly cheaper to promote. While Philip Morris USA spent almost $100 million to advertise the No. 1 Marlboro brand, Doral clocked in at a tiny $1.18 million--on retail sales of $2.07 billion. To its credit, Marlboro did have $11.6 billion in retail sales and a 25% share of the market, according to estimates by John Maxwell of Wheat First Securities in Richmond, Va.

Full-price players haven't given up. RJR is in the midst of re-energizing the No. 2 Winston brand. In 1991 the company spent $42.5 million, according to Leading National Advertisers, for the struggling brand. It's been repackaged in a fresh wrap. A smoother, flanker brand, Winston Select, has been added to appeal to younger smokers who generally choose Marlboro.

	Brand	Company Name	Sales (billions)	Media Expenditures (millions)
1	Marlboro	Philip Morris USA	$11.60	$99.8
2	Winston	R. J. Reynolds Tobacco Co.	3.37	42.5
3	Salem	R. J. Reynolds Tobacco Co.	2.43	7.8
4	Newport	Lorillard Inc.	2.11	41.9
5	Doral	R. J. Reynolds Tobacco Co.	2.07	1.18
6	Kool	Brown & Williamson Tobacco	2.07	12.1
7	Camel	R. J. Reynolds Tobacco Co.	1.8	8.4
8	Benson & Hedges	Philip Morris USA	1.44	15.3
9	Merit	Philip Morris USA	1.39	8.1
10	Virginia Slims	Philip Morris USA	1.26	20.9

Reynolds continues to struggle with Joe Camel. The cartoon character has bolstered Camel's share, but anti-smoking activists have repeatedly bashed the brand's reputation. In June, the American Medical Association staged a protest against Joe, following a December 1991 *Journal*

206

of the American Medical Association study that showed the character was a familiar to children as Mickey Mouse. Reynolds rebutted those studies with its own research.

Brown & Williamson has tested a campaign with a cartoon penguin. But it has yet to go national, fearing similar backlash.

Instead of creating new ad campaigns, Philip Morris has turned to promotions to boost its brands. This summer [1992] it introduced a five-pack of cigarettes to combat the high price of a full carton, which, including tax, can easily cost more than $21.

The industry leader is also trying to revive its Benson & Hedges cigarette by introducing a king-sized version of the tony brand. Unlike Doral and other discounters, PM is backing the original Benson & Hedges 100s with a sweepstakes program featuring upscale prizes.

While the U.S. market shrinks, tobacco's last best hope is in Europe, where the anti-smoking movement has yet to heat up. The former Communist bloc is an especially attractive possibility. So far, Philip Morris has made the biggest moves. The company has bought a major share in Czechoslovakia's tobacco industry and plans to use that position to launch into the former Soviet Union.

───────────

Source: Fara Warner, "Discount Durability," *Superbrands 1992*, p. 10.
© 1992 ADWEEK L.P. used by permission of BRANDWEEK.

───────────

____ 1. According to the article, Doral's pricing strategy seems to be to:
A. Cut prices on established products rather than on new brands.
B. Cut the prices during the high-volume season.
C. Realize this is a good way to freeze out new brands trying to enter the market.
D. Make frequent cuts because each one will bring successively larger gains in market position.
E. None of the above is correct.

____ 2. Doral's pricing scheme could be called a(n)_____strategy.
A. Discounter's   D. Market-skimming
B. Odd pricing   E. Freight absorption
C. One-price

PART 12K: Answers to Questions

PART 12D: Completion

1. pricing goal/base price/pricing strategies/ marketing mix
2. strategy
3. Market-skimming/high/new products
4. production capacities
5. Market-penetration/low
6. base/list
7. list price/larger amounts/one seller
8. dollars/units
9. noncumulative/cumulative
10. one/more/large orders
11. Cumulative/total volume
12. functional discounts/list price/marketing functions
13. cash discount/buyers
14. trade/quantity
15. percentage/time period/overdue
16. Seasonal discounts
17. winter/April 1
18. promotional services
19. Robinson-Patman
20. price/injury
21. marketability/quantity sold/various methods
22. price differential
23. services/allowances
24. Quantity
25. Trade
26. seller/buyer
27. uniform delivered/location
28. zone delivered
29. freight absorption
30. same/customers/quantities

31. flexible-price/different
32. bargaining
33. single-price
34. price of the package/dollars/cents
35. Unit pricing
36. Price lining
37. Odd pricing
38. leader pricing
39. leaders/loss leaders
40. leader pricing
41. manufacturers/list price
42. Price competition
43. Value pricing
44. Price wars
45. prices/market positions
46. demand curves
47. right/product differentiations/promotional activities

PART 12E: True-False Questions
1. T 2. T 3. F 4 T 5. F 6. T
7. F 8. T 9. F 10 T 11. F 12. T
13. F 14. T 15. T

PART 12F: Multiple Choice Questions
1. E 2. A 3. E 4. B 5. B 6. C
7. B 8. A 9. B 10. A 11. C 12. D
13. D 14. D 15. C

PART 12G: Matching Questions
a. 14 b. 18 c. 12 d. 19 e. 1 f. 16
g. 21 h. 5 i. 2 j. 15 k. 6 l. 11

PART FIVE

DISTRIBUTION

CHAPTER 13

CHANNELS OF DISTRIBUTION

PART 13A: Chapter Goals

After studying this chapter, you should be able to explain:

- The nature and importance of middlemen
- What a distribution channel is
- The sequence of decisions involved in designing a channel
- The major channels for consumer gods, business goods, and services
- Vertical marketing systems
- Intensity of distribution
- How to choose individual middlemen
- The nature of conflicts and control within distribution channels
- Legal considerations in channels management

211

PART 13B: Key Terms and Concepts

1. Middleman [362]

2. Merchant middleman [362]

3. Agent middleman [362]

4. Shifting of functions [363]

5. Distribution channel [363]

6. Direct distribution [367

7. Indirect distribution [367]

8. Multiple distribution channels [369]

9. Vertical marketing system [371]

10. Corporate vertical marketing system [371]

11. Contractual vertical marketing system [371]

12. Administered vertical marketing system [371]

13. Systems integrator [372]

14. Intensity of distribution [375]

15. Intensive distribution marketing system [376]

16. Selective distribution [376]

17. Exclusive distribution [376]

18. Channel conflict [377]

19. Horizontal conflict [377]

20. Scrambled merchandising [378]

21. Vertical conflict [379]

22. Slotting allowance [381]

23. Channel control [382]

24. Channel power [382]

25. Exclusive dealing [383]

26. Tying contract [383]

27. Refusal to deal [384]

28. Exclusive territory policy [384]

PART 13C: Summary

The job required of distribution is to get the product to its target market. Standing between the company and the consumer are a large group of independent businesses called middlemen [362]. Middlemen are ready to help the producer by performing activities and rendering services in connection with the purchase and/or sale of his products [362]. A channel of distribution may be defined as the set of people and firms involved in the flow of the title of a product as it moves from producer to consumer or business user [363].

The establishment of a channel of distribution involves four tasks. The first is to delineate the role of distribution within the marketing mix [365]. The next is to select the basic channel itself [365]. Elements such as the market, the product, the middlemen, and the company itself must be carefully weighed. The third is to determine the intensity of distribution; that is, how many middlemen will be used at each distribution level in a given market [366]. The final task is to select the individual middlemen and develop and foster the necessary cooperative relationship among them [366].

Forging and maintaining the links making up the channel gives rise to competitive conflicts in these distribution systems. They can be of a vertical nature (vertical conflict); that is, between retailer and wholesaler, between manufacturer and retailer, or between manufacturer and wholesaler [379]. Conflicts also exist on the same level of distribution (horizontal conflict), and generally arise from three sources: the market, middlemen, or manufacturers [377]. The main form of horizontal conflict has been the competition caused by scrambled merchandising [378]. Manufacturers, wholesalers, and retailers each have their own reasons, courses of action, and strategies in response to their environment. The newer vertical marketing systems offer significant economies of scale and increased coordination in distribution.

Channel members often strive for some control over other members. Depending on the circumstances, producers do not always dominate the channel--wholesalers and retailers can be channel managers too [382]. The most productive view is that all channel members see themselves as part of a system requiring cooperation.

PART 13D: Completion

1. Distribution's role within a marketing mix is to get the product to its _____.

2. A(n) _____ is a business firm that renders services directly related to the purchase and/or sale of a product as it flows from _____ to _____.

3. _____ actually take title to the products involved.

4. _____ do not take title but assist in the transfer of title.

5. It is one of the truisms in marketing that you can eliminate middlemen, but you can't eliminate _____.

6. Middlemen serve as _____ for their customers and as _____ for their suppliers.

7. A channel of distribution for a product consists of a set of _____ and _____ involved in the flow of the _____ to a product as it moves from producer to the ultimate consumer or business user.

213

8. A channel of distribution extends to the last person or organization that buys the product without making any significant change in its _____. When its form is altered and another product emerges, a new _____ is started.

9. In designing channels, a company wants a distribution channel that not only meets _____ needs but also provides an edge on _____.

10. The design requires four steps: (1) delineating the _____ of distribution, (2) selecting the _____of channel, (3) determining the _____of distribution (the number of middlemen used at the _____ and _____ levels in a particular territory), and (4) choosing specific _____.

11. In choosing specific channel members, a manufacturer needs to assess: (1) the _____, (2) the _____, (3) its own _____, (4) _____, (5) whether the middleman _____to the market the manufacturer wants to reach, and (6) whether the middleman's product _____, pricing _____, _____, and _____ are compatible with the producer.

12. A channel strategy should be designed within the context of an entire _____.

13. A channel consisting only of _____ and _____, with no middlemen providing assistance, is called _____ distribution.

14. In contrast, a channel consisting of _____, _____, and at least _____ level of middleman represents _____ distribution.

15. The most frequently used channels for consumer goods are: (1) _____-consumer; (2) producer-_____-consumer; (3) producer-_____- retailer-consumer; (4) producer-_____-retailer-consumer, and (5) producer-_____-wholesaler-_____ -consumer.

16. For business products they are: (1) _____-business user; (2) producer-_____-user; (3) producer-_____-user; and (4) producer-_____ -industrial distributor-_____.

17. For services: (1) _____-customer, and (2) producer-_____-producer.

18. A manufacturer may use multiple channels (also called dual distribution) either to reach _____ types of markets or to sell to different _____ within a(n) _____ market.

19. Differences in _____ of buyers or of geographic _____ often result in the use of more than one channel.

20. A significant trend is the use of producers of _____ channel systems to sell the same _____ to a(n) _____ market. This strategy aggravates _____.

21. A(n) _____ marketing system is a tightly coordinated distribution channel designed to achieve _____ efficiencies and _____ effectiveness.

22. Vertical marketing systems are characterized as _____, _____, and _____.

23. In a variation of an administered VMS, a(n) _____ pulls together all the products needed to present a business solution to a customer.

24. In a(n) _____ vertical marketing system, the production and marketing facilities are owned by the same company.

25. In _____ vertical marketing systems, independent firms are banded together by contracts to achieve the necessary efficiencies and effectiveness.

26. In _____ vertical marketing systems, the necessary coordination of production and marketing activities is achieved through the domination of one powerful _____ member or the shared power of _____.

27. Seven market considerations affecting choice of channels of distribution are: (1) type of _____; (2) number of potential _____; (3) geographic _____ of the market; (4) _____ size, (5) _____ considerations, (6) _____ considerations, and (7) _____ considerations.

28. Among the product considerations in channel selection are: _____ value, _____, and _____ nature of the product.

29. Three middlemen considerations affecting channel selection are: (1) _____ provided by middlemen; (2) _____ of desired middlemen; and (3) the _____ of middlemen toward a producer's _____.

30. Four basic company considerations affecting channel selection are: (1) desire for _____,(2) _____ provided by the seller, (3) ability of _____, and (4) _____ resources.

31. The producer has three major alternative courses of action in the field of distribution intensity: _____, _____, and _____.

32. Ordinarily the policy of intensive distribution is adopted by producers of consumer _____ goods.

33. Firms choose selective distribution to enhance the _____ of their products, strengthen customer _____, and/or improve _____.

34. Under a(n) _____ distribution policy, the supplier enters into an agreement with a particular _____ and/or _____ in a given market.

35. Under these arrangements, the middlemen are sometimes prohibited from handling a directly _____ line of products.

36. Under an exclusive distribution policy, a dealer is often willing to _____ the product aggressively because he realizes his future is tied to the success of the _____.

37. _____ exists when one channel member perceives another channel member to be acting in a way that prevents the first member from achieving its distribution objectives.

38. There are two types of conflict: _____ and _____.

39. Horizontal conflicts--those which occur on the same level of distribution--consists of: (1) competition between middlemen of the _____ and (2) competition between _____ of middlemen on the same level.

40. The main source of horizontal conflict is _____--the practice of diversifying a product assortment by adding merchandise lines not traditionally carried by this type of business.

41. The stimulus for scrambled merchandising among middlemen and for the crossing of traditional channel lines may come from three general sources: the _____, the _____ , or the _____.

42. The most severe conflicts in distribution systems, _____ conflicts, are conflicts among firms on different levels of the same channel.

43. A manufacturer wishing to bypass wholesalers can: (1) sell directly to _____ or (2) sell directly to _____.

44. Direct distribution is advantageous where the product: (1) is subject to physical or fashion _____, (2) is high _____, (3) is _____, and/or (4) requires _____ and _____ service.

45. There are several courses of action open to wholesalers to improve their competitive position: (1) improve _____; (2) provide _____ to retailers; (3) form _____; and (4) develop _____.

46. Some retailers are demanding a(n) _____ to place a manufacturer's product on store shelves.

47. A manufacturer can use several weapons in his efforts to dominate the retailer: build strong customer _____, establish one or more forms of _____ marketing systems, and _____ to uncooperative retailers.

48. In response, retailers can develop _____ loyalty among consumers, improve computerized _____, and form a(n) _____.

49. The ability to influence the behavior of other channel members is called _____.

50. Manufacturers argue that they should control the channel since they create the new _____ and need increasing _____ volume to achieve _____ of scale.

51. Retailers, on the other hand, argue that since they are closer to the _____, they know them better.

52. Channels of distribution should be treated as though each member is part of a(n) _____ designed to provide want-satisfaction to the customer.

53. A possible reason that manufacturers have problems with channels is that _____ is in charge of them.

54. Legal considerations in managing channels include _____ dealing, _____ contracts, _____ to deal, and exclusive _____.

PART 13E: True-False Questions

If the statement is true, circle "T"; if false, circle "F."

T F   1. Exclusive dealing contracts are illegal.

T F   2. The decision by a manufacturer to bypass the wholesaler must be made on noneconomic criteria because the wholesaler can always perform the traditional wholesaling functions at the lowest cost.

T F   3. A manufacturer can reduce his financial and managerial problems in marketing by establishing sales offices or branches.

T F   4. Channels of distribution should be determined basically by the buying habits of the ultimate customers for a given product.

217

T F   5. A company's distribution system should be flexible enough so that the use of one trade channel will not preclude the use of another.

T F   6. The longer the channel, the easier it is for a manufacturer to control the distribution of his product.

T F   7. The hardest job in setting up a channel of distribution is to select the appropriate middlemen, since it pretty well runs itself after that.

T F   8. A channel of distribution does not formally include banks, insurance companies, shipping companies, and storage firms.

T F   9. Competitive conflict, by definition, must be horizontal in nature.

T F 10. Scrambled merchandising may cause conflict on the same distribution level.

T F 11. The manufacturer is the one channel member who makes the decision regarding the selection of individual channel outlets.

T F 12. It is usually a bad idea for a manufacturer to use more than one channel of distribution.

T F 13. Manufacturers achieve greatest control over channels in a corporate vertical marketing system.

T F 14. If a manufacturer wishes to bypass his wholesaler, the only alternative which remains open to him is to sell directly to the retailer.

T F 15. Direct selling often places a greater financial burden on the producer.

PART 13F: Multiple Choice Questions

In the space provided write the letter of the answer that best fits the statement.

_____ 1. A policy of intensive distribution is most likely to be associated with:
    A. Expensive merchandise.   D. Fashion apparel.
    B. Agricultural equipment.   E. Convenience goods.
    C. Shopping goods.

_____ 2. Intensive distribution will most likely be used by a producer of:
    A. Tractors.   D. Furniture.
    B. Typewriters.   E. Women's apparel.
    C. Cleaning supplies.

___ 3. Probably the best distribution policy for a manufacturer of ball-point pens designed to sell for 98 cents throughout the nation is to:
   A. Sell directly to retailers, using exclusive agencies.
   B. Use wholesalers and intensive distribution.
   C. Establish sales offices and, through them, sell to retailers on an exclusive basis.
   D. Sell directly to retailers, using intensive distribution.
   E. Use wholesalers on an exclusive-agency basis.

___ 4. If there is a "traditional" channel of distribution for consumer goods, it is:
   A. Producer-consumer.
   B. Producer-wholesaler-retailer-consumer.
   C. Producer-retailer-consumer.
   D. Producer-agent-retailer-consumer.
   E. Producer-agent-wholesaler-industrial user.

___ 5. When selecting individual middlemen, the most important factor for a manufacturer to consider is:
   A. Does he sell to the market I want to reach?
   B. Does he have a modern facility?
   C. Will he advertise my product?
   D. Is he a discount retailer?
   E. Is he big?

___ 6. Most of the major manufacturers of grocery products generally use _____ distribution at the retail level.
   A. Intensive   D. Any of the above is desirable
   B. Selective   E. None of the above
   C. Exclusive

___ 7. A major cause of channel conflict on the same level of distribution has been the:
   A. Growth of scrambled merchandising.
   B. Desire of retailers to control the channels of distribution.
   C. Desire of wholesalers to control the channels of distribution.
   D. Manufacturers' dissatisfaction with wholesalers.
   E. Increase in self-service selling.

___ 8. Regarding channel leadership, the text takes the position that channel control should be:
   A. In the hands of producers, because they make the products.
   B. In the hands of retailers since they stand closest to consumers.
   C. Run by wholesalers since they stand between retailers and manufacturers.
   D. In the hands of retailers since they are in the best position to implement the marketing concept.
   E. A balance of power among all channel members.

9. What distribution policy would a manufacturer of high-fashion apparel most likely follow?
   A. Use all department stores as outlets.
   B. Use as many retail outlets as possible.
   C. Use all apparel shops as outlets.
   D. Use mail-order distribution.
   E. Limit the number of outlets.

10. Which statement best describes merchant middlemen?
    A. They do not take title, but they do actively assist in the transfer of title.
    B. They actually take title to the goods they are helping to market.
    C. They do not sell to other middlemen.
    D. While actually not taking title, they take possession.
    E. All of the above apply.

11. Of the following types of middlemen, which is the only one who takes title to the goods?
    A. A stockbroker.   D. A real estate broker.
    B. A selling agent.   E. A commission merchant.
    C. A merchant wholesaler.

12. The channel of producer-business user is most likely to be used by:
    A. A manufacturer of paper products for general office use.
    B. A manufacturer of safety goggles.
    C. A manufacturer of railroad tank cars.
    D. A manufacturer of dictating equipment intended for used by traveling sales people
    E. None of the above.

13. A channel of distribution does not formally include:
    A. Banks.   D. Storage firms.
    B. Insurance companies   E. Any of the above.
    C. Transportation firms.

14. Manufacturers achieve greatest control over channels in a(n) _____marketing system.
    A. Corporate vertical   D. Administered vertical
    B. Contractual vertical   E. Administered horizontal
    C. Contractual horizontal

15. A company consideration in choosing a distribution channel for a product is:
    A. Desire for channel control.   D. Financial resources.
    B. Services provided by seller.   E. All of the above.
    C. Ability of management.

PART 13G: Matching Questions

In the space provided write the number of the word or expression from column 1 that best fits the description in column 2.

1	2
1. Administered vertical	____ a. The dominant party in a multistage marketing system channel.
2. Agent middlemen	
	____ b. A channel system wherein the production and marketing facilities are owned by the same firm.
3. Channel conflict	
4. Channel control	
	____ c. Another name for multiple channels of distribution.
5. Channel of distribution	
6. Channel manager	____ d. An agreement requiring a customer to buy a product he does not want in order to get a desired product.
7. Contractual vertical marketing system	
8. Corporate vertical marketing system	____ e. The main cause of horizontal conflict.
9. Direct distribution	____ f. Examples are manufacturers' agents and brokers.
10. Dual distribution	
	____ g. The route taken by the title to a product as it moves from producer to consumer or business user.
11. Exclusive dealing	
12. Exclusive distribution	
	____ h. A business firm that renders services directly related to the purchase and/or sale of a product as it flows from producer to consumer.
13. Indirect distribution	
14. Intensive distribution	
15. Merchant middleman	____ i. A channel with no middlemen.
16. Middleman	____ j. Ordinarily the policy adopted by producers of consumer convenience goods.
17. Refusal to deal	
	____ k. A fee paid by manufacturers to place their product on store shelves.
18. Scrambled merchandising	
19. Selective distribution	

20. Slotting allowance

21. Vertical marketing system

22. Tying contract

PART 13H: Problems and Applications

1.   Changes will occur in the distribution system. William R. Davidson, late professor and chairman, Faculty of Marketing, The Ohio State University, selected the following six changes for discussion on the subject (see "Changes in Distributive Institutions," *Journal of Marketing*, vol. 34, no. 1, January, 1970).

        A.   Rapid growth of vertical marketing systems.
        B.   Intensification of intertype competition (also known as scrambled merchandising).
        C.   Increasing polarity of retail trade.
        D.   Acceleration of institutional life cycles.
        E.   Emergence of the "free-form" corporation as a major competitive reality in distribution.
        F.   The expansion of nonstore retailing.

Read the article and select for further study one of the changes Professor Davidson discusses. Select a metropolitan statistical area of your choice for study. What can you conclude about the "trend" in the metropolitan area you have selected for study? Write a report to your   instructor on your findings and conclusions.

2.   Visit a retail store. Talk with the owner or manager about the new product lines he has added to his product mix and those that he has dropped in the last five years. What can you conclude about scrambled merchandising? Write a one-page memo to your instructor reporting your findings and conclusions.

3.   Develop a schematic model of a vertical marketing system. Illustrate how your model would apply to Sears. What conclusions can you make about vertical marketing systems and conflict in distribution channels?

4.   Visit a retailer or distributor and find out what kind of working relationships they have with their suppliers in the following areas:
        A.   Promotional and managerial assistance
        B.   Sales manuals
        C.   Sales training courses

What can you conclude about the type of help offered? Write a memo to your instructor on your findings and conclusions.

5.   Can you eliminate the wholesaler function? Why or why not?

6.   You are the manufacturer of a new three-hole punch. Your product has been designed to sell at a retail price of $8.95.

   A. Determine what you need to know about the product, the market, and the application to establish a channel of distribution.
   B. Design a channel of distribution for the three-hole punch.
   C. Write a memo to your instructor justifying your channel of distribution. Your memo should cover market considerations, product considerations, company considerations, middlemen considerations, intensity of distribution, and selection of middlemen.

PART 13I: Exercise

Some years ago, American Tobacco Company was shaken to its foundations by the Surgeon General's reports linking cigarette smoking and cancer. It decided to diversify. American Tobacco bought the following corporations:

Franklin Life Insurance	Master Lock Co.
Jim Beam Brands Co. .	Titleist (golf balls)
Swingline, Inc. (staplers)	Moen (faucets)

In keeping with its new objectives, American Tobacco changed its name to American Brands. You, as Vice President for Marketing of American Brands, are reviewing the channels of distribution for each subsidiary. You are asking each subsidiary to give you a description of the two most common channels of distribution they utilize.

If there is duplication, you will demand that the subsidiaries involved combine their marketing effort by using the same advertising agency, channels of distribution, physical distribution system, and sales force.

1.   Draw the two channels of distribution for each subsidiary.

2.   Are there any duplications in the channels? If so, what do you think would be the effect of:
    A. Using the same advertising agency?
    B. Using the same distribution system?
    C. Combining the sales forces?

3.   What amount will each of the following middlemen demand in terms of markup?

223

A. Retailer _____
B. Wholesaler _____
C. Manufacturer _____

Use an average markup for each type of middleman as presented in the text. Also consult Appendix B on Marketing Mathematics.

PART 13J: A Real World Case: War in the Channels

Note to the reader: as added detail to the text's lead-in discussion regarding Goodyear's decision to sell their premium-priced tires through Sears, Roebuck & Co., consider the following article.

Goodyear Tire & Rubber Co. is learning something about independent dealers: they can fight back.

Last March [1991], the giant Akron, Ohio-based tire maker announced plans to sell Goodyear-brand tires through Sears, Roebuck & Co. auto centers beginning April 1. While the move is boosting Goodyear's market share, it also has begun to redo the company's exclusive dealer network.

Since the move, hundreds of Goodyear's 2,500 independent dealers have adopted other brands, according to distributors, analysts and dealers.

This could offset the volume gain from Sears. In the long run, it also could push consumers to low-end tires, weakening the Goodyear brand name and the premium prices the company hopes to command.

Goodyear's arrangement with Sears is an effort to follow consumers' move to cheaper chain stores, department stores and warehouse clubs. Their market share has grown 30% in the last five years as that of tire dealerships slipped 4%, according to Modern Tire Dealer, an industry publication.

Goodyear says that approach is working. The company's Goodyear-brand market share, which was an estimated 15% last year, is up one-percentage point this year. Part of this reflects Sears's inventory buildup, although Goodyear says that sales through dealers are "up significantly" and that it has seen "no increase" in the number of dealers carrying other brands.

But the move clearly gives independent dealers an incentive to look out for themselves and to make up for any sales that Sears may be taking away from them. While few dealers have picked up rival brands such as Michelin and Bridgestone, many have turned to cheaper no-name brands called "private labels" (some of which Goodyear makes through its Kelly-Springfield unit). The private brands offer dealers higher margins and lower their incentives to sell Goodyear tires.

Likewise, Sears has an inducement to lure customers with the Goodyear name and then push the store's Roadhandler and other private labels of its own.

Harry W. Millis, an industry analyst who runs Fundamental Research in Cleveland, says Goodyear's loss of business from dealers--who contribute most of the company's sales--will erase a third to half of the increase of 1.5 million to 2.5 million tires a year that it expects from Sears. He believes that "several hundred" Goodyear dealers have adopted private brands.

Shortly after the Sears announcement, Mike Gatto Inc., a large Goodyear dealer in Melbourne, Fla., adopted several private-brand tire lines. The new tires have reduced the dealer's sales of Goodyear-brand tires by 20%, but the dealer's profit margins have increased. "We sell what we think will give the customer the best value, and that's not necessarily Goodyear," says Vice President Pam Fitzgerald.

Northwest Tire & Service in Flint, Mich., added a private-brand line in April after the Sears announcement and plans to put up new signs soon. "The line of least resistance is to sell the cheapest thing you have," says owner Jim Faught.

Dealers adopting other brands range from Dobbs Tire & Auto, a 30-store St. Louis chain (where same-store sales of Goodyear-brand tires are off 10%) to Pinkerton Goodyear, a one-store operation in Butler, Pa. Metro 25, a Detroit-based tire distributor and retailer, says over 25 Goodyear dealers--about half the Goodyear dealers in the region--have approached the chain about becoming Metro 25 dealers. Metro sells Michelin, Uniroyal, Firestone and others.

"A lot of Goodyear dealers are coming out of the closet," says Lou DiPasqua, a former Goodyear executive who is now president of TBC Corp., which distributes the Multi-Mile, Cordovan and Sigma private brands. "They were quietly selling [private brands] anyway, but now they're advertising and displaying them vigorously." TBC, too, has seen an increase in business from Goodyear dealers.

Goodyear has had a bumpy ride with Sears, from the retailer's bad publicity involving accusations that it charged customers for unnecessary repairs, to objections from dealers. The dealers contend that Goodyear, despite earlier suggestions, has allowed Sears to sell a full line of tires, including the popular Aquatred, which dealers hoped to sell exclusively. So far, Sears hasn't ignited a price battle with dealers, as many had feared. But, says Jack McGrath, a consultant with Booz Allen & Hamilton, "the ballgame's not over."

Making matters worse for dealers, Groupe Michelin S.A. recently struck a sales agreement with Kmart Corp., and some believe Goodyear will eventually join Kmart, Montgomery Ward, or even the warehouses. Goodyear says it continually studies other distribution outlets.

_____

_____ 1. This article is a good example of:

A. Vertical conflict in channels.   D. Horizontal conflict in channels..

B. Direct distribution.   E. Intensive distribution.

C. Scrambled merchandising.

_____ 2. Goodyear is trying to set up a(n):

A. Corporate vertical marketing system.

B. Wholesaler sponsored voluntary chain.

C. Retailer-owned cooperative.

D. Franchise system

E. Administered vertical marketing system.

_____ 3. Regarding intensity of distribution, Goodyear has decided upon _____ distribution.

A. Intensive   B. Selective   C. Exclusive

PART 13K: Answers to Questions

PART 13D: Completion
1. target market
2. middleman/producer/consumer
3. Merchant middlemen
4. Agent middlemen
5. their functions
6. purchasing agents/sales specialists
7. people/firms/title
8. form/channel
9. customers'/competition
10. role/type/intensity/wholesale/retail/channel members
11. market/product/company/middlemen/ sells/mix/structure/promotion/customer service
12. marketing mix
13. producer/final customer/direct
14. producer/final customer/one/indirect
15. producer/retailer/wholesaler/agent/ agent/retailer
16. producer/industrial distributor/agent/agent/ user
17. producer/agent
18. different/segments/single
19. size/concentration
20. competing/brand/single/middlemen
21. vertical/operating/marketing
22. corporate/contractual/administered
23. systems integrator
24. corporate
25. contractual
26. administered/channel/two channel members
27. market/customers/concentration/order/ product/middleman/company
28. unit/perishability/technical
29. services/availability/attitude/policies
30. channel control/services/management/ financial
31. intensive/selective/exclusive
32. convenience
33. image/service/quality control
34. exclusive/wholesaling middleman/retailer
35. competing
36. promote/manufacturer
37. Channel conflict
38. horizontal/vertical
39. same type/different types
40. scrambled merchandising
41. consumer/middleman/producer
42. vertical channel
43. consumers/retailers
44. perishability/priced/custom-made/ installation/technical
45. internal management/management assistance/voluntary chains/middlemen's brands
46. slotting allowance
47. brand loyalty/vertical/refuse to sell
48. store/information systems/retailer cooperative
49. channel control
50. products/sales/economies
51. consumers
52. partnership
53. no one
54. exclusive/tying/refusal/territories

PART 13E: True-False Questions
1. F 2. F 3. F 4. T 5. T 6. F
7. F 8. T 9. F 10. T 11. F 12. F
13. T 14. F 15. T

PART 13F: Multiple Choice Questions
1. E 2. C 3. B 4. B 5. A 6. A
7. A 8. E 9. E 10. B 11. C 12. C
13. E 14. A 15. E

PART 13G: Matching Questions
a. 6 b. 8 c. 10 d. 22 e. 18 f. 2
g. 5 h. 16 i. 9 j. 14 k. 20

CHAPTER 14

RETAILING

PART 14A: Chapter Goals

After studying this chapter, you should be able to explain:

- The nature of retailing
- What a retailer is
- Types of retailers classified by form of ownership
- Types of retailers classified by marketing strategies
- Forms of nonstore retailing
- Trends in retailing

228

PART 14B: Key Terms and Concepts

1. Retailing (retail trade) [390]

2. Retailer [390]

3. Physical facilities [393]

4. Shopping center

    a. Convenience center [394]

    b. Neighborhood center [395]

    c. Community center [395]

    d. Regional center [395]

5. Corporate chain [396]

6. Independent retailer [397]

7. Contractual vertical marketing system [397]

8. Retailer cooperative [397]

9. Voluntary chain [397]

10. Franchising [397]

    a. Product and trade name franchising [397]

    b. Business format franchising [398]

11. Franchise system [398]

12. Department store [400]

13. Discount retailing [401]

14. Discount house [401]

15. Supercenter [402]

16. Limited-line store [402]

17. Off-price retailer [403]

18. Factory outlet [403]

19. Category-killer store [403]

20. Supermarket retailing [364]

21. Supermarket [404]

22. Convenience store [405]

23. Warehouse club (wholesale club) [405]

24. Hypermarket [406]

25. Nonstore retailing [406]

26. Direct selling

    a. Door-to-door selling [408]

    b. Party-plan selling [408]

27. Telemarketing [409]

28. Automatic vending [409]

29. Direct marketing

    a. Direct mail [410]

    b. Catalog retailing [411]

    c. Televised shopping [411]

30. Green retailing   [412]   32. Wheel of retailing   [413]

31. Power center   [413]

PART 14C: Summary

Retailers are businesses that sell goods and services to people who are buying for personal, nonbusiness reasons [390]. They serve as purchasing agents for consumers and sales specialists for wholesalers and manufacturers [390]. They try to anticipate customers' wants, develop appropriate assortments, and arrange for financing if required [391].   Most retailers are small. This, however, does not have to be a disadvantage since they can be more flexible and responsive to changing consumer needs [393].

Retail ownership can be classified by form of ownership [396]. The independent stores have been able to survive the corporate chain competitive advantage by forming contractual vertical marketing systems [397]. One type, the contractual franchise system, includes two main types of franchising systems: product and trade name, and business format [397-398].

Retailers can also be classified by key marketing strategies: how each responds to assortments, price levels, and customer-service levels [399].   The major types discussed were department stores, discount houses, limited-line stores (including specialty stores, off-price retailers, and category-killer stores), supermarkets, convenience stores, warehouse clubs, and hypermarkets [399-406].   Some 15 percent of retail sales takes place away from stores. The forms of nonstore retailing are direct selling, telemarketing, automatic vending, and direct marketing [406-411].

Retailers need to carefully select target markets and plan their marketing mixes. Besides product assortments, price, promotion, and customer services, decisions must also be made regarding physical facilities. Specific decisions relate to location, design, and layout of the store [393].

The retailing is not a static structure. Major forces cause change in the complex, dynamic fabric that is retailing. These forces are explained in a theory called the wheel of retailing [413]. No type of retail institution will succeed over a long period of time if its principal method of operation involves a reduction in the ability to service customers.

PART 14D: Completion

1. _____(or _____) consists of the sale, and includes all activities directly related to the sale of goods and services, to the ultimate consumer for _____, _____ use.

2. A(n) _____ is any business enterprise that sells something to ultimate consumers for nonbusiness use.

3. In order to serve as _____ for their customers and as _____ for their suppliers, retailers anticipate customers' _____, develop _____ of products, acquire market _____ and _____.

4. The ease of entry into _____ results in fierce _____ and better _____ for the consumer.

5. The primary reason for retailers' existence must be based upon their ability to cater to the _____.

6. Compared to wholesalers, retailers have _____ sales, have _____ rates of merchandise turnover, and buy _____quantities of merchandise so their overhead costs are spread over a smaller base of operations.

7. While most retailers are very small, there is a high degree of _____ in retailing.

8. Firms operating retail stores must consider three aspects of physical facilities: (1) _____, (2) _____, and (3) _____.

9. A(n) _____ consists of a planned grouping of retail stores that lease space in a physical structure usually owned by a single organization and that can accommodate multiple tenants.

10. The four major types of shopping centers are _____ centers, _____ centers, _____ centers, and _____ centers.

11. Retailers may be classified on the following bases: (1) form of _____, and (2) marketing _____.

12. A(n) _____ is an organization of two or more centrally owned and managed stores generally handling the same lines of _____.

13. While technically two or more units constitute a chain, ____ units is a more reasonable minimum number.

14. _____ differentiates corporate chains from contractual vertical marketing systems.

15. Due to _____ management, individual units in a chain typically have little autonomy.

16. While having many outlets allows chain stores to _____, their standardization makes them _____.

17. Although independents have traditionally had _____ than chain stores, this is difficult to prove.

18. In a(n) _____ marketing system, _____ owned firms join together under a contract specifying how they will operate.

19. The three types are _____, _____ chains, and _____ systems.

20. A(n) _____ is formed by a group of small retailers who agree to establish and operate a(n) _____.

21. A(n) _____ is sponsored by a(n) _____ who enters into a contract with _____.

22. The first two types enable _____ to compete effectively with large, strong chains, and provide members with _____ in various areas.

23. A franchise is a system under which a(n) _____ provides the right to use a(n) _____ plus management assistance in exchange for payments from a(n) _____.

24. Within this broad definition we find two main types of franchising systems: _____ and _____ name, and _____.

25. The focus for the first is _____; for the second, how the _____.

26. Franchising also provides a franchisor with a means for _____ since the franchisees provide the capital when they buy franchises.

27. Because they have their own money at stake, franchisees are _____ to work _____ and adhere to the parent company's _____.

28. The advantages to franchisees are that: (1) they can use the _____ well-known trade _____, which helps to _____, and (2) various forms of _____ _____ are provided to _____ prior to and after opening the outlet.

29. In retailing, the marketing mix emphasizes product _____, _____, _____, _____, and _____.

30. A department store is a large-scale retailing institution that has a very _____ and _____

232

product assortment, prefers not to compete on the basis of _____, and offers a(n) _____ variety of customer services.

31. The discount house is a large-scale retailing institution that has a _____ and _____ product assortment, emphasizes _____ price, and offers relatively few _____.

32. A new type of discount house is the _____, a combination discount house and grocery store.

33. Limited-line stores have a(n) _____ but _____ product assortment and its customer services _____ from store to store.

34. Specialty stores offer a very _____ product assortment, often concentrating on a specialized _____, or even a(n) _____ of a specialized product line.

35. Off-price retailers, who position themselves _____ discount houses in terms of price, offer _____ and _____ product assortments, emphasize _____ prices, and offer few customer services.

36. Factory outlets, a special type of _____, are owned by _____ and usually sell a single manufacturer's _____ items as well as regular merchandise typically at lower prices than charged by other retailers.

37. Category-killer stores (so called, since they are designed to destroy all _____ in a specific product category) offer a(n) _____ but very _____ assortment, emphasize low prices, and offer _____ to _____ customer services.

38. As a method, supermarket retailing features several related product lines, a(n) _____ degree of _____, largely _____ checkouts, and _____ prices.

39. As a type of institution, a supermarket has a moderately _____ and moderately _____ product assortment spanning groceries and some _____ items, and offers relatively few customer services.

40. _____ are a larger version of the supermarket and offer more _____ and more _____ on food items than does a conventional supermarket.

41. A(n) _____ is a very large-scale retailing institution that has a very _____, moderately _____ assortment, emphasizes _____ prices, and offers _____.

42. _____ offer convenience-oriented groceries and non-foods, have _____ prices than found in most other grocery stores, and offer _____ customer services.

233

43. A recent innovative discount institution, the _____ or _____, is both a wholesaler and a retailer, and offers very _____ but very _____ product assortments, extremely _____ prices, and _____ customer services.

44. Nonstore retailing includes _____, _____, _____, and _____.

45. _____ is _____ contact between a sales person and a consumer away from a retail store.

46. The two major types are _____, and _____.

47. _____ refers to a sales person initiating contact with a(n) _____ and also closing a sale over the telephone.

48. _____ can extend a firm's market by reaching customers where and when it is not feasible for stores to do so.

49. Direct marketing includes _____, _____ retailing, and _____ shopping.

50. In "green marketing," many retailers have begun programs related to the "4 R's": _____, _____, _____, and _____.

51. Seven highly significant trends are emerging in retailing: (1) changing _____ and _____ structure, (2) expanding _____ technology, (3) emphasis on lower _____ and lower _____, (4) accent on _____ and _____, (5) focus on _____, (6) added _____, and (7) continuing growth of _____.

52. The _____ provides a predictive model of how retail institutions experience and respond to evolutionary changes in the market place.

PART 14E: True-False Questions

If the statement is true, circle "T"; if false, circle "F."

T F   1. Warehouse clubs deal strictly at retail.

T F   2. Most retailing establishments are very small.

T F   3. Catalog retailing has been declining over the past 20 years.

T F 4. Because specialty stores handle a wide line of merchandise, they usually have an excellent assortment.

T F 5. Discount retailing has led to a revision of traditional retail profit margins.

T F 6. Nonstore sales may be made by either producers or retailers selling to middlemen.

T F 7. One advantage of door-to-door selling is its low cost.

T F 8. A franchise is a system under which a franchisor provides the right to use a trademark plus management assistance in opening and operating a business in exchange for payments from a franchisee.

T F 9. "Category-killer stores" are called that because they offer the ultimate in a specific product category.

T F 10. The largest shopping center is the community center.

T F 11. It is easy to prove that independents have higher prices than chain store operators.

T F 12. Franchising is not included in contractual vertical marketing systems.

T F 13. The focus of the product franchising system is on what is sold.

T F 14. Retailing may be done by any marketing institution.

T F 15. Central ownership is the key factor that differentiates corporate chains from contractual vertical marketing systems.

PART 14F: Multiple Choice Questions

In the space provided write the letter of the answer that best fits the statement.

____ 1. The assembly of goods for dispersion to ultimate consumers is a fundamental service provided by:
  A. Direct marketing.   C. Convenience stores.   E. Any of the above.
  B. Factory outlets.   D. Department stores.

____ 2. In terms of size, the largest store is the:
  A. Convenience store.   D. Supermarket.
  B. Warehouse club.   E. Supercenter.
  C. Hypermarket.

____ 3. Which statement best describes specialty stores?
  A. They carry a wide assortment of products.
  B. They carry a deep assortment.
  C. They have four divisions: merchandising, sales promotion, store operation, and accounting control.
  D. They carry a limited variety of products.
  E. They welcome price competition.

____ 4. The largest shopping center is the _____ center.
  A. Convenience   C. Neighborhood   E. None of the above.
  B. Community   D. Regional

____ 5. All of the following are retail transactions EXCEPT:
  A. A farmer sells produce to consumers at a roadside stand.
  B. A sporting goods store sells baseballs to a local, minor league, professional baseball club.
  C. A man buys, at the factory, a large air conditioner for his home.
  D. A woman buys, for use at home, a case of Kleenex from a wholesaler and pays the wholesale price.
  E. A student buys a milkshake.

____ 6. Which statement best describes a franchise system?
  A. The connecting link between franchisor and franchisee is a contract.
  B. It is an association of independent retailers, initiated and sponsored by a wholesaler for the purpose of assuring the wholesaler a series of profitable retail outlets for his products.
  C. It is an organization instituted and sponsored by a group of independent retailers who establish and operate a wholesale warehouse.
  D. The formal tie is stock ownership in the cooperative warehouse.
  E. It is most prevalent in the grocery field.

____ 7. Which statement best describes the function of retailers?
  A. The function of retailers is to make other middlemen's jobs easy.
  B. The function of retailers is to make the consumer's buying job as easy and convenient as possible.
  C. Retailers perform the service of purchasing agent for manufacturers.
  D. Retailers perform the function of transporting and storing goods.
  E. Retailers perform the function of drop-shipping.

____ 8. If chains are able to sell at lower prices than independents, the reason may be the chains':
  A. Specialization of management.   D. Development of their own brands.
  B. Division of labor.   E. All of the above are reasons.
  C. Greater buying power.

236

9. Any of the following could cause the wheel of retailing to turn EXCEPT:
  A. Entrance into the market of a high-price, high-cost retailer.
  B. Initially, the established retailers ignore the new entrant.
  C. Consumers begin to flock to the new entrant.
  D. The new entrant begins to trade up, causing costs to rise.
  E. Rising costs invite the entrance of another retailer to begin the wheel anew.

10. Most retail establishments in the United States are classified as:
  A. Corporations.   C. Corporate chains.   E. Franchises.
  B. Small.   D. Cooperative chains.

11. All of the following are characteristics of discount house operations EXCEPT:
  A. Low markup.   D. Wide assortment of goods.
  B. Low prices.   E. A minimum of customer services.
  C. Broad assortment of goods.

12. The warehouse club has all the following characteristics EXCEPT they:
  A. Are only open to members.
  B. Emphasize very low prices.
  C. Have very large shopping spaces.
  D. Carry a very deep assortment.
  E. Carry a very broad assortment.

13. The first decision regarding facilities should be:
  A. Location.   C. Positioning.   E. Defining marketing mix.
  B. Design   D. Layout.

14. All of the following are emerging trends in retailing EXCEPT:
  A. Changing demographics.   D. More emphasis on productivity.
  B. More experimentation.   E. Continued growth of nonstore retailing.
  C. Less reliance on computers.

15. The retail store with a very broad and deep assortment of merchandise, a wide array of customer services, and an unwillingness to compete on the basis of prices is the:
  A. Convenience store.   D. Department store.
  B. Specialty store.   E. Category-killer store.
  C. Discount house.

PART 12G: Matching Questions

In the space provided write the number of the word or expression from column 1 that best fits the description in column 2.

1		2

1. Automatic vending

2. Category-killer store

3. Contractual vertical marketing system

4. Convenience stores

5. Corporate chain

6. Department store

7. Direct marketing

8. Direct selling

9. Discount retailing

10. Factory outlet

11. Franchise system

12. Green retailing

13. Hypermarket

14. Limited-line stores

15. Nonstore retailing

16. Off-price retailers

17. Retailer cooperative

18. Retailing

19. Shopping center

20. Supercenter

21. Supermarkets

____ a. So called because it eliminates competition.

____ b. A retailing innovation begun in Europe.

____ c. Includes retailer cooperatives, voluntary chains, and franchise systems.

____ d. Stores selling branded items below list price.

____ e. All activities relating to the sale of products to the ultimate consumer for personal, nonbusiness use.

____ f. Includes direct selling and direct marketing.

____ g. Formed by a group of small retailers who agree to establish and operate a wholesale operation.

____ h. A special type of off-price retailer owned by a manufacturer.

____ i. A combined retail and wholesale operation.

____ j. Eleven or more outlets under the same management.

____ k. Stores that feature limited product assortments, small size, higher prices, and long hours.

____ l. A theory of evolutionary change in retailing.

238

22. Telemarketing

23. Voluntary chain

24. Warehouse club

25. Wheel of retailing

PART 14H: Problems and Applications

1.   "Franchising is a relatively recent phenomenon in American business, having started just after World War II." Would you agree with this statement? Why? Research the origins of franchising and report your findings to your instructor.

2.   Go the latest issue of "Survey of Buying Power," published annually by *Sales & Marketing Management* magazine. List the five top states by total retail sales and percent of U. S. total.

State	Total Retail Sales Dollars	Percent of U.S. Total
A.		
B.		
C.		
D.		
E.		

*Review Appendix B on Marketing Arithmetic in the text.

3.   *What are the percentage markups on cost which correspond to the following percentage markups on selling price?
   A. 15%   B. 22-1/2%   C. 33-1/3%   D. 66-2/3%

4.   *What are the percentage markups on selling price which correspond to the following percentage markups on cost?
   A. 15%   B. 33-1/3%   C. 400%   D. 50%

5.   *A retailer with annual net sales of $12,000,000 maintains a markup of 66-2/3 percent based on cost. Her expenses average 35 percent. What is her gross margin and net profit in dollars?

6.   What types of retail outlets are located on your campus? Classify them as to product lines carried. Are there any off-price outlets? Why do you suppose this is so?

239

7.   Have department stores in your community abandoned the one price system and are they bargaining with customers in their sales of appliances? Conduct an informal investigation and report your findings to your instructor.

8.   Assume you and a friend have been planning on opening a men's clothing store.   What would be a good estimate of net operating profit after income taxes?   Answer: _____. Assume you have forecasted sales at $294,000.   Calculate your profit after income taxes on this sales volume. Answer:_____.

9.   Trace the trade channel for bread. Where does it start? Where does it end? Remember from Chapter 13 that when a product's form is altered, another product emerges and a new channel is started.

10.   Draw a model of the wheel of retailing as it applies to discount gasoline retailing. What conclusions can you make?

11.   Why have discount houses been successful? How do you account for the rapid increase in the number of warehouse clubs?   Write a memo to your instructor on either of these subjects.

PART 14I: Exercise

In Chapter 1, the classical economic theory of production was discussed. It was defined as the creation of utility. Utility is the ability of a good or service to satisfy a human need. Marketing, an important component of production, creates utility as well.

In the matrix below, place the number of the creator of the utility under the appropriate utility classification. For instance, in the first example, the manufacturer creates all five utilities, while the retailer creates three.

Creator of the Utility: 1. Manufacturer;   2. Wholesaler;   3. Retailer;   4. Consumer

Situation	Time	Place	Possession	Form	Image
1. A retailer buys from a manufacturer's sales branch on consignment.	1,3	1,3	1	1	1,3
2. A manufacturer sells through its factory outlets.					
3. A small retailer buys from a wholesaler who buys from a manufacturer.					

	Situation	Utilities				
		Time	Place	Possession	Form	Image
4.	Penney's buys goods made especially for them and sells them through their catalog on a credit card.					
5.	A McDonald's franchisee sells cheeseburgers to customers.					
6.	You buy a CD from the Columbia Record Club on a credit card.					
7.	You buy an audiotape from a record store which buys direct from the producer of the tape.					
8.	You pay for a blood transfusion at your local hospital. They obtained the blood from a donor at no cost through their own blood bank.					
9.	You buy a ticket from a travel agency for a flight next week and pay cash.					
10.	You buy a candy bar in a vending machine owned by a vending machine operator.					

PART 14J: A Real World Case: Picky Customers

CHICAGO--Retail experts say changing attitudes among American consumers are dividing buyers into two distinct groups, where the differences go beyond mere economics.

"There are two societies emerging, and they will shop very differently," says C. W. "Bill" Ress, a Columbus, Ohio, consultant and market researcher, who addressed a recent gathering of the International Council of Shopping Centers in Chicago.

Shoppers in the 1990s will be increasingly polarized into upscale and downscale categories, and the middle-market retailers who have previously fared so well will likely be the ones to suffer, he said.

And, he said, these changing attitudes will affect the way people shop and present retailers with their greatest challenges since World War II, said Ress and others attending the conference.

"It will be a large up-market and a large down-market and less of a middle market in between," Ress said.

"We're already seeing something called the Enhancement Sacrificial Syndrome, buyers who go off the deep end to have things they can't afford and then end up cutting back to pay for it," Ress said. "Thus, the mink coat customer may be the same customer who is buying the cheapest groceries at the outlet store."

"In the two markets, the up-market wants efficient delivery. The upscale market is also very home-centered, so there will be a lot of money spent on or in the home in the 1990s," he said.

"The down-market shopper very likely wants to be entertained in the mall. They are more tuned in to styles and looks if they are young and are tuned off to new ways of shopping if they are older," he said.

Just adding amusement features to malls and other retail projects, a development trend that has accelerated in recent years, will not energize shoppers, developers and analysts said. "Shopping has become less fun," Ress said. "In the 1970s, my research showed that 82 percent of the population said they enjoyed going shopping even if they were not out to buy anything. Today, only 18 percent say they like to just go out shopping without a need or destination in mind."

"The majority of people are somewhat apathetic about shopping, but it doesn't mean they are antagonistic. So efficiency becomes the important thing. They have little loyalty to brands and even less to stores."

That means retailers will have to stay on their toes.

"The shopper of the 1990s will be concerned about time and convenience. We must make it easier for consumers to make quicker choices," said David Hocker, president of the International Council of Shopping Centers.

"We must address these demographic changes to survive," he said.

James Kaplan, a Chicago retail leasing specialist, said that there has been a change in the kind of tenants populating shopping centers in the last few years.

"There are a lot more non-traditional users going into centers, like dentists, weight-loss centers, and storefront insurance companies. It's a lot more service-oriented," he said.

Changing lifestyles play a large role in the success of retailers in smaller shopping centers, he said.

"For example, a center we are leasing in Forest Park [Illinois] is anchored by a Blockbuster Video. Then we leased to a TCBY yogurt store, a Subway sandwich shop and a bagel place. It's

242

because of lifestyle: People want a tape, then they'll pick up something to eat, some dessert, then go home," Kaplan said. "There are a ton of these neighborhood convenience-type centers coming on line today," he said.

But for traditional retailers, the trends translate into slower growth for the decade, Ress predicted, although sales could pick up steam near the end of the 1990s.

Retailers can expect to see only about 2 or 2-1/2 percent growth per year, on average, he said, with productivity per square foot of shop space falling as well.

"All of the forces that have driven retail growth--like pent-up demand, the baby boomers and women in the work force--have been used up. We've had all the growth we are going to get from them," Ress said.

"Instead, there will be more experienced, less enthusiastic audiences in retail stores. And more experienced consumers demand more value. Their behavior will be more personal and more unpredictable," Ress told an audience of about 700 developers, retailers and retail leasing agents.

"Consumers are increasingly unforgiving. If you don't get it right the first time, they won't be back. And they are more willing to trade off stores. They know what they need, and they will find a store that offers it," he said.

And if they can't find a store they like, consumers are happy to turn to alternatives.

"Our surveys show 52 percent of the people shop by catalog or are willing to do some shopping by catalog. Catalog shopping is growing twice as fast as in-store sales. And the most successful are the up-scale catalog operations," Ress said.

"On the positive side, I think the problems in the department store industry will shake out very quickly now. The department store business seems to have a great future in the 1990s," Hocker said. "There are a lot of aggressive retailers looking to make deals."

One segment of the market retailers are sure to continue to pursue is the dual-income family. But Ress cautions that the market "will not be like 'L.A. Law' where the couple earns $300,000. These will be people with good incomes who work hard for it." And incomes will be spread thinner in the coming decade.

"There will be both a voluntary and involuntary redistribution of income in the 1990s," Ress said. "On the voluntary side, people will be more interested in activities than in acquisitions. If you open up your closet and see it's full, you're more likely to go skiing than go out and shop for more apparel."

"On the involuntary side, medical costs will be soaring, we will spend money to fight the drug

243

war, and we will spend more on social support systems like jails and schools. The reality of it is that if we have a relatively slow-growing economy and retail spending is getting less of it, it equals a sluggish market."

_____

_____

___ 1. According to the article, changing lifestyles are forcing the greatest changes in which type of shopping center?
    A. Convenience.   C. Regional.   E. None of the above.
    B. Neighborhood.   D. Community.

___ 2. Which of the following trends in retailing did the article emphasize?
    A. Changing demographics.
    B. More experimentation.
    C. More reliance on computers.
    D. Changing industry structure.
    E. Continuing growth of nonstore retailing.

PART 14K: Answers to Questions

PART 14D: Completion
1. Retailing/retail trade/personal/ nonbusiness
2. retailer
3. purchasing agents/sales specialists wants/assortments/information/financing
4. retailing/competition/values
5. consumer
6. smaller/lower/smaller
7. concentration
8. location/design/layout
9. shopping center
10. convenience/neighborhood/community/ regional
11. ownership/strategies
12. corporate chain/products
13. 11
14. Central ownership
15. centralized
16. standardize/inflexible
17. higher prices
18. contractual vertical/independently
19. retailer cooperatives/voluntary/franchise
20. retailer cooperative/wholesale warehouse
21. voluntary chain/wholesaler/interested retailers
22. independent retailers/management assistance
23. franchisor/trademark/franchisee
24. product/trade/business format
25. what is sold/business is run
26. rapid expansion
27. highly motivated/hard/proven format
28. franchisor's/name/attract customers/ management assistance/franchisees
29. assortment/price/location/promotion/ customer services
30. broad/deep/price/wide
31. broad/shallow/low/customer services
32. supercenter
33. narrow/deep/vary
34. narrow/product line/part
35. below/narrow/deep/low
36. off-price retailer/manufacturers/clearance
37. competition/narrow/deep/few/moderate
38. high/self-service/centralized/competitive
39. broad/deep/nonfood
40. Superstores/products/selling space
41. hypermarket/broad/deep/low/some services
42. Convenience stores/higher/few
43. warehouse club/wholesale club/broad/ shallow/low/few
44. direct selling/telemarketing/automatic vending/direct marketing
45. Direct selling/personal
46. door to door/party plan
47. Telemarketing/shopper
48. Vending machines
49. direct mail/catalog/televised
50. reducing/recycled/recycling/reusing
51. demographics/industry/computer/prices/ costs/convenience/service/productivity/ experimentation/nonstore retailing
52. wheel of retailing

PART 14E: True-False Questions
1. F   2. T   3. F   4. F   5. T   6. F
7. F   8. T   9. T   10. F   11. F   12. F
13. T   14. T   15. T

PART 14F: Multiple Choice Questions
1. E   2. C   3. D   4. D   5. B   6. A
7. B   8. E   9. A   10. B   11. D   12. D
13. A   14. C   15. D

PART 14G: Matching Questions
a. 2   b. 13   c. 3   d. 16   e. 18   f. 15
g. 17   h. 10   i. 24   j. 5   k. 4   l. 25

CHAPTER 15

WHOLESALING AND PHYSICAL DISTRIBUTION

PART 15A: Chapter Goals

After studying this chapter, you should be able to explain:

- The nature and justification of wholesaling and the role of wholesaling middlemen
- Differences across three categories of wholesaling middlemen
- Major types of merchant wholesalers, agent wholesaling middlemen, and manufacturers' sales facilities, and the services they render
- What physical distribution is
- The systems approach to physical distribution
- How physical distribution is used to strengthen a marketing program and reduce marketing costs
- The five subsystems within a physical distribution system: inventory location and warehousing; materials handling; inventory control; order processing; and transportation
- Trends in wholesaling and physical distribution

246

PART 15B: Key Terms and Concepts

1. Wholesaling [420]
2. Wholesaling middleman [420]
3. Merchant wholesaler [423]
4. Agent wholesaling middleman [423]
5. Manufacturer's sales facility [423]
   a. Manufacturer's sales branch [423]
   b. Manufacturer's sales office [423]
6. Full-service wholesaler [425]
7. Truck jobber [426]
8. Drop shipper [426]
9. Manufacturers' agent [426]
10. Broker [428]
11. Commission merchant [429]
12. Auction company [429]
13. Selling agent [429]
14. Import-export agents [429]
15. Physical distribution (logistics) [429]
16. Systems approach to physical distribution [431]
17. Total cost concept [432]
18. Time utility [433]
19. Place utility [433]
20. Physical distribution management [434]
21. Inventory location and warehousing [434]
22. Warehousing [435]
23. Distribution center [435]
24. Private warehouse [435]
25. Public warehouse [435]
26. Materials handling [435]
27. Containerization [435]
28. Inventory control [436]
29. Economic order quantity (EOQ) [436]
30. "Just-in-time" concept [436]
31. Order processing [437]
32. Transportation [438]
33. Modes of transportation [438]
34. Intermodal transportation [439]
35. Piggyback service [439]
36. Fishyback service [439]
37. Freight forwarder [439]
38. Service wholesaler [441]

PART 15C: Summary

Wholesaling is the sale, and all activities directly related to the sale, of goods and services to parties for resale, use in producing other goods and services, or operating an organization [420]. In a broad sense then, all sales are either wholesale sales or retail sales. The difference depends on the buyer's purpose in buying--is it a business or a nonbusiness intended use? [420]

Wholesaling middlemen act as purchasing agents for retailers and business users [421]. They often render to customers and suppliers all or some combination of the following services: buying, selling, subdividing, transportation, creating assortments, warehousing, financing, risk taking, market information, and management services and advice [425]. Wholesalers who offer all ten of the services are called full-service wholesalers. Agent wholesaling middlemen, manufacturers' agents, selling agents, brokers and commission merchants do not take title or possession of the goods [426]. They are, in general, specialists in selling.

The category of agents and brokers has declined over the years, being replaced by manufacturers' sales facilities [423]. Agent wholesaling middlemen (manufacturers' agents, brokers, commission merchants, and others) remain strong in certain industries and in certain geographical locations where the market is still too small for manufacturers to send in their own sales force.

For the future, wholesalers will face continuing challenges to their roles in distribution. In order to succeed, they will need to address emerging trends in distribution and develop appropriate marketing strategies [440].

Physical distribution is the flow of products from sources of supply to the firm and thence from the firm to its customers. From the economic standpoint, physical distribution creates place utility by transportation and time utility by storage [433]. Through prudent warehouse location and inventory management, the firm can maintain a level of customer service necessary to hold present customers and attract new ones.

Physical distribution should be considered as a total system of business action [432]. This unfortunately is far from the present state of affairs in many businesses, where firms will examine only one or two aspects of physical distribution to the exclusion of others, thereby causing operational and organizational fractures. The systems concept encompasses the total cost concept to the management of physical distribution wherein management attempts to give the appropriate level of customer service consistent with the lowest cost of the total of the elements involved in moving and handling the product [432].

In its fullest development, physical distribution for a manufacturer would involve not only the flow of finished goods from the end of the production line to the customer, but also the flow of raw materials from their source of supply to the beginning of the production cycle. Similarly, middlemen would manage the flow of goods into their own shelves as well as to the customer's home or store. This task may be divided into five parts: determine the inventory locations and establish a warehousing system [434]; establish a materials-handling system [435]; maintain an inventory control system [436]; establish a procedure for processing orders [437]; and select the method of transportation [438]. It is important to approach these activities not as individual problems to be solved, but as subsystems of the whole--the physical distribution system.

PART 15D: Completion

1. _____ and _____ are often misunderstood and criticized by consumers.

2. Wholesaling, or wholesale trade, includes the _____, and all activities directly related to the _____, of goods or services to parties for resale, use in _____ other goods and services, or _____ an organization.

3. The only real criterion for distinguishing between wholesale and retail sales is the purchaser's intended use of the _____.

4. Economically, wholesalers justify themselves by having _____ that create economies of _____ and _____.

5. The volume of wholesale trade _____ the volume of retail trade.

6. Wholesaling middlemen vary greatly in: (1) the _____ they carry, (2) the _____ they sell to, and (3) their methods of _____.

7. All wholesaling middlemen are grouped into three broad categories: (1) _____ _____ , (2) _____ wholesaling middlemen, and (3) manufacturers' _____.

8. _____, who form the largest segment of wholesaling firms, are _____ and take _____ to the merchandise they handle.

9. Agent wholesaling middlemen such as manufacturers' agents and brokers do not _____to goods--instead they actively help in negotiating their _____ or _____ on behalf of other firms.

10. Manufacturers' sales facilities are owned and operated by a(n) _____ and are physically _____ from manufacturing plants.

11. A manufacturer's _____ carries a stock of the product being sold.

12. A manufacturer's _____ does not.

13. A(n) _____ is an independent merchant wholesaler that generally performs a full range of wholesaling activities.

14. Wholesalers render the following ten basic services to their customers and to producers: (1) _____--they act as purchasing agents for their customers; (2) _____ --they buy from many suppliers to develop an inventory matching the needs of customers; (3) _____--a wholesaler buys in truckload quantities and resells smaller lots; (4) _____ -- provides a sales force for producers to reach small businesses; (5) _____--they provide quick and frequent delivery; (6) _____--they store products that are nearer customers' locations; (7) _____--they provide credit; (8) _____--wholesalers usually take title to merchandise; (9) _____; and (10) _____ _____--they assist customers, especially small retailers in various areas of management.

15. Special types of merchant wholesalers include _____ and _____ .

16. The _____ is a merchant wholesaler that carries a line of perishable products and delivers them by truck to retail stores.

17. _____, who do not actually handle their products, sell merchandise for delivery directly from the producer to the consumer.

18. Agent wholesaling middlemen are distinguished from merchant wholesalers in two important respects: agent middlemen _____ to the merchandise, and they typically perform _____ .

19. An emerging trend is that _____ are likely to gain at the expense of agent wholesaling middlemen and manufacturers' sales facilities.

20. Based on sales volume, there are six types of agent wholesaling middlemen: (1) _____--commissioned by a manufacturer to sell part or all of the producer's product in a geographic territory; (2) _____--agent middlemen whose prime responsibility is to bring buyers and sellers together and provide marketing information to either party; (3) _____--sellers in a local market who consign shipments to a commission merchant in a central market and who, in turn, is responsible for selling prices, handling, and selling the goods; (4) _____--agent middlemen who provide auctioneers and the physical facilities for displaying products; (5) _____--independent middlemen who are used essentially in place of a manufacturer's entire marketing department; and (6) _____--facilitators who bring buyers and sellers from different countries together.

21. _____ consists of all the activities concerned with moving the right amount of the right products to the right place at the right time.

22. Some people use another name for physical distribution: _____.

23. The task of physical distribution may be divided into five subsystems: (1) inventory _____ and _____, (2) _____, (3) _____, (4) _____, and (5) _____.

24. A major reason for increased interest in physical distribution management is that physical distribution _____ are substantial.

25. Since deregulation, transportation firms have been able to decide which _____ and levels of _____ would best satisfy their target markets.

26. By treating physical distribution activities as a total _____, rather than as a set of fragmented parts, business can take a significant stride toward greater efficiency.

27. Implicit in the total cost concept in physical distribution is the thought that management should strive for an optimum balance between _____ and _____ for the entire physical distribution system.

28. The strategic use of physical distribution may enable a firm to strengthen its marketing position by providing more _____ and reducing _____ costs.

29. A good _____ will improve the distribution service a firm gives its customers.

30. It may also reduce distribution _____.

31. The value of storage is the fact that it creates _____ utility.

32. Storage is essential when there is a(n) _____ in the timing of production and _____.

33. The main function of transportation in physical distribution is to add _____ to products through the creation of _____ utility.

34. The _____, or _____, schedule is the carrier's price list.

35. Physical distribution management involves decisions regarding inventory _____ and _____, _____, _____, and _____.

36. Warehousing includes such functions as _____, _____, and _____ products and preparing them for _____.

37. A distribution center is planned around _____ rather than transportation facilities.

38. This new distribution system has lowered distribution costs by reducing the number of _____, pruning _____, and eliminating _____ conditions.

39. Public warehouses offer _____ and _____ facilities to any individual or company.

40. The warehouse building should be included in a list of materials-handling equipment along with _____, _____ trucks, and other _____.

41. _____ is a cargo handling system that involves a shipment of products in large containers of metal or wood.

42. The main goals of inventory control are to minimize the _____ and _____ in inventories while filling customers' orders _____, _____, and _____.

43. Improvements in computer technology have enabled management to shorten the _____ time and to reduce substantially the level of _____.

44. The _____, or _____ , is the volume at which inventory-carrying cost plus the order-processing cost are at a minimum.

45. The "just-in-time" concept involves _____ just in time for use in production and then _____ just in time for sale.

46. In addition to establishing procedures for handling and financing orders efficiently, decisions should be made about the following matters: _____, _____ granting, _____ preparation, and collection of _____.

47. The five basic forms of transportation are: _____, _____, _____, _____ , and _____.

48. When two or more modes of transportation are used to move freight, this is called _____ transportation.

49. "Piggyback" services involve transporting loaded truck trailers on _____.

50. "Fishyback" service transports loaded trailers on _____ or _____.

51. The main function of a freight forwarder is to consolidate _____ shipments or _____ shipments from several shippers into _____ or _____ quantities.

252

52. Although freight forwarders do not have their own transportation equipment, _____ firms do.

53. In the future, _____ are likely to continue to grab a larger share of total wholesale trade away from agent wholesaling middlemen and manufacturers' sales facilities.

54. In order to gain strength in the field of physical distribution, some firms are forming _____.

PART 15E: True-False Questions

If the statement is true, circle "T"; if false, circle "F."

T F   1. Agent wholesaling middlemen generally either act as a substitute for a manufacturer's sales force or serve as an additive to the sales force.

T F   2. A manufacturer sometimes uses manufacturers' agents along with his own sales force.

T F   3. Manufacturers' agents typically do not carry merchandise stocks.

T F   4. Selling agents are used in place of a manufacturer's entire marketing department.

T F   5. A commission merchant is really not a merchant but an agent wholesaling middleman.

T F   6. There is little or no economic justification for the existence of wholesalers.

T F   7. There has been a gradual increase in the total sales of agents and brokers nationally.

T F   8. Agent wholesaling middlemen take title to the merchandise.

T F   9. Warehouses create place utility but not time utility.

T F 10. Enclosing a shipment of goods in a container of some sort and then transporting the goods unopened until they reach their destination is known as "piggyback service."

T F 11. "EOQ," "Easiest Order Quotient," is a measure of the best way to ship something.

T F 12. In terms of total intercity ton-miles carried, railroads lead the other forms of transportation.

T F 13. In a nutshell, freight forwarders make money by consolidating l.c.l. shipments from several shippers into carload or truckload quantities.

T F 14. For many products, the largest single group of operating expenses is physical distribution costs.

T F 15. A properly designed logistics system can reduce total costs and increase net profits, but it ordinarily cannot help to increase sales volume.

PART 15F: Multiple Choice Questions

In the space provided write the letter of the answer that best fits the statement.

____1. An example of a wholesaling transaction is:
   A. A farmer sells a truckload of manure to a suburban homeowner for a new lawn.
   B. A homeowner buys a case of Heinz Ketchup at a wholesale price.
   C. A Dodge dealer sells a new car to a traveling salesperson for her personal use.
   D. A grocery store sells Scotch Tape to the gift shop next door.
   E. None of the above.

____2. The annual volume of wholesale trade always exceeds total annual retail sales because:
   A. Many products sold by retailers are bought directly from manufacturers and thus never through a wholesale establishment.
   B. Wholesaling middlemen sell to industrial users as well as to retailers.
   C. Retail unit prices are higher than wholesale prices.
   D. Wholesalers deal in larger quantities.
   E. Wholesaling middlemen are not used in the marketing of some products.

____3. The services of full-service wholesalers are most important to manufacturers in connection with:
   A. The performance of the advertising function.
   B. Selling to chain-store organizations.
   C. Aggressive personal selling activities at the point of final sale.
   D. Securing distribution in small and scattered outlets.
   E. Selling to department stores.

____4. The elimination of middlemen from the channel of distribution results in:
   A. Higher marketing costs for consumer goods.
   B. Lower marketing costs for convenience goods.
   C. A shift in basic functions within the channel of distribution.
   D. Greater marketing efficiency in most cases.
   E. Higher profits for those remaining in the channel.

254

____5. All of the following marketing institutions are considered wholesaling establishments EXCEPT:
  A. Manufacturers' agents.
  B. Manufacturers' sales branches.
  C. Chain-store warehouses.
  D. Mail-order houses.
  E. Commission merchants.

____6. Which of the following functions would be eliminated in a channel of distribution if goods were sold directly by manufacturers to retailers?
  A. Advertising
  B. Financing inventory
  C. Storage function
  D. Transportation
  E. None of the above

____7. Wholesaling involves:
  A. Sales made for resale.
  B. Sales to business users.
  C. Sales made from one producer to another.
  D. Any sale not for personal, nonbusiness use.
  E. Any of the above.

____8. Full-service wholesalers provide:
  A. Warehousing.
  B. Sales forces.
  C. Delivery.
  D. Credit.
  E. All of the above.

____9. If an executive is using the total cost concept, this means that he or she must take into account the cost of:
  A. Packing and crating.
  B. Insurance.
  C. Transportation.
  D. Pilferage and theft.
  E. All of the above.

____10. Which of the following modes of transportation carries the greatest ton-miles volume of intercity freight?
  A. Pipelines.
  B. Airlines.
  C. Barges on rivers.
  D. Motor trucks.
  E. Railroads.

____11. In comparing modes of transportation, the MOST expensive mode is by:
  A. Air.
  B. Rail.
  C. Oil pipeline.
  D. Highway.
  E. Water.

___12. A physical distribution system is LEAST likely to be concerned with:
   A. Determining inventory locations.
   B. Determining specifications of products to be purchased by manufacturers for production uses by middlemen for resale.
   C. Establishing a materials-handling system.
   D. Selecting a method of transportation.
   E. Determining the optimum quantity in which products should be ordered.

___13. Physical distribution includes:
   A. Inventory location.   D. Transportation.
   B. Materials handling.   E. All of the above.
   C. Inventory control.

___14. A benefit flowing from a just-in-time inventory system is:
   A. Purchases can be in small quantities thereby releasing funds for other uses.
   B. Maintenance of low inventory levels of parts.
   C. Maintenance of low inventory levels of finished goods.
   D. Delivery schedules can be shortened and made more flexible and reliable.
   E. All of the above.

___15. All of the following statements regarding EOQ are correct EXCEPT:
   A. As order sizes increase, inventory carrying costs decrease.
   B. As order sizes increase, order-processing costs decrease.
   C. The optimum order quantity is usually larger than the EOQ.
   D. In order to balance minimum inventory costs with its desired level of customer service, EOQ would be smaller than the actual order quantity.
   E. EOQ is the point where the order processing curve crosses the inventory carrying cost curve.

PART 15G: Matching Questions

In the space provided write the number of the word or expression from column 1 that best fits the description in column 2.

1	2
1. Agent wholesaling middleman	____ a. The sale, and all activities directly incident to the sale of goods or services to parties for resale, for use in making other goods and services, or operating an organization.
2. Auction company	
3. Broker	
4. Commission merchant	____ b. An establishment owned by a producer that carries merchandise stock.

256

5. Containerization

6. Distribution center

7. Drop shipper

8. EOQ.

9. Fishyback service

10. Freight forwarder

11. Full-service wholesaler

12. Import-export agent

13. Intermodal transportation

14. Inventory control

15. "Just in time" concept

16. Manufacturers' agent

17. Manufacturers' sales branches

18. Manufacturers' sales offices

19. Materials handling

20. Merchant wholesalers

21. Physical distribution

22. Piggyback service

23. Place utility

24. Public warehouse

25. Selling agent

26. Time utility

_____ c. A middleman whose prime responsibility is to bring buyers and sellers together.

_____ d. Merchant wholesalers who carry a selected line of perishable products and deliver them by truck to retail stores.

_____ e. A wholesaler engaged in arranging shipmentsdirect from producers to consumers.

_____ f. An establishment authorized by a manufacturer to sell part or all of the producer's products in a restricted territory.

_____ g. Agent middleman who provides auctioneers and the physical facilities for displaying and inspecting products.

_____ h. The management of the physical flow of products, and the development and operation of efficient flow systems.

_____ i. Facilities planned around markets rather than transportation requirements.

_____ j. Value created by having goods in the appropriate locations for use or sale.

_____ k. The process of examining all costs of physical distribution rather than considering the costs separately.

_____ l. Functions such as assembling, dividing, and storing products and preparing them for reshipment.

_____ m. Transporting loaded trailers on barges or ships.

_____ n. A marketing institution developed through the years to serve firms that ship l.c.l.

257

27. Total cost concept   ____ o. The volume at which the inventory
                                                carrying cost plus the order-processing
28. Truck jobber   cost is at a minimum.

29. Warehousing

30. Wholesaling

PART 15H: Problems and Applications

1.   Differentiate among the terms merchant wholesaler, distributor, and wholesale transaction.

2.   Why may a wholesaler be described as a marketing specialist?

3.   Why should changes in buying behavior and population influence the management of existing channels or the design of new ones?

4.   Visit a freight forwarding company in your community. Find out what services they offer their customers. Assume that you have half a carload of standard two-drawer steel file cabinets to ship from San Francisco to St. Louis. Find out the class rate, the transit time, the terms of shipment, and the total cost of transportation by rail. You will find freight forwarding companies listed in the Yellow Pages of a telephone directory. Report your findings in a memo to your instructor.

5.   Manufacturers, wholesalers, and retailers perform overlapping functions. Listed below are the typical functions performed by each. Based on the functions, make a case for the economic justifications of wholesalers.

Manufacturer Functions	Wholesaler Functions	Retailer Functions
Designing	Buying	Buying
Making	Selling	Selling (display)
Selling	Creating assortments	Creating assortments
Pricing	Subdividing	Subdividing
Promoting	Transportation (delivery)	Delivery
Branding	Warehousing (stock)	Stocking
	Financing	Financing
	Risk taking	Risk taking
	Managerial services	Promoting
	Market information	

258

How can you measure the economic value of each function performed by this wholesaler? Why does it have value to manufacturers, retailers, and consumers? Write a memo, no more than two pages, typed, detailing your case.

6. What is the nature of demand for farm products and what role does physical distribution play in the marketing of farm products?

7. What specific functions are performed by a:

Drop Shipper	Commission Merchant	Broker	Selling Agent

What conclusions can be made?

8. In physical distribution, perhaps the most universally recognized element of customer service is the order cycle--that is, the time elapsed from the placement of the order to the receipt of the good. After picking a product known to you, trace the elements of the order cycle from placement to delivery. Can the cycle be shortened? An approach to this problem can be found in Victor P. Buell (ed.), *Handbook of Modern Marketing, 2d ed.*, McGraw-Hill, New York, 1986.

9. In your college or university you will find the following publications:
Traffic Management
Traffic World
Transportation and Distribution
Transportation Journal
Transportation Quarterly

Find an article in one of the magazines on any subject discussed in this chapter. Write a memo to your instructor which summarizes the main point or points of the article. Another good source for this assignment is the marketing abstracts section of any issue of the *Journal of Marketing*.

11. The text notes that "just-in-time" inventory control, purchasing, and production scheduling

have been practiced by Japanese producers. Which Japanese producers are involved and how do they do it? Could American carmakers' price disadvantage with the Japanese be narrowed by adopting this technique? If so, how?

12.   Estimate the cost of carrying an average inventory valued at $100,000 for one year. Compute the specific cost for:

	% of Total Cost	Amount
Storage facilities	__%	$_____
Taxes and insurance	__%	_____
Materials handling and recordkeeping	__%	_____
Interest on investment	__%	_____
Depreciation, obsolescence, and shrinkage	__%	_____
Total	__%	$_____

You will find a set of suggested percentages for these items in A. W. Frey (ed.), *Marketing Handbook, 2d ed.*, Ronald Press, New York, 1965, ch. 21, p. 9.

13.   Write a memo to your instructor on "How Inventory Control Reduces Cost." Present several examples. You will find a good introduction to the subject in George W. Aljian, *Aljian's Purchasing Handbook, 4th ed.*, McGraw-Hill, New York, 1982, sec. 12. See also *Marketing Handbook* (cited in problem 10), ch. 21, p. 9.

PART 15I (a): Exercise

How does one select a wholesaler?

This exercise describes four situations involving different types of manufacturers who are seeking distribution. You are to select the wholesaler which would be most appropriate and justify your choice.

Types of wholesalers
1.   Merchant or full-service wholesalers.
2.   Wholesalers such as truck jobbers and drop shippers.
3.   Agent wholesaling middlemen such a manufacturer's agent, selling agents, brokers, and commission merchants.

  1.   Axel Stordahl has operated a Douglas fir stud mill outside Medford, Oregon, for a number of years. He sells directly to lumber yards and builders in the area. Lately, Axel has given consideration to selling his studs in the booming Sacramento, California, housing market, some 300 miles south. He is seeking a local wholesaler who: (a) handles other wood products, (b) calls on lumber yards and the leading builders, and (c) grants credit to his customers and can arrange for delivery of the lumber.

Type of wholesaler needed _____
Justification _____
_____
_____

2.   Joao and Paulo Gilberto, recent millionaire immigrants from Brazil, have developed a guarana-flavored soft drink they call "La Bomba."   While guarana-flavored drinks are the most popular in Brazil (cakes, ice cream--even lipstick is flavored with it), they are virtually unknown in the U.S. They want to go "the Coke route" by making the syrup and selling it to licensed bottlers who will do everything else except advertise.

Type of wholesaler needed _____
Justification _____
_____
_____

3.   Big Sucker Pump Co. of Louisville, Kentucky, has been an established and beloved Midwestern household pump manufacturer for over 80 years. Their sales west of Denver have been minuscule. George "Red" Diamond, the new sales manager, wants to change all that. He is in San Francisco seeking distribution. He would prefer a single, well-established West Coast distributor and is willing to give extraordinary markups and even sell on consignment if he can get the right company.

Type of wholesaler needed _____
Justification _____
_____
_____

4.   Professor Henderson Hobbs, starting with a generations-old family recipe for mead (honey-fermented wine), has built a part-time hobby into a full-fledged business. He does not wish to resign his professorship but senses that the business has to continue growing or he will be forced to sell it. Since calling on customers takes so much time, he has decided to turn that task over to wine merchants in his three largest markets: Chicago, Milwaukee, and Detroit.

Type of wholesaler needed _____
Justification _____
_____
_____

PART 15I (b): Exercise

As traffic manager for Vulcan Custom Metal of Miami, Florida, you are faced with deciding how

261

to ship a 65-ton scroll press from Allied Machine Mfg. in Seattle, Washington, to your plant in Miami. Time is of the essence since you have a number of orders that could be filled at less cost with this new machine. You estimate it will cost Vulcan $540 per day in lost profits from the time you place the order with Allied. Since Allied demands payment in 10 days, you estimate it will cost Vulcan $275 per day in lost interest thereafter.

You have pulled together the following figures to try to analyze the total cost of distribution using four alternative methods of moving the press to Miami.

What mode of transportation should you use to ship the press?

	Motor	Rail	Piggyback	Air
1. Freight cost	$8.50/cwt	$5.00/cwt	$5.80/cwt	$14.20/cwt
2. Local delivery freight cost	-	.65/cwt	-	1.30/cwt
3. Crating and preparation charges	$1,850.00 (4 days)	$3,800.00 (8 days)	$3,800.00 (8 days)	$120.00 (1 day)
4. Uncrating and setup charges	$100.00 (2 days)	$320.00 (4 days)	$320.00 (4 days)	$40.00 (1 day)
5. Insurance	$1,580.00	$1,820.00	$1,820.00	$1,200.00
6. Days in transit	8 days	18 days	16 days	1 day

Notes: 1. Allied has a rail spur--you don't.
2. Neither of you is near the airport.
3. Cwt = 100 pounds.

PART 15J: A Real World Case: The Old Santa Fe Trail

The Plaza in Santa Fe provides an appealing mixture of the old and the new. Galleries exhibit a variety of modern art. Indian craftsmen sell jewelry, pottery and weavings reflecting ancient designs next to stores displaying goods as standardized as anything to come out of Adam Smith's pin factory. And the Plaza, with its prehistoric secrets, has caught the attention of archaeologists searching for remnants of the past. The Plaza was the western terminus of the Santa Fe trail, and it is the Trail that captures an economist's attention.

The Santa Fe trail teaches some of the greatest objects lessons of economics to be found in

American history. These simple lessons concern middlemen and competition and are not yet understood by either our country's people or its politicians. Our only folk wisdom about middlemen is enshrined in the strident call to "cut out the middleman." In the popular view, middlemen are parasites who have somehow horned their way into a trading chain, raising costs of consumer goods and earning undeserved profits. The implication then, is that consumers would be better off if these scoundrels could be eliminated.

The history of the Santa Fe Trail starkly exposes the fallacies in anti-middleman reasoning. In the early 1800s, Santa Fe was a city isolated on the distant northern frontier of the Spanish empire in the New World. Its people would have found it costly, if not impossible, to produce the whole range of manufactured goods that Europeans and Americans enjoyed. Thus the citizens of Santa Fe stood to benefit from trade with outsiders. However, it would have been prohibitively costly for them to deal directly with European manufacturers. They turned instead to middlemen, traders who came up the Royal Highway--El Camino Real--from the port city of Vera Cruz.

These circumstances reveal the first important truth about middlemen. Middlemen arise when there are barriers to trade. The barriers may be geographic, linguistic, informational or may be related to the costs of performing specialized business functions on a small scale. Whatever the source, barriers make it costly for people to trade. Middlemen are economic agents who specialize in overcoming barriers at lower cost than is possible for the would-be traders.

For many years the people of Santa Fe had a limited choice of middlemen. The central administrators of the Spanish empire tightly regulated their citizens' trade with the rest f the world. These administrators allowed only Spanish and Mexican traders to haul goods to Santa Fe. El Camino Real was long and difficult, and traders used primitive means to transport goods. Prices in Santa Fe reflected the high transportation costs. Still, the people of Santa Fe bought the trade goods, despite the cost.

Over the years American fur traders and other explorers who wandered into Santa Fe observed the high prices. They carried this information with them back to the Independence-St. Louis area, the jumping-off spot for the frontier. American merchants and traders knew a profit opportunity when they saw one and made numerous attempts to open trade with Santa Fe from the early nineteenth century. The Spanish administrators, however, insisted on a Spanish and Mexican monopoly of Santa Fe trade and turned away or jailed American traders. The Spanish administration used government to eliminate a whole group of middlemen. How costly this was to the people of Santa Fe became apparent a few years later. Change for American middlemen came in 1821 when a Mexican revolution overthrew the Spanish government and installed a Mexican one. The new government welcomed Americans, both as settlers and as traders.

William Becknell led the first pack train of traders from the United States to Santa Fe. The American traders undercut the prices of the El Camino Real traders and quickly sold their goods. When Mr. Becknell and a few companions returned to the frontier town of Franklin, near St. Louis, their pack animals were laden with silver coin. Legend has it they flamboyantly slashed open the rawhide bags and spilled silver on the streets of Franklin for all to see. A precise calculation of this trading venture is not possible, but it is reported that one investor of $60 received a $900 payoff from Mr. Becknell.

This episode points out the second important truth about middlemen. High profits for middlemen cannot be taken as evidence that consumers have been exploited. Mr. Becknell and his traders benefited rather than exploited the consumers of Santa Fe. They made profits because they offered Santa Fe buyers lower prices than they had ever seen before and because their costs of doing business were lower than those of the El Camino Real traders.

Mr. Becknell quickly struck again. The following spring he set out with a new party of men and a small wagon train loaded with $3,000 worth of trade goods. The party was threatened by buffalo stampedes, Indians, and shortages of water, but they eventually arrived at the Plaza in Santa Fe. They sold everything, including the wagons and reportedly earned 2,000 percent on their investment. It is "obscene" profits like this that lead politicians and social critics to conclude that someone has been exploited. The easily visible gains of the middleman obscure the degree to which consumers benefit in such a situation. But benefit they do, as shown by their willingness to buy and by the fact that American traders undercut the prices of the established traders.

Trade is a mutually beneficial activity, a positive sum game. Nobody trades expecting to be hurt. Put another way, Karl Marx was wrong when he categorized trade as unproductive labor. Trade creates value, and all parties generally share in the new value. All parties gain from trade, and no one's gains come at the expense of anyone else. This is the third lesson from the Santa Fe Trail.

The fourth lesson followed quickly. Mr. Becknell's profits were highly visible--spilling coins about the public streets seems a touch indiscreet--and other entrepreneurs organized wagon trains. These traders pushed across the Santa Fe Trail to the Plaza, eager to outdo Mr. Becknell, who took three wagons across in 1822. By the count of Josiah Gregg, 26 wagons and $35,000 in merchandise traveled the Trail in 1824, and 130 wagons with $250,000 in goods in 1831.

In the face of this increased supply of trade goods, competition among traders forced prices down. Mr. Gregg noted that prices fell faster than the volume of trade grew. In a few years, profit on investment fell into the 20 percent to 40 percent range, and Mr. Gregg added that it was frequently under 10 percent.

This is the fourth lesson of the Santa Fe Trail: Competition among middlemen will assure that most of the gains from trade ultimately go to consumers. High profits in the early days of the Trail signaled new firms to enter the business of carting goods across the prairies. New entrants in the market drove prices down until the Santa Fe trade offered only normal profits. In the early days of the trade, the traders captured most of the gains. But the market reversed that situation; when the trade had reached equilibrium, it was consumers who benefited most from trade.

The fifth lesson the Santa Fe Trail is that if any cutting out of middlemen is desirable, the market will do it. Government intervention to control middlemen is likely to be counter-productive. More efficient American middlemen cut the original Spanish and Mexican middlemen out of the market. Later, several natives of Santa Fe entered the trade and prospered, apparently driving out some American middlemen who did not understand as clearly which goods would sell in Santa Fe. Further, the pressure of competition led large traders to start dealing directly with American manufacturers, thus cutting the St. Louis-Independence merchants out of the trading chain. These changes in trade reduced costs and eventually rebounded to the advantage of consumers. In contrast, the Spanish government's policy of cutting out the middlemen created the opposite effect. By cutting American middlemen out of the Santa Fe trade, the Spanish bureaucrats raised prices and thus harmed the consumer of Santa Fe.

The lessons of the Santa Fe Trail provide insight about the global collapse of socialism. In a sense, Mr. Marx and other socialist thinkers were the ultimate advocates of cutting out middlemen. They argued that the workers produced output. Capitalists were parasitic middlemen who got rich by imposing themselves between the workers and the consumers. If only these middlemen could be eliminated, the worker-consumers would reap the benefits of their labor.

The failures of 70 years of socialism show, however, the workers' economic situation worsens when capitalist entrepreneurs, executives, managers, financiers, marketers and other middlemen are eliminated. When the former socialist nations convert to market systems, these middlemen will rise again. When they do, so will consumer welfare.

———————

Source: Richard B. Coffman, "The Old Middleman Trail," *The Margin*, March/April, 1991, pp. 12-13. Reprinted by permission of *The Margin*.

———————

___ 1. What sort of middlemen is this article emphasizing?
    A. Merchant wholesaler.   D. Manufacturer's sales office.
    B. Agent wholesaling middleman.   E. Manufacturer's agent.
    C. Manufacturer's sales branch.

___ 2. The article emphasizes which of the following wholesaler functions?
    A. Buying   C. Warehousing   E. All of the above.
    B. Subdividing   D. Transporting

PART 15K: Answers to Questions

PART 15D: Completion
1. Wholesaling/physical distribution
2. sale/sale/producing/operating
3. good or service
4. skills/scale/transaction
5. exceeds
6. products/markets/operation
7. merchant wholesaler/agent/sales facilities
8. Merchant wholesalers/independently owned/title
9. take title/sale/purchase
10. manufacturer/separated
11. sales branch
12. sales office
13. full-service wholesaler
14. buying/creating assortments/subdividing/ selling/transportation/warehousing/ financing/risk taking/market information/ management assistance
15. truck jobbers/drop shippers
16. truck jobber
17. Drop shippers
18. do not take title/fewer services
19. merchant wholesalers
20. manufacturers' agents/brokers/commission merchants/auction companies/selling agents/import-export agents
21. Physical distribution
22. logistics
23. location/warehousing/materials handling/ inventory control/order processing/ transportation
24. costs
25. rates/services
26. system
27. costs/profit
28. customer satisfaction/operating
29. logistics system
30. costs
31. time
32. imbalance/consumption
33. value/place
34. rate/tariff
35. location/warehousing/materials handling/ inventory control/transportation
36. assembling/dividing/storing/reshipping
37. markets
38. warehouses/excessive inventories/ out-of-stock
39. storage/handling
40. conveyor belts/forklift/mechanized equipment
41. Containerization
42. investment/fluctuations/promptly/ completely/accurately
43. order-delivery/inventories
44. economic order quantity/EOQ
45. buying in small quantities/producing in quantities
46. billing/credit/invoice/past-due accounts
47. railroads/trucks/water vessels/pipelines/ airplanes
48. intermodal
49. railroad flatcars
50. barges/ships
51. less-than-carload/less-than-truckload/ carload/truckload
52. package-delivery
53. merchant wholesalers
54. logistic alliances

PART 15E: True-False Questions
1. T 2. T 3. T 4. T 5. T 6. F
7. F 8. F 9. F 10. F 11. F 12. T
13. T 14. T 15. F

PART 15F: Multiple Choice Questions
1. D 2. B 3. D 4. C 5. D 6. E
7. E 8. E 9. E 10. E 11. A 12. B
13. E 14. E 15. A

PART 15G: Matching Questions
a. 30 b. 17 c. 3 d. 28 e. 7 f. 16 g. 2
h. 21 i. 6 j. 23 k. 27 l. 29 m. 9 n. 10
o. 8

266

PART SIX

PROMOTION

CHAPTER 16

THE PROMOTIONAL PROGRAM

PART 16A: Chapter Goals

After studying this chapter, you should be able to explain:

- The components of promotion and how they differ
- The role promotion plays in an organization and in the economy
- How the process of communicating relates to effective promotion
- The concept and design of the promotional mix
- The promotional campaign
- Alternative promotional budgeting methods
- Regulation of promotion

PART 16B: **Key Terms and Concepts**

1. Promotion	[456]	14. Hierarchy of effects	[463]
2. Personal selling	[456]	15. Push strategy	[466]
3. Advertising	[456]	16. Pull strategy	[466]
4. Sales promotion	[456]	17. Campaign	[468]
5. Public relations	[456]	18. Campaign theme	[469]
6. Publicity	[457]	19. Promotional budgeting methods	[470]
7. Communication process	[457]	20. Federal Trade Commission Act	[473]
8. Encoding	[457]	21. Wheeler-Lea Amendment	[473]
9. Decoding	[457]	22. Substantiation	[473]
10. Feedback	[457]	23. Consent decree	[473]
11. Noise	[457]	24. Cease-and-desist orders	[473]
12. Promotion and the demand curve	[459]	25. Corrective advertising	[473]
13. Promotional mix	[462]	26. Robinson-Patman Act	[474

PART 16C: Summary

The marketer's objective is to advance his product or service in rank or position until it is the customer's first choice. Promotional activities are concerned with the methods the marketer can use to make his product or service first choice among a target group of consumers [456].

The marketer develops his promotional mix, which consists of five elements: advertising, personal selling, sales promotion, publicity, and public relations [456-457]. The promotional mix is a subsystem of the marketing mix, introduced earlier, and discussed throughout the text.

The two most widely used methods of promotion are personal selling and advertising. The communication process is central to any method of promotion [457]. A communication process requires four elements: a message, a source of the message, a communication channel, and a receiver of the message [457]. However, to refine the process into workable form, the message must be encoded (symbolized) and the receiver of the message must decode the message (the symbol) [457].

The promotional manager will coordinate his activities (advertising, personal selling, and sales promotion) around a campaign [468]. Factors influencing a promotional mix include funds available, nature of the market, nature of the product, and stage of the product's life cycle [462-468]. Methods used in determining the promotional appropriation include some relation to income, task or objective, use of funds available, and following the competition [470-472].

Marketers cannot go hogwild. They are constrained in their promotional efforts by federal regulations, principal among which are the Federal Trade Commission Act [473], its Wheeler-Lea Amendment [473], and the Robinson-Patman Act [474]. State and local legislation, the activities of private organizations, and the advertising industry itself help to regulate aspects of promotion [474-475].

PART 16D: Completion

1. Basically, promotion is an attempt at _____.

2. Promotion is the element in the organization's _____ that is used to _____, _____, and _____ the market for a product and/or organization selling it in hopes of influencing the recipients' _____, _____, or _____.

3. The promotional tools making up the promotional mix include the following ingredients:
   (1) _____, (2) _____, (3) _____, (4) _____, and (5) _____.

4. _____ is the presentation of a product to a prospective customer by a representative of the selling organization.

5. _____ is impersonal mass communication that the sponsor has paid for and in which the sponsor is clearly identified.

6. _____ is demand stimulating activities designed to supplement _____ and facilitate _____.

7. _____ is a planned effort by a company to influence public attitudes and opinions about the company and its products.

8. _____, a nonpersonal form of promotion, is not paid for by the company benefiting from it.

271

9. Fundamentally, a communications process requires only four elements: (1) a(n) _____, (2) a(n) _____, (3) a(n) _____ , and (4) a(n) _____.

10. Information must first be _____ into a transmittable form.

11. The symbols must then be _____ and given _____ by the receiver.

12. The receiver then formulates a(n) _____.

13. The response serves as _____.

14. _____ is any external factor that interferes with successful communication.

15. Three characteristics of imperfect competition are: (1) _____ differentiation, (2) _____ buying behavior, and (3) _____ market information.

16. In terms of economic theory, the essential purpose of promotion is to change the location and shape of the _____ for a firm's product.

17. It is hoped that promotion also will affect the demand _____ for the product, making demand more _____ in the face of a price increase and more _____ when the price goes down.

18. Sales promotion is needed: (1) to disseminate _____, (2) for _____, and (3) to remind consumers about the _____ and its potential to _____.

19. A company should treat personal selling, advertising, and other promotional activities as a(n) _____ effort within the total marketing program.

20. They must also be coordinated with activities in _____, _____, and _____.

21. Promotion should also be strongly influenced by a firm's overall strategic _____.

22. The _____ is a firm's combination of personal selling, advertising, sales promotion, publicity, and public relations needed to achieve its marketing objectives.

23. The four basic factors that should influence management's decisions with respect to its promotional mix are: (1) the _____ market, (2) the nature of the _____, (3) the stage of the product's _____, and (4) the amount of _____ available for promotion.

24. In terms of readiness to buy, consumers move through six stages, called the _____

_____, which include awareness, knowledge, liking, preference, conviction, and purchase.

25. The nature of the firm's market influences the company's promotional mix in at least four of its aspects: (1) readiness to _____ , (2) _____ scope of the market, (3) _____ _____, and (4) _____ of the market.

26. The most important _____ attributes that play a role in a promotional strategy are: (1) _____ value, (2) degree of _____, and (3) pre- and post-sale _____.

27. When a product is in the introductory stage of the product life cycle, the promotional strategy is to _____ prospective buyers and show them how it will _____ them.

28. Professor Neil H. Borden suggested five criteria which may serve as guides for management in deciding whether the firm should use advertising to increase the demand for its product: (1) the _____ trends for the product should be favorable; (2) there should be considerable opportunity to _____ the product; (3) the product should have _____ qualities; (4) powerful _____ should exist for the product; and (5) the firm must have _____ to support an advertising program.

29. Promotion aimed at middlemen is called a(n) "_____" strategy, while promotion aimed at end users is referred to as a(n) "_____" strategy.

30. Using a(n) _____ strategy means that a channel member will direct its promotion primarily at the _____ who are the next link forward in the distribution channel.

31. When a(n) _____ strategy is used, the marketer directs the promotional efforts at end users--usually the _____.

32. A campaign is a coordinated series of _____ built around a(n) _____ and designed to reach a(n) _____ goal in a defined _____.

33. The total promotional campaign can be subdivided into five parts: _____, _____, _____, _____ , and _____.

34. A campaign revolves around a(n) _____ or _____. This _____ permeates all promotional efforts and tends to _____ the campaign.

35. In order for a promotional campaign to be successful, the efforts of the groups handling _____, _____ , _____ , _____ and _____, and _____ must be _____ effectively.

36. The four basic methods for determining the budget allocation for promotion are: (1) relation

273

to _____, (2) use of all _____ available, (3) following the _____, and (4) task or _____ .

37. Two promotional appropriation methods used in relation to income are: _____ of money per unit, and percentage of past or anticipated _____.

38. By setting promotional expenditures on the basis of sales, management is saying that promotion is a(n) _____ of sales; in fact, it is a(n) _____ of sales.

39. The task or objective approach in determining the promotional budget involves the following steps: (1) deciding what the promotional program _____, and (2) determining what the _____ of promotion must be.

40. This is sometimes called the _____.

41. Since a primary objective of promotion is to sell something for persuasion, the potential for _____ exists.

42. The two major pieces of federal legislation regulating promotional activities are the _____ and the _____.

43. The Federal Trade Commission Act and its Wheeler-Lea Amendment have the greatest influence on regulating promotional messages in _____ commerce.

44. Loopholes in the Federal Trade Commission Act led to the enactment of the _____ in 1938.

45. The Federal Trade Commission may force a firm to remove advertising deemed deceptive from circulation using a(n) _____ order.

46. Another enforcement activity, _____, paid for by the offending firm, is intended to _____ the misunderstanding left in consumers' minds as a result of the allegedly false ads.

47. Since corrective ads have proved to be only _____ in eliminating false impressions, their use has been curtailed.

48. The Robinson-Patman Act has two sections relating to price discrimination involving _____.

49. It states that the seller must offer the promotional services, or payment for them, on a(n) _____ equal basis to ____ competing customers.

50. The Printer's Ink model statute of 1911 is intended to establish "truth in advertising" in
_____.

51. The "_____" restrict the activity of sales people who represent firms located outside the affected city and who sell door to door, or call on business establishments.

PART 16E: True-False Questions

If the statement is true, circle "T"; if false, circle "F."

T F 1. Feedback in communications is important because it allows the receiver a chance to judge how well a message is received.

T F 2. The Robinson-Patman Act is mainly concerned with price discrimination.

T F 3. More is spent on personal selling than any other type of sales promotion.

T F 4. In terms of demand elasticity, it is hoped that promotion will make demand elastic in the face of a price increase.

T F 5. An example of noise in communications is competitive advertising.

T F 6. Another name for the task or objective method of budgeting is the buildup method.

T F 7. All that is necessary to successfully advertise a product is money.

T F 8. "Green River" ordinances restrict the practices of sales people.

T F 9. Primary demand refers to the idea that people will not buy a product they do not need no matter how excellent the advertising.

T F 10. Marketing and selling are synonymous.

T F 11. The federal agency responsible for enforcing promotional activities is the Federal Trade Commission.

T F 12. Point-of-purchase display is a form of sales promotion.

T F 13. Based on the unit value of the product, high price implies a need for personal selling; low price, for advertising.

T F 14. Promotion aimed at middlemen is called a "pull" strategy.

275

T F 15. Sales promotion should serve to coordinate advertising and personal selling efforts in a company.

PART 16F: Multiple Choice Questions

In the space provided write the letter of the answer that best fits the statement.

____ 1. In a marketing communications system, an example of the element of noise is:
   A. A sales talk.
   B. Competitors' newspaper ads.
   C. The action taken by a company.
   D. The consumer's interpretation of an ad.
   E. Research done to get consumers' reaction.

____ 2. In the promotional mix of a firm, advertising will be emphasized more than personal selling when the firm:
   A. Has a limited local market.
   B. Has limited financial resources.
   C. Is selling industrial, installation-type products.
   D. Sells unbranded products.
   E. Sells to many customers in many different industries.

____ 3. For which of the following products would personal selling most likely be used?
   A. Bread. B. Office supplies. C. Computers. D. School supplies. E. Toothpaste

____ 4. Setting the promotional appropriation as a percentage of sales expected for the coming period has a major weakness in that it:
   A. Has not received very wide acceptance.
   B. Does not allow a company to judge its selling costs in relation to sales income.
   C. Is complicated to determine.
   D. Acts as a noncontrollable fixed expense.
   E. Results in promotion being a result of sales, rather than a cause of sales.

____ 5. All of the following deal with interstate commerce EXCEPT:
   A. "Green River" ordinances.   C. Federal Trade Commission Act.
   B. Robinson-Patman Act.   D. Wheeler-Lea Amendment.

____ 6. Neil Borden's concept of "advertisability" includes all of the following factors EXCEPT:
   A. Favorable primary demand.   D. Hidden product features.
   B. Rational buying motives.   E. Differentiated product.
   C. Adequate financing.

___ 7. A nonpersonal form of unpaid demand stimulation is called:
   A. Test marketing.   C. Publicity.   E. Public relations.
   B. Advertising.   D. Sales promotion.

___ 8. The nature of marketing influences is felt:
   A. In the geographic scope of the market.
   B. By the type of customers.
   C. By the concentration of the market.
   D. All of the above.
   E. None of the above.

___ 9. All of the following are considered to be within the scope of sales promotion EXCEPT:
   A. Window display in a department store.
   B. Distribution of product samples by mail.
   C. Product exhibition at an industrial trade show.
   D. Training program for retail sales people.
   E. Trading stamps.

___ 10. The federal law that stipulates that a seller must offer promotional services and facilities, or payments for them, on a proportionally equal basis to all competing customers is the:
   A. Federal Trade Commission Act.   C. Wheeler-Lea Amendment.
   B. Robinson-Patman Act.   D. "Green River" ordinances.

___ 11. The central idea or focal point of an advertisement is its:
   A. Theme. B. Medium. C. Campaign. D. Copy. E. Message.

___ 12. The most money is spent on which form of promotion?
   A. Personal selling.   C. Sales promotion.   E. Public relations.
   B. Advertising.   D. Publicity.

___ 13. In strategic market planning, promotion should be coordinated with:
   A. Personal selling.   C. Pricing.   E. All of the above.
   B. Product planning.   D. Advertising.

___ 14. A "pull" strategy would probably be used in marketing:
   A. High fashion garments.   D. Custom computer services.
   B. A new cookie.   E. Structural steel.
   C. Earth movers.

___ 15. The most widely used method of determining the promotional budget is:
   A. Relation to sales.   D. Task.
   B. Use of all available funds. E. Objective.
   C. Follow competition.

PART 16G: Matching Questions

In the space provided write the number of the word or expression from column 1 that best fits the description in column 2.

1   2

1. Advertising

        ___ a. The most strategic combination of advertising, personal selling, sales promotion, and other promotional tools to meet company sales goals.

2. Buildup method

3. Campaign

        ___ b. Tells the sender whether a message was received and how it was perceived by the destination target.

4. Corrective advertising

        ___ c. A coordinated series of promotional efforts built around a single theme and designed to reach a predetermined goal.

5. Decoding

6. Encoding

        ___ d. The promotional appeal dressed up in a distinctive, attention-getting form.

7. Federal Trade Commission Act

8. Feedback

        ___ e. Brand demand.

9. "Green River" Ordinances

        ___ f. Another name for the task or objective means of determining the promotional budget.

10. Noise

        ___ g. Established the FTC.

11. Personal selling

        ___ h. A penalty imposed by the FTC.

12. Primary demand

        ___ i. A promotion strategy aimed at end users.

13. Promotion

        ___ j. The most money is spent on this type of sales promotion.

14. Promotional mix

15. Publicity

        ___ k. Getting a favorable "plug."

16. Public relations

        ___ l. Changing an idea into words, pictures, or both.

17. "Pull" strategy

18. "Push" strategy

19. Robinson-Patman Act

20. Sales promotion

21. Selective demand

22. Theme

23. Wheeler-Lea Amendment

PART 16H: Problems and Applications

1.   In recent years, the changing pattern of retail distribution, with its increased emphasis on the use of self-service selling and automatic vending machines, has pointed to the need for greater use of sales promotion. Write a memo to your instructor on this subject.

2.   Is the task of stimulating primary demand ever finished? Prepare a memo on this subject. In your memo, take a position.

3.   When should manufacturer-retail cooperative advertising be used? Write a memo to your instructor for a specific product or service, taking the position that cooperative advertising should be used. Review the textbook discussion in Chapter 18 on this subject before you select a specific good or service.

4.   Select any charitable organization that operates in your area. How do they go about promoting their organization to acquire the funds necessary for their operation?

5.   In a memo to your instructor, develop a complete promotional strategy for a new film in the "Indiana Jones" series.

6.   In a schematic form, illustrate the relationships and differences found among the following items:
   A. Promotion   C. Sales promotion
   B. Advertising   D. Personal selling

7.   Select a product currently being sold by a company in your area. Find out the relative importance placed upon each aspect of the promotional mix in selling that product. Prepare a memo for discussion with your classmates.

8.   Research the type of promotional campaign that was used to stimulate primary demand for a product that is relatively new in our society, e.g., solar heating systems, CD players, food processors, or portable computers.

9.   Review the discussion under "When should personal selling be the main ingredient?" For

each item mentioned (see your text under the heading, "Determining the Promotional Mix"), rate the following companies.

<u>The Boeing Co.</u>   <u>A.B.C. Encyclopedia Co.</u>

        Yes   No   Yes   No

1. _____ _____   1. _____ _____
2. _____ _____   2. _____ _____
3. _____ _____   3. _____ _____
4. _____ _____   4. _____ _____
5. _____ _____   5. _____ _____
6. _____ _____   6. _____ _____
7. _____ _____   7. _____ _____

PART 16I (a): Exercise

Table 16-1 relates the promotional strategy to the product life-cycle stage. Listed below are several products and/or brands. Beside each, indicate which promotional strategy each marketer will most likely utilize.

1. Coca-Cola.

2. A computer with the capability of making a home burglar-proof.

3. Burger King's "Whopper."

4. Standard-sized black-and-white television set.

5. Miniaturized black-and-white television set.

6. Wheaties.

7. A new diet soft-drink.

8. Chevrolet Camaro.

PART 16I (b): Exercise

1. Professor Neil Borden listed five elements that serve as guides in determining the "advertisability" of a product. Assuming the fifth criterion--sufficient funds to support an effective advertising program--has been met by the producers, evaluate the following products on the other four criteria.

	Primary Demand?	Product Differentiation?	Hidden Qualities?	Emotional Buying Motives?
1. "Real" cigarettes	_____	_____	_____	_____
2. "Lite" beer (Miller)	_____	_____	_____	_____
3. "Micrin" mouthwash	_____	_____	_____	_____
4. Table grapes	_____	_____	_____	_____
5. "Vote" toothpaste	_____	_____	_____	_____
6. "Sun-Maid" raisins	_____	_____	_____	_____
7. "Listerol" disinfectant spray	_____	_____	_____	_____
8. Red delicious apples	_____	_____	_____	_____
9. "Softswirl" instant pudding	_____	_____	_____	_____
10. "Texaco" heating oil	_____	_____	_____	_____

2. Which of the items, in your judgment, do not meet Borden's "advertisability" test, and therefore should not be advertised? Why?

PART 16I (c): Two Communications Exercises

Communications Exercise 1:

Your instructor will select five volunteers to stand in front of the class (do not be afraid to volunteer--you will not be embarrassed).

The instructions are as follows: "Take a plain sheet of 8-1/2 X 11 inch paper; hold it straight out in front of you with both hands. I want to caution you. You cannot ask any questions. Now, close your eyes. Fold the paper in half. Tear off the upper left-hand corner of the paper. Fold the paper in half again. Now, tear off the lower left-hand corner of the paper. Fold the paper in half again. Now, tear off the lower right-hand corner of the paper. For the last time, fold the paper in half. Tear off the upper right-hand corner of the paper. Now, open your eyes, and unfold the paper."

What does this exercise have to do with communications?

Communications Exercise 2:

The instructions are as follows:

"Take a plain sheet of 8-1/2 X 11 inch paper and listen carefully to what I am about to relate to you. You may wish to diagram what follows."

281

"You are a school bus driver. You leave the school yard and drive northeast for 10.5 miles where you pick up four children. You then drive five miles south where you pick up five children. You then drive east for 9.2 miles where you pick up six children plus one bully. You drive southwest for 16 miles where you pick up eight children. Finally, you drive north for 11.2 miles back to the school yard where you unload the children."

"How old is the bus driver?"

PART 16J: A Real World Case: David and Goliath

Last year [1991], Quick's Candy Inc. shipped millions of its gourmet lollipops to U.S. troops during operation Desert Storm. It was a tall order for the tiny Buchanan (Mich.) company, which had to deliver the huge quantity with military precision. But then, company founder Howard E. Quick knows all about that: He's been selling to Kmart for three years.

Retailing may be increasingly dominated by giant chains and mammoth manufacturers, but Quick's, with sales of about $3.5 million, shows how small suppliers can survive. "Small vendors can move quickly, and if they can execute a quality product, they'll still be a viable source," says Jim Glime, Kmart's manager for business development.

Quick's lollipops, retailing for 50 cents to 65 cents apiece and in flavors from piña colada to black currant, sold briskly in some Kmart test stores. Now, nine-year-old Quick's supplies all 2,400 Kmart stores in the U.S. and Canada. It's investing $2 million in new equipment that will triple candy output.

Besides producing a tasty lollipop, the family-run confectioner also works hard to make Kmart's life easy. Quick's invested $15,000 in computer systems that let it monitor inventories at Kmart's 12 distribution centers. When supplies run low, Quick's automatically replenishes inventories, with no prior approval from Kmart. It's only one of 250 Kmart vendors with that capability ...

The trouble is, many small suppliers fear their niche with the big retailers is rapidly shrinking. For starters, few small companies can make the kind of investments in production capacity it takes to serve the giants. Worse, the power retailers are cutting back the number of their suppliers in the name of efficiency. Some retailers aim to pare their vendor lists by 10% a year for the next several years, says Philip H. Kowalczyk, management consultant at Kurt Salmon Associates ...

Sometimes speed, quality, and flexibility aren't enough. WalMart cut Quick's from 700 to 100 stores when it found a cheaper lollipop, says Howard Quick. He's now fighting to regain the business. But to avoid overdependency on the big retailers, Quick's is also beefing up sales to other outlets, such as schools, groceries, and the military. Still, for Quick's and other small suppliers, the fastest way to grow is to tie their fates to the power retailers--and hang on for dear life.

___ 1. The article about Quick's suggest that their gourmet lollipops probably meet all of Neil Borden's criteria for advertisability EXCEPT:
   A. Favorable primary demand.   D. Hidden product features.
   B. Emotional buying motives.   E. Differentiated product.
   C. Adequate financing.

___ 2. Quick's primarily uses _____ in its promotional strategy.
   A. Personal selling   D. Publicity
   B. Advertising   E. Public relations
   C. Sales promotion

___ 3. Although the article does not specifically mention it, Quick's probably uses a _____ strategy.
   A. Push   B. Pull

PART 16K: Answers to Questions

PART 16D: Completion
1. influence
2. marketing mix/inform/persuade/remind/ feelings/beliefs/behavior
3. personal selling/advertising/sales promotion/ publicity/public relations
4. Personal selling
5. Advertising
6. Sales promotion/advertising/personal selling
7. Public relations
8. Publicity
9. message/source of this message/ communication channel/receiver
10. encoded
11. decoded/meaning
12. response
13. feedback
14. Noise
15. product/emotional/less-than-complete
16. demand curve
17. elasticity/inelastic/elastic
18. information/persuasion/availability/satisfy
19. coordinated
20. product planning/pricing/distribution
21. marketing plan
22. promotional mix
23. target/product/life cycle/money
24. hierarchy of effects
25. buy/geographic/type of customers/ concentration
26. product/unit/customization/service
27. inform/benefit
28. primary demand/differentiate/hidden/ emotional buying motives/sufficient funds
29. push/pull
30. push/middlemen
31. pull/ultimate consumers
32. promotional efforts/single theme/specific/ period of time
33. advertising/personal selling/sales promotion/public relations/publicity
34. theme/central idea/theme/unify
35. advertising/personal selling/sales promotion/publicity/public relations/ physical distribution/coordinated
36. sales/funds/competition/objective
37. fixed amount/sales
38. result/cause
39. must accomplish/cost
40. buildup method
41. abuse
42. Federal Trade Commission Act/ Robinson-Patman Act
43. interstate
44. Wheeler-Lea Amendment
45. cease-and-desist
46. corrective advertising/correct
47. marginally successful
48. promotional allowances
49. proportionally/all
50. intrastate commerce
51. "Green River" ordinances

PART 16E: True-False Questions
1. T   2. T   3. T   4. F   5. T   6. T
7. F   8. T   9. T   10. F   11. T   12. T
13. T   14. F   15. T

PART 16F: Multiple Choice Questions
1. B   2. E   3. C   4. E   5. A   6. B
7. C   8. D   9. D   10. B   11. A   12. A
13. E   14. B   15. A

PART 16G: Matching Questions
a. 14   b. 8   c. 3   d. 22   e. 21   f. 2
g. 7   h. 4   i. 17   j. 11   k. 15   l. 6

```
┌─────────────────────────────────────┐
│                                      │
│                                      │
└─────────────────────────────────────┘
┌─────────────────────────────────────┐
│                                      │
│           CHAPTER 17                 │
│                                      │
└─────────────────────────────────────┘
┌─────────────────────────────────────┐
│                                      │
│   PERSONAL SELLING AND               │
│   SALES MANAGEMENT                   │
│                                      │
│                                      │
│                                      │
│                                      │
│                                      │
│                                      │
│                                      │
└─────────────────────────────────────┘
```

PART 17A: Chapter Goals

After studying this chapter, you should be able to explain:

- The part that personal selling plays in our economy and in an organization's marketing program
- The variety of personal selling jobs
- The changing patterns in personal selling
- The major tasks in staffing and operating a sales force
- Key issues in evaluating a sales person's performance

PART 17B: Key Terms and Concepts

1. Personal selling [480]
2. Retail-store selling [481]
3. Outside sales forces [481]
4. Telemarketing [482]
5. Professional sales person [482]
6. Role ambiguity [482]
7. Role conflict [483]
8. Driver-sales person [483]
9. Inside order-taker [483]
10. Outside order-taker [483]
11. Missionary sales person [483]
12. Sales engineer [483]
13. Creative sales person [483]
14. Order-taker [484]
15. Sales-support personnel [484]
16. Order getter [484]
17. Selling center [484]
18. Systems selling [485]
19. Relationship selling [485]
20. Prospecting [487]

21. Qualifying [488]
22. Preapproach in selling [488]
23. Sales presentation [488]
24. AIDA [488]
25. Canned sales talk [489]
26. Closing a sale [489]
27. Trial close [489]
28. Meeting objections [489]
29. Postsale activities [490]
30. Sales-force selection [491]
31. Sales training program [492]
32. Motivating sales people [494]
33. Sales compensation plan [494]
34. Salary [494]
35. Commission [494]
36. Combination compensation plan [495]
37. Evaluating rep's performance [495]
38. Quantitative evaluation bases [496]
39. Qualitative evaluation bases [496]

PART 17C: Summary

Personal selling is the major promotional method used in American business whether measured by the number of people employed, total expenditures, or percentage of sales [480]. Sales jobs are different from other jobs in a company because sales people service their customers, build goodwill, sell the company's products, and train their customers' sales people [480].

There is a wide variety of sales jobs, ranging from driver-sales person to the sales engineer, each requiring different levels of creative selling [483].

There are four steps to selling a product [487-490]. The first is prospecting, or identifying potential sales customers. In the next step, prospects are qualified to determine their interest in buying and their capability to buy. The third step is the sales presentation. Often this takes the form of "AIDA," that is, creating attention, generating interest, stimulating desire, and requesting action [488]. The last step involves postpurchase activities designed to reduce cognitive dissonance and increase the likelihood of repeat business.

Given the selling job, strategic sales-force management requires a number of specific activities. These activities include selecting sales people, forecasting sales, preparing sales budgets, establishing sales territories, and setting sales quotas [490]. Evaluations are based on both quantitative and qualitative factors [496]. The quantitative factors can be viewed in terms of a set of output factors and a set of input factors. Some output factors which ordinarily are quite useful as evaluation bases are sales volume, gross margin, orders, closing rates, and accounts [496]. Some useful input measures are calls per day, direct selling expenses, and nonselling activities [496].

Sales compensation consists of both financial and nonfinancial rewards. Financial rewards are classified as straight salary, straight commission, and the most common type, a combination of the two [494-495].

PART 17D: Completion

1. _____ is the personal communication of information to persuade _____ to buy _____.

2. Personal selling occurs in nearly every _____.

3. Personal selling is the major promotional method used to increase _____ by offering _____ to customers over the _____.

4. Personal selling is likely to be the most important promotional method when the: (1) market is _____; (2) product has a(n) _____ unit value or is _____ in nature; (3)

product must be fitted to a(n) _____ needs; (4) sale involves a(n) _____; (5) product is in the _____ stage of its life cycle; and (6) firm lacks funds to _____ adequately.

5. Major limitations of personal selling are its _____ and management's inability to get the _____ needed to do the job.

6. Generally, there are two types of personal selling: where the _____ come to the _____ (_____ selling); and where the _____ go to the _____ (also called _____ sales forces).

7. Some firms have sales forces that go to the customer, but not in person. This is called _____.

8. The _____ sales person does a total selling job which includes _____customers, building _____, selling _____, and _____ customers' sales people.

9. In performing these activities, the sales person often encounters role _____ and role _____.

10. This is because the best interests of the _____ conflict with the _____ interest of the _____ or the _____.

11. Sales jobs include: (1) _____, (2) _____ order-taker, (3) _____order-taker, (4) _____ sales people, (5) _____, and (6) people who engage in _____ of goods and services.

12. Sales jobs differ from other jobs in that: (1) the sales force is largely responsible for implementing a firm's _____; (2) sales people represent their _____ to customers; (3) sales people operate with little direct _____; and (4) sales jobs frequently involve considerable _____ and time away from _____.

13. Four emerging patterns in personal selling are selling _____ , _____ selling, _____ selling, and _____.

14. A selling center is a group of people representing not only a(n) _____ department, but such functional areas as _____, _____, and _____.

15. Systems selling means selling a(n) _____ of related goods and services.

16. Relationship selling is the process of developing a(n) _____ relationship with selected _____ over time.

17. Relationship selling involves creating _____; that is, using _____, behaving _____, displaying _____, being _____, and displaying _____.

18. Telemarketing is growing because: (1) some customers _____ it, and (2) many marketers find it increases selling _____.

19. The steps involved in the personal sales process are: (1) identifying or _____ the buyers; (2) _____ the individual prospect, or _____; (3) <u>sales</u> presentation, and (4) _____ services.

20. Qualifying the prospect involves determining whether he or she has the necessary _____, purchasing _____, and _____ to buy.

21. Presenting the sales message often involves a technique whose acronym is _____.

22. The trial close is important because it gives sales people a way of testing the prospect's willingness to _____.

23. In the final stage of the selling process--postsale activities--the sales person's job is to minimize the customer's postpurchase anxiety or _____.

24. Management of the personal selling function begins with: (1) the setting of _____ and (2) planning sales-force _____ such as _____ sales, preparing sales _____, establishing sales _____, and setting sales _____.

25. Effective sales-force management begins with a qualified _____.

26. _____, or personnel selection, is the most important management activity in any organization.

27. A recruiting system involves three steps: (1) prepare a written _____, (2) recruit an adequate number of _____, and (3) select the _____ from among the applicants.

28. When sales people are hired, the first task is to integrate them into the company family; in other words, _____ them into the company.

29. To set up a training program involves answering the following questions: (1) What are the _____? (2) Who should do the _____? (3) What should be the _____? (4) _____ should training be done? and (5) What _____ should be used?

289

30. To compensate their sales forces, companies offer both _____ and _____ rewards.

31. Financial rewards may be _____ monetary payments (salary or commission), or _____ monetary compensation (paid vacations, pensions, and insurance plans).

32. Three widely used methods of compensating a sales force are: straight _____, straight _____, and a(n) _____ plan.

33. The ideal way to develop a combination compensation plan is to balance the best features of both the _____ and _____ plans with as few of their drawbacks as possible.

34. Both _____ and _____ factors should be used as the bases for performance evaluation.

35. A sales person's quantitative performance should be evaluated on the basis of both his _____ (_____) and his _____(_____).

36. Some quantitative performance output factors which ordinarily are quite useful as evaluation bases are: (1) _____ as measured by products, customer groups, etc.; (2) sales volume as a percentage of _____ or _____; (3) _____ as measured by product line or customer group; (4) _____, evaluated by number of orders and average size of order; (5) _____ rate; and (6) _____--percentage of accounts sold, or number of new accounts.

37. Some useful input factors to measure are: _____ per day, _____ selling expense, and _____ activities.

38. Qualitative factors include: (1) knowledge of _____, (2)_____ management, (3) _____ relations, (4) _____ appearance, and (5)_____ and _____.

PART 17E: True-False Questions

If the statement is true, circle "T"; if false, circle "F."

T F   1. "Creative selling" usually is associated with a retailer's sales people.

T F   2. A good recruiting system operates continuously.

T F   3. The major limitation to personal selling is its cost.

T F   4. A selling center is also known as team selling.

T F 5. It is important that only quantitative and not qualitative factors be used as the basis for performance evaluation.

T F 6. An effective selling job does not end when the order is written up.

T F 7. The sales person has essentially one goal--that of persuasion.

T F 8. Missionary sales people sell religious supplies to retail stores.

T F 9. Good sales people automatically become good sales managers.

T F 10. Some sales output factors are calls per day, displays set up, and number of training meetings held with dealers or distributors.

T F 11. The conscientious sales person, in order to be thorough, always goes through the "AIDA" steps with all his prospects.

T F 12. The most important job facing the sales manager is selecting sales people.

T F 13. Hiring sales people is simple: just look for tall, good-looking, well dressed, aggressive males.

T F 14. Compared to all the other promotional techniques, personal selling has greater flexibility.

T F 15. The most common compensation method is straight commission.

PART 17F: Multiple Choice Questions

In the space provided write the letter of the answer that best fits the statement.

___ 1. All of the following are advantages of personal selling as compared with other promotional tools EXCEPT:
   A. More flexible in its operation.
   B. Can reach more prospects at a lower cost per prospect.
   C. Specific objections and questions can be answered immediately.
   D. Market effort can be pinpointed.
   E. Its goal is to actually make a sale.

___ 2. AIDA happens during the _____ stage of the personal selling process.
   A. Preparation   C. Preapproach   E. Postsale
   B. Prospecting   D. Presentation

____ 3. An inventor of an expensive and complicated scientific instrument will most probably choose which of the following as the principal promotional tactic?
   A. Technical publicity.
   B. Personal selling.
   C. Business journal advertising.
   D. Trade journal advertising.
   E. A direct mail campaign.

____ 4. Personal selling involves:
   A. Making sales presentations.
   B. Explaining product benefits.
   C. Analyzing the terms of sale.
   D. Following up the sale.
   E. All of the above.

____ 5. A sales person works 5 days a week, makes 140 calls, gets 60 orders, and has a total sales volume of $15,000 for the week. Which of the following is closest to her closing average?
   A. .333   B. .430   C. .400   D. .250   E. .230

____ 6. Refer back to question 5. What is the sales person's daily call rate?
   A. 7   B. 3   C. 2-1/2   D. 7-1/2   E. None of the above

____ 7. The sales person is usually engaged in reducing cognitive dissonance during the _____ stage of the personal selling process.
   A. Preparation   C. Preapproach   E. Postpurchase service
   B. Prospecting   D. Presentation

____ 8. The sales job where the sales person does not solicit orders, but instead builds goodwill and performs other promotional activities will probably be held by:
   A. Driver-sales person.
   B. Inside order-taker.
   C. Sales engineers.
   D. Missionary sales people.
   E. Creative sales people.

____ 9. According to the text, the most important activity in managing a sales force is:
   A. Personnel selection.   C. Personnel followup.   E. Personnel direction.
   B. Planning.   D. Personnel training.

____10. The straight-salary plan of compensating sales people has the advantage of:
   A. Offering a maximum of security to the sales person.
   B. Giving management control over a rep's efforts.
   C. Catering to the customer's best interests.
   D. Offering stability of earnings for the sales person.
   E. All of the above.

____11. The promotional technique offering the greatest flexibility is:
   A. Advertising.   C. Sales promotion.   E. Public relations.
   B. Personal selling.   D. Publicity.

___12. Using telecommunications equipment as part of the "going to the customer" category of personal selling is known as:
    A. Selling centers.   C. Team selling.   E. Telemarketing.
    B. Systems selling.   D. Relationship selling.

___13. The first task of the sales person is to:
    A. Present the sales message.   D. Close the sale.
    B. Identify prospects.   E. Deal with cognitive dissonance.
    C. Meet objections.

___14. A good recruiting system:
    A. Operates continuously.
    B. Is systematic in reaching and exploiting all appropriate sources of applicants.
    C. Provides a flow of qualified applicants in numbers greater than the firm's needs.
    D. All of the above.
    E. None of the above.

___15. A sales person can be evaluated on:
    A. A quantitative basis.   D. The basis of outputs.
    B. A qualitative basis.   E. Any of the above.
    C. The basis of inputs.

PART 17G: Matching Questions

In the space provided write the number of the word or expression from column 1 that best fits the description in column 2.

1	2
1. AIDA	___ a. Personal communication of information to persuade a customer to buy.
2. Combination compensation plan	
	___ b. An example is a retail clerk standing behind a counter.
3. Driver-sales person	
4. Inside order-taker	___ c. Problems that flow from the different tasks sales people are called upon to perform.
5. Missionary seller	
	___ d. The portion of the personal selling process involved with reducing cognitive dissonance.
6. Outside order-taker	
7. Personal selling	___ e. A compensation plan used where great incentive is needed to get the sales.

293

8. Postpurchase services   ___ f. A sales presentation method.

9. Prospecting   ___ g. The most common type of compensation plan.

10. Role ambiguity   ___ h. A group of people representing a sales department as well as finance, production, and research and development.

11. Role conflict

12. Sales engineer

13. Selling center

14. Straight commission

15. Straight salary

16. Telemarketing

PART 17H: Problems and Applications

1. Why do sales people probably need more tact, diplomacy, and social poise than other employees on their same level in the organization?

2. Why can a "canned" sales talk be effective?

3. You work for a wholesale company that sells its products to retail outlets. Assume you have a new product that you wish to present to your retail account. How would you go about doing this?

4. Select two firms with field sales forces. Make an appointment with the sales manager of each to discuss "the task of integrating a new sales person into the company family." Evaluate your findings. Based on your two findings, what conclusions can be made? Write your instructor a memo on your findings and conclusions.

5. Explain why a sales person, when compensated under the straight salary method, can consider the best interests of the customer.

6. Under the straight commission plan, why is there always a danger that the sales person will oversell a customer, high-pressure him, or otherwise incur his ill will?

7. Why do a substantial number of companies let their sales people pay all their own expenses from their own salaries or commissions?

294

8.	Explain why a high closing average (orders divided by calls) may be camouflaging a low average-order size or a high sales volume on low-profit items.

9.	Explain how the "trial close" gives the sales person an indication of how near the prospect is to a decision.

10.	Do you agree that a successful traveling sales person would do as well selling strictly over the telephone? What personality factors do you think a successful telemarketer should have?

11.	Talk to sales managers of three companies that sell their products over the telephone. What do they look for when hiring a person for telephone sales? Write a one- or two-page summary of your findings for your instructor.

12.	Spend a day with a sales person, preferably one who calls on accounts in your area. Write a summary of his or her activities.

13.	Can a sales person lose a sale by talking too much? Why?

14.	Talk to a sales person who sells products to retail stores. Besides writing orders for his product, does he have any other duties expected of him? Discuss this with your classmates.

PART 17I: Exercise

Listed below are six sales positions and three types of compensation plans. The eight companies described are seeking sales people. First identify the type of sales position they require and then the most appropriate compensation plan. Justify your selection.

Sales Position

a. Driver-sales person
b. Inside order-taker
c. Outside order-taker
d. Missionary sales person
e. Sales engineer
f. Creative seller

Compensation Plan

a. Straight salary
b. Straight commission
c. Combination

1.	Insurance company concentrating on selling insurance to doctors serving their internships.

Type _____ Compensation _____

Justification: _____

_____

2.   Bottle manufacturer specializing in designing custom wine bottles for large wineries.

   Type _____ Compensation _____

   Justification: _____

   _____

3.   Hosiery manufacturer that wholesales its products in supermarkets using its own fleet of trucks.

   Type _____ Compensation _____

   Justification: _____

   _____

4.   Snack food concessionaire at a football stadium.

   Type _____ Compensation _____

   Justification: _____

   _____

5.   Drug wholesaler dispensing free samples and product information to doctors.

   Type _____ Compensation _____

   Justification: _____

   _____

6.   Water-filter manufacturer desiring to assist dealers in setting up point-of-purchase displays.

   Type _____ Compensation _____

   Justification: _____

   _____

7.   Department store popcorn and candy counter.

   Type _____ Compensation _____

   Justification: _____

   _____

8.   A water-heater manufacturer's newly developed solar system for heating water desiring to have it specified in architects' and mechanical engineers' plans.

Type _____ Compensation _____
Justification: _____
_____

PART 17J: Real World Case: Selling Shenanigans

Faster repairs. Spiffy showrooms. "Loaner cars" when vehicles are in the shop. Caring salespeople. Birthday cards. Friendly receptionists.

These, some car dealers believe, are the ways to satisfy their customers. They might as well be polishing the hubcaps on a jalopy. For all their efforts to make customers happy, neither dealers nor auto makers are willing to address the core of car buyers' dissatisfaction: the suspicion that they're being ripped off. Car shoppers know that anywhere they go, list prices are going to be as padded as a weightlifter on steroids, and they'll have to haggle. "We've got a legalized con game out there, in some ways," says Richard D. Recchia, executive vice-president at Mitsubishi Motors Corp.

Other auto makers share Recchia's irritation. Despite their sophisticated new marketing approaches, carmakers have little control over the buyer's experience at the point of sale. On the surface, that's not much different from the challenge facing marketers of toothpaste or televisions. But where a toothpaste or TV buyer might shrug off overpaying by 4 cents or $40, a car buyer is less sanguine about being taken to the tune of $400. And shoppers who feel comfortable in a supermarket enter a car showroom as if they were stepping into a war zone where they'll have to do battle.

Some shoppers enter the fray armed with invoice printouts from Consumer Reports or with advice from an array of manuals on negotiating car prices. Others hire mercenaries--car brokers, who promise to use their skills to get a better price than a mere amateur could. Such stratagems are popular because, after all, Americans don't want to haggle, right?

BAZAAR WORLD. Except when they want to. Americans shopping for electronic goods or major appliances can go to Glitzy's Department Store and pay the price on the tag, or to Wacky Wally's Warehouse and try to talk it down. And many car shoppers want to horse-trade before they have picked out their new car. The buyer has this trade-in, see, which clearly is worth more than the dealer is offering--just get a load of that baby's interior ...

So for all that Americans claim to hate haggling, they're partly responsible for the souklike atmosphere at dealerships. Carmakers have tried simply offering lower prices. When General Motors Corp. introduced its GM10 coupes last year, it offered a low sticker on the Buick Regal and a higher price, but with rebates almost immediately, on the Oldsmobile Cutlass Supreme. The Regals languished on the lots, while the Oldsmobiles--similar cars at comparable prices--sold at a steady clip.

297

Still, the car bazaar is largely the creation of Detroit and its dealers. Just like department stores, Detroit has taught drivers to expect a sale. Chrysler Vice-Chairman Gerald Greenwald admits that carmakers pad their price tags to limit the margin damage they'll suffer later, when they offer rebates.

Carmakers complain that dealers are sullying the industry's reputation, but manufacturers do their part to flummox the customer, too. American Honda Motor Co. refused to let its Acura dealers set up showrooms next door to a Honda shop. That was partly to help build a distinct brand image for Acura. But it also kept Honda shoppers from easily learning that they could get the supposedly more prestigious Acura Integra for less money than some Honda Preludes.

SOMETHING EXTRA. The marketplace should offer a choice to those consumers who don't want to play the industry's various shell games. Some car buyers wouldn't mind paying the tagged price, or maybe even more, if they felt that they were getting something extra in the deal. That might be superior service, with a promise of a free loaner vehicle if their car needs repairs, or even being treated with respect in the showroom. Instead, they have almost no choice: all dealers claim to compete on price. And they don't even do that well, given the typical car buyer's suspicion that the dealer is trying to take them for more than one kind of ride.

The system needs to change. But over the years, states passed laws to protect dealers from carmakers, and those laws now defend the status quo against retailing innovation. Manufacturers, preferring the loyalty of small dealers, have resisted the rise of superdealers who are big enough to carve out brand images for themselves. But keeping dealers weak is silly. "Bloomingdale's can be famous, and it doesn't harm the dressmaker who sells dresses there," notes Sidney J. Levy, chairman of the marketing department at Northwestern's Kellogg School.

It won't be easy for dealers--or anyone else--to unlearn the ways cars have been sold for more than 40 years. Dealers will have to stop their constant hawking of supposedly low prices and develop new retailing strategies that respect the buyers' intelligence. Manufacturers will have to relinquish some of their power over dealers. And buyers will have to stop demanding big bucks on their trade-ins if they want dealers to stop inflating the price of the car on the lot. But those who are willing to change will ultimately win the customer-satisfaction sweepstakes. Only then will buying a car be as pleasurable as driving off in one.

Source: James B. Treece, "Dealing with a Car Dealer Shouldn't Be So Demeaning," *Business Week*, June 12, 1989, p. 83. Reprinted from June 12, 1989, issue of *Business Week* by special permission, copyright © 1989 by McGraw-Hill, Inc.

___1. Which of the following personal selling tasks was specifically mentioned in the article as being objectionable to consumers?
A. Explaining product benefits.
B. Arranging the terms of the sale.
C. Responding to objections.
D. Demonstrating the proper operation of the product.
E. Answering questions about the product.

___2. The jobs of car dealers' sales people include all the following features EXCEPT:
A. They represent their organizations to the outside world.
B. They usually have profit responsibility.
C. They operate with little direct supervision.
D. They must travel a considerable amount.
E. They have direct sales responsibility.

PART 17K: Answers to Questions

PART 17D: Completion
1. Personal selling/somebody/something
2. human interaction
3. profitable sales/want-satisfaction/long run
4. concentrated/high/technical/individual customer's/trade-in/introductory/advertise
5. high cost/quality of people
6. customers/sales people/across-the-counter/ sales people/customers/outside
7. telemarketing
8. professional/servicing/goodwill/products/ training
9. ambiguity/conflict
10. customers/short-run/sales person/company
11. driver-sales person/inside/outside/ missionary/sales engineers/creative selling
12. marketing strategy/company/supervision/ traveling/home
13. centers/systems/relationship/telemarketing
14. sales/finance/production/research and development
15. total package
16. mutually beneficial/customers
17. trust-builders/candor/dependably/ competence/consumer oriented/likability
18. prefer/efficiency
19. prospecting/qualifying/preapproach/sales/ postsale
20. willingness/power/authority
21. AIDA
22. buy
23. cognitive dissonance
24. sales goals/activities/forecasting/budgets/ territories/quotas
25. sales manager
26. Staffing
27. job description/applicants/best qualified
28. assimilate
29. goals of the program/training/content of the program/When and where/instructional methods
30. financial/nonfinancial
31. direct/indirect
32. salary/commission/combination
33. straight-salary/straight-commission
34. quantitative/qualitative
35. input/efforts/output/results
36. sales volume/quota/territorial potential/ gross margin/orders/closing/accounts
37. calls/direct/nonselling
38. products/time/customer/personal/ personality/attitude

PART 17E: True-False Questions
1. F 2. T 3. T 4. T 5. F 6. T
7. F 8. F 9. F 10. F 11. F 12. T
13. F 14. T 15. F

PART 17F: Multiple Choice Questions
1. B 2. D 3. B 4. E 5. B 6. E
7. E 8. D 9. A 10. E 11. B 12. E
13. B 14. D 15. E

PART 17G: Matching Questions
a. 7 b. 4 c. 10 d. 8 e. 14 f. 1
g. 2 h. 13

CHAPTER 18

ADVERTISING, SALES PROMOTION, AND PUBLIC RELATIONS

PART 18A: Chapter Goals

After studying this chapter, you should be able to explain:

- The nature of advertising, what it means to the individual firm, and its importance in our economy
- Characteristics of the major types of advertising
- How advertising campaigns are developed and advertising media are selected
- What sales promotion is and how to manage it
- The role of public relations and publicity in the promotional mix

PART 18B: Key Terms and Concepts

1. Advertising [502]

2. Consumer advertising [504]

3. Business-to-business advertising [504]

4. Product advertising [504]

5. Institutional advertising [504]

6. Direct-action advertising [504]

7. Indirect-action advertising [505]

8. Primary-demand advertising [505]

9. Selective-demand advertising [505]

10. Pioneering advertising [505]

11. Demand-sustaining advertising [505]

12. Differential advantage [505]

13. Comparative advertising [505]

14. Advertising campaign [506]

15. Cooperative advertising [507]

16. Vertical cooperative advertising [507]

17. Advertising allowance [507]

18. Horizontal cooperative advertising [508]

19. Attention [508]

20. Influence [508]

21. Appeal [509]

22. Execution [509]

23. Advertising media [509]

24. Cost per thousand (CPM) [511]

25. Direct tests [516]

26. Indirect tests [516]

27. Advertising recall [516]

28. Pretests [517]

29. Advertising agency [518]

30. Sales promotion [519]

31. Trade promotion [519]

32. Consumer promotion [519]

33. Public relations [513]

34. Publicity [524]

PART 18C: Summary

Advertising consists of all activities involved in presenting to an audience a nonpersonal, sponsored-identified message regarding a product or organization [502]. This message is called an advertisement; it is disseminated through one or more media and is paid for by an identified sponsor [503]. The types of advertisements may be focused on consumers or businesses, may be called product and institutional advertising, and may call for direct or indirect action. Other useful classifications include primary and selective demand, pioneering, public service, comparative, and cooperative advertising [504-506].

Fundamentally, the only purpose of advertising is to sell something--a good, service, person, or place. The development of the advertising campaign requires defining objectives, establishing a budget, creating a message, selecting media, and evaluating the advertising message. The initial planning involves setting the specific goal, selecting a central theme, and determining the total promotional appropriation [506-517]. Media selection involves an analysis of specific media circulation data, message requirements, costs of the various media, characteristics of each of the media, and time and location of the buying decision. It may also require evaluation of the cooperative programs and promotional aids offered by the media.

The effectiveness of advertising is difficult to measure. Each of the various measurement devices has enjoyed some degree of success. In general, however, there is still a long way to go before really effective evaluation tools and techniques are developed for advertising [515-516].

A firm can use an advertising agency, have its own advertising department, or use a combination of both [517]. In the final analysis, the "organizational setup" will depend on costs, qualified personnel, and functions performed by the advertising activities.

Sales promotion, the third major promotional tool, and the one which is used to coordinate and supplement the advertising and personal selling programs, has increased in importance over the years [519]. Sales promotion should receive the same importance that a firm gives to its advertising and personal selling efforts. Objectives must be established with their appropriate strategies. A separate budget must be set up. After selecting the appropriate promotional tool, the strategic plan is implemented. Finally, the entire effort should be evaluated [522-523].

The final promotional methods discussed were publicity and public relations. Publicity is any promotional communication regarding an organization and/or its products where the message is not paid for by the firms benefiting from it [524]. Publicity is part of public relations [524]. Typically these two promotional activities are handled in a department separate from the marketing department in a firm. Nonetheless, all the management care that goes into advertising and personal selling should also be applied to a publicity campaign [525].

PART 18D: Completion

1. Advertising consists of all _____ involved in presenting to an audience a(n) _____ sponsor-identified _____ about a(n) _____ or _____.

2. The importance of advertising in the U.S. economy is reflected in that, in 1991, total advertising expenditures were over _____, more than _____ the amount spent in 1981.

3. The three top media in 1991 (in order of dollar volume) were: _____, _____, and _____.

4. Expenditures for personal selling far _____ those for advertising.

5. Advertising can be classified according to: (1) the _____ (consumers or businesses), (2) _____ is being advertised (product or institution), and (3) the _____ (primary or selective demand).

6. Ads are directed at either _____ or _____.

7. Two additional bases for classifying types of advertising are: _____ and _____.

8. Product advertising focuses on a specific _____ or _____.

9. Institutional advertising is designed either to present information about the _____ or to build _____.

10. Institutional advertising may be subdivided into the following two categories: _____ advertising and _____ advertising.

11. _____ advertising is that type which is designed to stimulate demand for a(n) _____ of a product.

12. _____ advertising is used when the product is in the _____ phase of its life cycle.

13. This is called _____ advertising.

14. It is also used by _____ to stimulate the demand for their _____ product.

15. This is called _____ advertising.

16. _____ advertising essentially pits one brand against another.

17. The objective of selective demand advertising is to increase the demand for a brand by emphasizing its special _____ and _____.

18. _____ advertising, a type of _____ advertising, either _____ (naming a rival brand), or _____ points out differences between the brands.

19. A(n) _____ campaign consists of all tasks involved in transforming a(n) _____ into a planned coordinated advertising program to reach a specific _____ for a product or brand.

20. Before designing the campaign, management must: (1) know who the _____ is, (2) establish the overall promotional _____, (3) set the promotional _____, and (4) determine the overall promotional _____.

21. The real goal of advertising is to _____--a good, service, person, or place.

22. Advertising is seldom used alone but is part of an overall strategy that may include _____, _____, and other _____.

23. Once the promotional budget is established, it must be _____ among the various _____ composing the overall promotional program.

24. _____ promotes products of two or more firms that share the cost of the advertising.

25. _____ advertising involves firms on _____ levels of distribution.

26. Another type of vertical cooperative advertising uses a promotional allowance called a(n) _____.

27. _____ advertising involves a group of firms on the same level of distribution.

28. An ad must, first, attract and hold the _____ of the intended audience, and second, _____ that audience in the desired way.

29. Messages have two components: the _____ and the _____.

30. The ad's _____ is the benefit that the individual will receive as a result of accepting the message.

31. _____ is combining in a convincing way the feature or device that gets attention with the appeal.

32. The three levels of decision that must be examined in the selection of advertising media are: (1) _____ of medium that may be used, (2) the specific _____ within each type, and (3) which specific _____ will be used.

33. General factors influencing media choice include: (1) _____ of the ad, (2) audience _____, (3) requirements of the _____, (4) _____ and _____ of the buying decision, and (5) media _____.

34. Media choices are influenced both by the _____ of the specific advertisement and by the _____ of the entire program.

35. Media circulation must fit the _____ distribution patterns of the product.

36. The advertiser should select the medium which will reach the prospective customer near the _____ and _____ where the buying decision will be made.

37. The cost of the media to be used should be considered in relation to the amount of _____ available and the _____ of the media.

38. The characteristics of the six major types of media--_____, _____, _____, _____, _____, and _____ advertising--must be weighed against product attributes before a specific medium is selected.

39. An item of merchandise implanted with the advertiser's name, message, or logo and given free is _____ advertising.

40. Emerging media include: (1) _____, (2) _____, (3) product _____, and (4) _____ media.

41. It is difficult to evaluate the effectiveness of advertising because: (1) ads have different _____ , (2) ads can have an effect over _____ , and (3) _____ problems exist.

42. _____ and _____ tests can be used to measure ad effectiveness.

43. Television ads that are tested before they are presented to the general public are called _____.

44. In organizing for advertising, management can: (1) develop a(n) _____ advertising department, (2) use a(n) _____ advertising agency, or (3) use _____.

45. When advertising is a substantial part of the marketing mix, a firm usually has its own
   _____.

46. A(n) _____ is an independent company that provides specialized advertising services and may also offer more general marketing assistance.

47. Many advertising agencies are becoming _____ because they often offer services heretofore performed by other outside _____ or by the _____ themselves.

48. There are several reasons why an advertising department is established when the company uses an advertising agency: (1) the department acts as a(n) _____ between the agency and the firm, (2) the department approves the agency's _____ and _____ and assumes the responsibility for preparing and administering the advertising _____, (3) it coordinates advertising with _____, and (4) the department may handle direct-mail advertisements, dealer displays, and other activities ordinarily not performed by the _____.

49. Sales promotion is defined as demand stimulating devices intended to supplement _____ and to improve _____.

50. The two categories of sales promotion are _____ promotions and _____ promotions.

51. In recent years, sales promotion has been the _____ growing method of promotion.

52. Sales promotion is becoming more popular because of: (1) _____ results, (2) _____ pressure, (3) state of buyers' _____ , and (4) low quality of _____ selling.

53. The _____ for sales promotion should be set in the course of determining the appropriation for the _____.

54. In selecting the proper sales promotion tools, the target audience--business _____ or _____, _____, or the producer's own _____ --must be determined.

55. Sales promotion directed at end-users includes: _____, _____, _____ or _____, _____, _____ and _____, _____ displays, product _____, _____ and _____ , and advertising _____.

56. Public relations is a management _____ designed to favorably influence attitudes toward a(n) _____, its _____, or its _____.

57. Three reasons for public relations being relegated to step-child status in most organizations

are: (1) the _____ does not even handle them, (2) the term is used loosely by both _____ and the _____, and (3) only in recent years have organizations come to realize the _____ of good public relations.

58. Public relations activities typically are designed to build or maintain a favorable _____ for an organization and a favorable _____ with the organization's various "publics."

59. Publicity is either: (1) a(n) _____ appearing in a mass medium, or (2) a(n) _____ that is delivered by a person in a speech or an interview.

60. The benefits of publicity are: (1) it is not "_____ " on an audience, (2) it is lower _____ than advertising or personal selling, (3) it increases _____ , (4) it provides more _____ , and (5) it is more _____.

61. The disadvantages include: (1) loss of _____ over the message, (2) limited _____ , and (3) the _____.

PART 18E: **True-False Questions**

If the statement is true, circle "T"; if false, circle "F."

T F   1. More money is spent in television than in any other major advertising medium.

T F   2. One of the advantages of publicity is that it is free.

T F   3. Outdoor advertising lends itself well to the introduction of new and unique products.

T F   4. A large portion of the total advertising dollar is being spent to measure advertising's effectiveness.

T F   5. Advertising is both a process and a product.

T F   6. In most organizations, publicity and public relations are relegated to step-child status behind personal selling and advertising.

T F   7. An airline advertisement listing the benefits of flying first class is an example of product advertising as opposed to institutional advertising.

T F   8. Demand sustaining advertising is usually done by trade associations such as egg and milk producers.

T F   9. An example of horizontal cooperative advertising is a group of shop-owners at a

308

ski resort running a joint monthly ad in a ski magazine.

T F 10. The sponsor is openly identified in advertising.

T F 11. In terms of annual dollar expenditures for advertising, newspapers are the most important class of media in the United States.

T F 12. Probably the most difficult type of advertising to evaluate is that intended to build goodwill, create a favorable company image, or influence attitudes.

T F 13. The Federal Trade Commission has determined that comparative ads are illegal.

T F 14. Sales promotion campaigns are used to stimulate responses in ultimate consumers but not in middlemen.

T F 15. Evaluating advertising is simple--if the ad budget doubles and sales double, one can conclude that the advertising caused the sales gain.

PART 18F: Multiple Choice Questions

In the space provided write the letter of the answer that best fits the statement.

_____1. When the Beef Industry Council advertises, "Beef--it's what's for dinner," they are creating _____ advertising.
A. Primary demand   C. Pioneering   E. Comparative
B. Selective demand   D. Demand sustaining

_____2. Based on annual expenditures by all advertisers, the second most important advertising medium in the United States is:
A. Television. B. Radio. C. Magazines. D. Newspapers. E. Direct mail.

_____3. The marketing saying "it's the final three feet that counts" emphasizes the importance of:
A. Advertising.   C. Market segmentation.   E. Branding.
B. Sales promotion.   D. Public relations.

_____4. Which of the following advertising slogans appeals most to rational buying motives?
A. "When you care enough to send the very best."   D. "Just do it."
B. "Catch the wave."   E. "More shaves per blade."
C. "Oh, what a feeling!"

_____5. The most personal and selective of the advertising media is:
A. Newspapers. B. Direct mail. C. Outdoor. D. Magazines. E. Television.

_____6. All of the following are considered within the scope of sales promotion EXCEPT:
  A. A window display in a department store.
  B. The distribution of product samples by mail.
  C. A product exhibition at an industrial trade show.
  D. An offer of merchandise premiums with purchase of other products.
  E. A training program for retail sales people.

_____7. When the Lincoln Division of Ford advertises that its cars cannot possibly be confused the way Oldsmobile, Buick, and Chevrolet are, it is using _____ advertising.
  A. Primary demand   C. Comparative   E. Selective demand
  B. Public service   D. Illegal

_____8. Based upon the total volume of advertising expenditures, the most important medium is:
  A. Newspapers. B. Direct mail. C. Outdoor. D. Magazines. E. Television.

_____9. Advertising that takes place during the introductory stage of a product's life cycle is called:
  A. Primary demand.   C. Pioneering.   E. Comparative.
  B. Selective demand.   D. Demand sustaining.

_____10. The distribution of a new product sample to consumers door-to-door is an example of:
  A. Marketing research.   C. Sales promotion.   E. Personal selling.
  B. Publicity.   D. Advertising.

_____11. All of the following are benefits of publicity EXCEPT:
  A. Higher cost than advertising or personal selling.   D. More information.
  B. Greater credibility than advertising.   E. Timeliness.
  C. Increased readership.

_____12. All of the following are limitations of publicity EXCEPT:
  A. Loss of control over the message.   D. Publicity is free.
  B. Limited exposure.   E. None of the above.
  C. No guarantee the publicity will ever be used.

_____13. Public relations and publicity have been relegated to step-child status behind personal selling, advertising, and sales promotion because of management's lack of attention to:
  A. Organizational structure. C. Adverse publicity.   E. Any of the above.
  B. Inadequate definitions.   D. Unrecognized benefits.

_____14. Budweiser's "friends know when to say when" campaign against drunk driving is an example of _____ advertising.
  A. Product   C. Customer-service   E. Primary demand
  B. Direct-action   D. Public service

___15. Quicker, more measurable sales results are produced by:
   A. Public relations.   D. Sales promotion.
   B. Publicity.   E. Advertising.
   C. Personal selling.

PART 18G: Matching Questions

In the space provided write the number of the word or expression from column 1 that best fits the description in column 2.

1	2
1. Advertising	___ a. All activities involved in presenting to a group a non-personal sponsor-identified message regarding a product or organization.
2. Advertising agency	
3. Advertising allowance	___ b. An example is the Starch Readership Test.
4. Advertising campaign	
5. Advertising media	___ c. Advertising designed to stimulate demand over a long period of time.
6. Business-to-business advertising	
7. Comparative advertising	___ d. Advertising designed to create a proper attitude toward a seller and to build goodwill.
8. Consumer advertising	
9. Cooperative advertising	___ e. The means by which advertising messages reach consumers.
10. Customer service advertising	___ f. When an advertiser mentions rival brands by name in his ad.
11. Demand sustaining advertising	
12. Direct-action advertising	___ g. An attempt to stimulate generic demand for a product.
13. Direct tests	___ h. A firm's broad communications effort intended to influence various groups' attitudes toward the firm.
14. Indirect-action advertising	
15. Indirect tests	___ i. Advertising sponsored by trade groups.
16. Institutional advertising	___ j. Advertising designed to improve the quality of life.

311

17. Pioneering advertising

18. Primary demand advertising

19. Product advertising

20. Public relations

21. Public service advertising

22. Publicity

23. Sales promotion

24. Selective demand advertising

____ k. Advertising used in the introductory stage of a product's life cycle.

____ l. An independent firm established to render specialized services in advertising.

PART 18H: Problems and Applications

1.   Should television advertising shown during children's programming on Saturday mornings be curtailed? If so, in what way? Write a memo to your instructor stating the pros and/or cons of your point of view.

2.   Should the Federal Trade Commission prohibit the use of TV program ratings? Discuss.

3.   Advertising expenditures have been reported by eight media: direct mail, radio, yellow pages, magazines, television, newspapers, outdoor advertising, and the business press. Go to the latest *Statistical Abstract of the United States* and find the indices of national advertising expenditures by media. What can you conclude about trends of national advertising expenditures by media between 1970 and the present? Write a memo to your instructor reporting your findings.

4.   Find out what amount of revenue magazines have received by type of product between 1970 and the present. Do this for automotive products, including accessories, equipment, and consumer services. What factors have accounted for this change?
      Note: You will find magazine advertising revenue reported by type of product in the *Statistical Abstract*.

5.   Find an example of each of the following types of advertising:
      A. Institutional (retail or manufacturer).
      B. Direct- and indirect-action product.
      C. Customer service advertising.
      D. Primary and selective demand product.

E. Comparative.

F. Vertical and horizontal cooperative advertising.

6.   Talk to the advertising manager of a television station. What restrictions does he or she place on advertising that will be accepted? Do they look for deceptive advertising? Prepare a summary of your findings for your instructor.

7.   What are the advantages and disadvantages of each of the following advertising media?

A. Newspapers

B. Television

C. Direct mail

D. Magazines

E. Radio

F. Business papers

G. Outdoor advertising

H. Yellow pages

8.   Do you think advertising is really an institution of abundance? Take a position. Write a one-page memorandum stating your position.

9.   Select two radio stations in your community, a large one and a small one. Evaluate their programming statements as reported in the latest edition of Standard Rate & Data Service, *Spot Radio Rates and Data*, and Standard Rate & Data Service, *Spot Radio Small Markets Edition*. Do you agree with what they report as their target audience? Make a comparison of the two stations' target audiences. What conclusion can be drawn from your comparison?

10.   Get a copy of a local "throw-away" newspaper and try to find examples of sales promotion. Make a report for your instructor.

11.   What effect do you think the Tylenol and Excedrin scares have had on the public relations efforts of Johnson & Johnson and Bristol-Myers, the manufacturers?

PART 18I (a): Exercise

DeBeers tells us that "a diamond is forever," General Electric "brings good things to life," and Diet Pepsi grunts "Uh huh!" Copywriters wrack their brains in an attempt to develop corporate slogans for "image" advertising purposes. How successful are they? Probably not too successful, as your performance on this little quiz will attest. In fact, there are some advertising specialists who claim that these slogans are so much wasted space and that they even distract from the main message of an ad. See: "Better Understanding Through Quizzes," *Wall Street Journal*, December 9, 1982, p. 33. For a more complete listing, see: Laurence Urdang and Ceila Dame Robbins (eds.), *Slogans, First Edition* (Detroit, MI: Gale Research Co., 1984).

Directions: Beside each slogan, write the number of the advertiser of that slogan.

	Advertiser		Slogan
1.	American Express	____ A.	Because so much is riding on your tires..
2.	Apple Computer	____ B.	A different kind of company. A different kind of car.
3.	AT&T	____ C.	Don't leave home without it.
4.	BMW	____ D.	Get _____. It pays.
5.	Chevrolet	____ E.	The heartbeat of America.
6.	Digital Equipment	____ F.	I love what you do for me.
7.	General Electric	____ G.	Innovation working for you.
8.	Hewlett-Packard	____ H.	It just feels right.
9.	Lexus	____ I.	The open advantage.
10.	Mazda	____ J.	The power of the pyramid is working for you.
11.	Merrill Lynch	____ K.	The power to be your best.
12.	Metropolitan Life	____ L.	The quality goes in before the name goes on.
13.	Michelin	____ M.	Quality means the world to us.
14.	Motorola	____ N.	The relentless pursuit of perfection.
15.	Saturn	____ O.	The right choice.
16.	3M	____ P.	There is a better way.
17.	Toyota	____ Q.	A tradition of trust.
18.	Transamerica	____ R.	The ultimate driving machine
19.	Xerox	____ S.	We bring good things to life.
20.	Zenith	____ T.	We document the world.

PART 18I (b): Exercise

Celebrities are often used to sell products. See if you can match the celebrities with the products or sponsors they are associated with.

	Celebrity		Product or Sponsor
1.	Larry Bird	a. ___	Ace Hardware
2.	Christie Brinkley	b. ___	American Express
3.	Ray Charles	c. ___	Beef Industry Council
4.	Jimmy Conners	d. ___	Chrysler
5.	Bill Cosby	e. ___	Cover Girl
6.	Lee Iacocca	f. ___	Diet Coke
7.	Elton John	g. ___	Diet Pepsi
8.	Michael Jordan	h. ___	Dorito Tortilla Chips
9.	Jay Leno	i. ___	Isotoner Gloves

10. John Madden   j. ___ Jell-O
11. Karl Malden   k. ___ Kmart
12. Dan Marino   l. ___ La Victoria
13. Robert Mitchum   m. ___ Nike
14. Arnold Palmer   n. ___ Nuprin
15. Jacqueline Smith   o. ___ Pennzoil Motor Oil
16. Lee Trevino   p. ___ Wheaties

PART 18I (c): Exercise

Evaluate an advertisement you have clipped from a newspaper or magazine by answering the following questions. Bring the ad to class with you.

1. Type of advertisement--product or institutional.

_____

2. Objectives of the advertisement.

_____
_____
_____

3. What physical and psychological appeals are being made?

_____
_____
_____

4. List all the media in which you have seen this ad appear.

_____

5. Evaluate the elements making up the ad--the copy, illustrations, and layout.

_____
_____
_____
_____

6. Based on the ad, would you buy or not buy this product? In case of an institutional ad, has your opinion of the firm changed as a result of this ad?

_____
_____
_____

315

PART 18J: A Real World Case: Advertising and Zen

Man, woman. Birth, death. Infinity." Dr. Zorba

An intriguing exercise, this juxtaposition of opposing forces in the universe. TV watchers were enthralled by it in 1960, and they still are 30 years later.

Water, rocks. Cars, no cars. Genius, buffoonery. Infiniti.

The contemporary transcendental contradiction comescourtesy of those marketing Zenmasters at Hill, Holliday, Conners, Cosmopulos, Marina del Rey, whose work for the Infiniti line of luxury cars has paradox coming out the yin and yang.   Having introduced the concept of carless car advertising, having used raw nature as a backdrop to discuss technological refinement, having become the objects of national ridicule and gloried in it, now they have achieved the ultimate: Brilliant advertising that is terrible. Stupid advertising that is ingenious. Perfect advertising, mired in flaws.

"We look at it and do not see it." Lao Tzu

The introductory campaign mesmerized and infuriated viewers, generating unprecedented new-product awareness, but also resentment and scorn--all because there was no picture of the car. Now, finally, we see the car. Sixty- and 30-second versions of two spots--one called "Power" and one called "Exterior styling"--end of the mystery at last. Sort of. In the 60-second "Power," the car is on camera for 36.3 seconds, in full view for 1 second.

"It is the vague and elusive. Meet it and you will not see its head. Follow it and you will not see its back." Lao Tzu

The first shot uses the wavy camera effect, so you can't quite register the whole profile. Another shot is a driver's-eye view, revealing only 25 percent of the steering wheel and half the dash. The third shot depicts the car sloshing through what appears to be surf--none too powerfully, by the way.

"And the gilded car of the day, His glowing axle doth allay/In the steep Atlantic stream." John Milton

A $40,000 gilded car, looking for all the world like a $19,000 Thunderbird, as writer/narrator Bill Heater intones: "It was the goal of Infiniti to design a luxury car with superior power and performance, a luxury sedan that doesn't compromise performance for comfort, or a luxury feel for raw power." Superimposed on the screen, meanwhile, are Infiniti's power specifications--278 horsepower, 32 valves, and so forth.

"Fine words and an insinuating appearance are seldom associated with true virtue." Confucius

316

I am prepared to stuff 278 horses and 32 valves down Heater's throat, if that's what it takes to rid the world of his ostentatiously understated voice-over delivery. His laid-back shtick is more annoying than Madge the manicurist in high shrill. But wait, we're soon back to nature: a lightning flash on the dusky horizon. Thus are the conventional aspects of the advertising married to the harmonious universe imagery of the introductory campaign. Yin and yang merge to a glorious whole.

"To see a world in a grain of sand/And a heaven in a wild flower,/Hold infinity in the palm of your hand/And eternity in an hour." William Blake

The key word would be eternity, which is how long this commercial makes 60 seconds seem. These natural and technical components may mesh in terms of man's communion with the universe, but in terms of coherent advertising, the effect is disjointed in the extreme. All of which is to say: This is horrible advertising, embarrassing selfparody, irritating beyond description. And it is also captivating nearly beyond compare, so bracing is this work that its screaming flaws are muted. Excessive or no, style and technique and the cultivation of the unexpected amount to powerful advertising.

"The first time I saw (the Infiniti ads), I thought, 'That's a nice-looking car. It looks a lot like rocks and trees.'" Stan Freberg

How much advertising, after all, immediately permeates the public psyche? You can't be a national punch line unless you are in the nation's thoughts. Inscrutability captured the public's imagination during Infiniti's introduction. Style and iconoclasm, however forced, will take over from here. As Confucius said: "The people may be made to follow a path of action, but they may not be made to understand it."

RATING * * *   The rating system uses four stars to represent excellent, three for notable, two for mediocre and one for pathetic.

_____

Source: Bob Garfield, "Infiniti: A Contradiction in Advertising," *Sacramento Bee*, February 19, 1990, p. D5. Reprinted by permission of Crain Communications.

_____

____1. The Infiniti ad campaign used _____ advertising.
    A. Primary demand   D. Comparative
    B. Selective demand   E. Public service
    C. Illegal

____2. The Infiniti ad campaign is an example of _____ advertising.
    A. Direct-action   D. Product
    B. Comparative   E. Institutional
    C. Cooperative

PART 18K: Answers to Questions

PART 18D: Completion

1. activities/nonpersonal/paid-for message/ product/organization
2. $126 billion/twice
3. newspapers/television/direct mail
4. exceed
5. target audience/what/object sought
6. consumers/businesses
7. product/institutional
8. product/brand
9. advertiser's business/goodwill
10. customer service/public service
11. Primary demand/generic category
12. Primary demand/introductory
13. pioneering
14. trade associations/industry's
15. demand sustaining
16. Selective demand
17. features/benefits
18. Comparative/selective demand/directly/ indirectly
19. advertising/theme/goal
20. target audience/goals/budget/theme
21. sell something
22. personal sellling/sales promotion/ tools
23. allocated/activities
24. Cooperative advertising
25. Vertical cooperative/different
26. advertising allowance
27. Horizontal cooperative/same
28. attention/influence
29. appeal/execution
30. appeal
31. Execution
32. type/category/media vehicles
33. objectives/coverage/message/time/location/ cost
34. purpose/goals
35. geographic
36. time/place
37. funds/circulation
38. newspapers/television/direct mail/radio/ magazines/outdoor
39. specialty
40. yellow pages/informercials/placement/ place-based
41. objectives/time/measurement
42. Direct/indirect
43. pretests
44. internal/outside/both
45. advertising department
46. advertising agency
47. integrated agencies/specialists/advertisers
48. liaison/plans/advertisements/budget/ personal selling/agency
49. advertising/personal selling
50. trade/consumer
51. fastest
52. short-run/competitive/expectations/retail
53. budget/total promotional mix
54. users/households/middlemen/sales force
55. coupons/cash rebates/premiums/gifts/free samples/contests/sweepstakes/point-of- purchase/demonstrations/trade shows/ exhibitions/specialities
56. tool/organization/products/policies
57. marketing department/business/public/value
58. image/relationship
59. news story/endorsement
60. forced/cost/readership/information/ timely
61. control/exposure/expense

PART 18E: True-False Questions
1. F 2. T 3. F 4. F 5. T 6. T
7. T 8. T 9. T 10. T 11. T 12. T
13. F 14. F 15. F

PART 18F: Multiple Choice Questions
1. D 2. A 3. B 4. E 5. B 6. E
7. C 8. E 9. C 10. D 11. A 12. D
13. E 14. D 15. D

PART 18G: Matching Questions
a. 1 b. 15 c. 14 d. 16 e. 5 f. 7 g. 18
h. 20 i. 11 j. 21 k. 17 l. 2

318

PART SEVEN

MARKETING IN SPECIAL FIELDS

```
┌─────────────────────────────┐
│                             │
│                             │
└─────────────────────────────┘
```

CHAPTER 19

**SERVICES MARKETING
BY FOR-PROFIT AND
NONPROFIT
ORGANIZATIONS**

PART 19A: Chapter Goals

After studying this chapter, you should be able to explain:

- What services are and are not
- The importance of services in our economy
- The characteristics of services, and the marketing implications in these characteristics
- The attitudes of service organizations--for-profit and nonprofit--toward marketing
- The concept of donor markets and client markets in nonprofit organizations
- Planning a market mix for services marketing
- The future of services marketing

PART 19B: Key Terms and Concepts

1. Services [537]

2. Classification of services [537]

3. Types of nonprofit organizations [537]

4. Services characteristics

    a. Intangibility [539]

    b. Inseparability [540]

    c. Heterogeneity [540]

    d. Perishability [540]

    e. Fluctuating demand [540]

5. Donor (contributor) market [543]

6. Client (recipient) markets [543]

7. Market segmentation in services marketing [544]

8. Product planning for services [545]

9. Branding of services [547]

10. Service quality [547]

11. Pricing structure for services [548]

12. Distribution system for services [550]

13. Promotion of services [551]

14. Service encounter [552]

PART 19C: Summary

In a broad sense, there is no difference between the marketing of goods and the marketing of services. In actual practice, however, there are significant differences. It is hard to ignore the service areas of the economy since about half of what we spend goes for services. In addition, about 90 percent of the new jobs created in the past twenty years were in the service fields. Not only are services of considerable importance in today's economy, the prospects are that they will continue to grow relative to the goods sector of the economy [536].

Although a definition of services was provided early in the chapter, there is little agreement as to the definition or the scope of the service field [536]. The distinctive characteristics of services are intangibility, inseparability from the seller, heterogeneity, perishability, and a widely fluctuating demand [539-541]. These features have several implications for marketers.

The growth in services has not been matched by a growing acceptance of the marketing concept on the part of service managers. Service organizations have been slow to adapt and change relative to consumer wants and needs [541].

Most nonprofit organizations must deal with two markets: the donor or contributor market, and clients, the recipients of the organization's money or services. As a result, nonprofit organizations must develop two separate marketing programs, one to attract and retain resources from donors, and the other to serve its clients.

Probably the biggest problem facing service industries in the future is to increase their productivity [555]. Another major problem is how to maintain a high and consistent level of quality [556]. The answers to both these issues for both profit and nonprofit organizations lie in investing in education and training programs for employees, investments in technology, and job restructuring so that each worker can become more efficient by accomplishing more in less time [557].

PART 19D: Completion

1. Cause-related marketing is a strategy whereby a(n) _____ hooks up with a(n) _____.

2. Usually a company implements its cause-related marketing strategy with one of three form of sponsorship: (1) _____, (2) _____ support plus conditional _____, and (3) donations tied to _____.

3. Questions arise as to whether the company's goals should be _____ (sell more products) or _____ (donate to a favorite cause).

4. In order to implement a cause-marketing strategy effectively, management should make it clear from the start that the objective is to make _____ for the company.

5. In the broadest sense, it is probably true that _____ marketing and _____ marketing are the same.

6. In practice, the strategies and tactics used in the marketing of _____ frequently are not appropriate for _____ marketing.

7. The text defines services as _____, _____ activities that are the main object of a transaction designed to provide _____ to customers.

8. The U.S. is moving beyond the industrial economy stage to the point where it is becoming the world's first _____.

9. About ___ percent of the jobs that will be created between 1986 and 2000 will be in service industries.

10. Most of this growth will not be in _____ jobs. In fact, the fastest growing occupational category has been in "_____, _____, and _____."

11. Services also make up _____ of consumer expenditures.

12. Spending for _____ services has increased more rapidly than spending for _____ services.

13. While nonprofit marketing is becoming increasingly important, frequently a large part of the money collected by a nonprofit organization goes to cover _____, rather than to serve the intended markets.

14. When nonprofit organizations fail to do an effective marketing job, there are additional _____ and _____ costs.

15. The general characteristics of services are: _____, _____, _____, _____ and _____.

16. The promotional program must concentrate on the _____ to be derived from the service, rather than the service itself.

17. Four promotional strategies are: _____, _____, _____ _____, and _____.

18. Services often cannot be _____ from the person of the seller. Also, given services are often created, dispensed, and consumed _____.

19. Because of service heterogeneity, the service company has problems of consistency of _____ and _____.

20. Services are _____ and cannot be _____.

21. Executives in service firms have not been _____ oriented.

22. Two reasons for a lack of a marketing orientation are: (1) the sellers think of themselves as _____ or _____, not as _____ of the service; and (2) top managers of service companies have failed to recognize how important _____ is to the _____ of the firm.

23. Most _____ organizations were not at all comfortable with the idea of marketing since they did not understand the concept of a(n) _____ program.

24. Nonprofit organizations have been _____ than profit-seeking organizations in employing modern management techniques.

25. A marketing program is developed in the same way in any organization--goods or services,

324

for-profit or nonprofit: (1) _____ and _____ the target markets, (2) design and implement _____ strategies to reach those markets in order to (3) achieve the organization's _____.

26. Nonprofit organizations must aim at two markets: (1) _____--contributors of money, labor, or materials to the organization, and (2) _____--the recipients of money and services from the organization.

27. Since nonprofit organizations must deal with two markets, they must develop _____ distinct _____.

28. Selecting target markets is _____ whether a firm is marketing a good or a service, is a for-profit organization or a nonprofit one.

29. Marketers of services must make strategic decisions regarding (1) what services they will _____, (2) what _____strategies they will adopt, (3) what _____ (branding and warranty) the services will have, and (4) how they will manage service _____.

30. Many service firms have become successful by recognizing a previously unrecognized or unsatisfied _____.

31. The key to selecting the services to offer is for an organization to decide (1) what "_____" it is in, and (2) what _____ it wants to serve.

32. The assortment of benefits donors can expect include: (1) making donors _____ or relieving their _____feelings, (2) supporting their favorite _____, (3) providing them with a(n) _____, (4) contributing to their _____ in reference groups, and (5) supporting their _____.

33. Service-mix strategies include _____ the service line, _____ the service mix, _____ the service offerings, and managing the _____.

34. In some respects, product planning is easier for _____ than for _____.

35. Services _____ is a problem because maintaining consistency of quality is difficult.

36. The _____ is a key factor in determining a firm's success.

37. Quality is defined by the _____ and not by the _____ of a service.

38. Management must strive to maintain service quality consistently at or above the level of _____.

39. As part of its service quality, a firm should design and operate an on going _____ program.

40. In an effort to improve quality, some service firms have begun a(n) _____ _____(_____) program. For these programs to work, companies must be patient and look for results over the _____.

41. Price determination for _____ is critically important: (1) because they are _____, (2) because they cannot be _____, and (3) because of the fluctuating _____.

42. Pricing in nonprofit organizations is different from pricing in a for-profit firm. In the donor market, nonprofit organizations do not set the price (the _____). It is set by _____.

43. In the client market, some nonprofit organizations face the same _____, and can use the _____, as profit-seeking firms.

44. _____are widely used in marketing services as are _____(flexible) pricing strategies.

45. Many service organizations have abandoned a strategy of avoiding _____ and have begun to move through three identifiable pricing stages: (1) price is barely mentioned in _____, (2) the seller uses a(n) _____ strategy to target a given market at a specific price, and (3) competition occurs as firms stress _____ _____ in their advertising.

46. Designing a distribution system in a nonprofit or for-profit organization involves two jobs: (1) to select the _____, and (2) to provide for the _____ _____ of the product.

47. Channels for most services are _____ and _____ because a service cannot be separated from its _____.

48. The only other frequently used channel includes one _____.

49. A(n) _____ is essential when a service is distributed directly from producer to consumer, especially today since consumers are so convenience oriented.

50. Nonprofit organizations try to provide arrangements in locations to make _____ contributions easy and convenient.

51. _____ is the one part of the marketing mix that services marketers are most familiar with and most adept at.

52. _____ plays a dominant role in the promotional programs of most service firms.

53. A(n) _____ is a customer's interaction with any service employee or with any tangible element such as a service's physical surroundings.

54. Advertising, which has been used in many service fields in years past, is now expanding into _____ firms, including legal, accounting, and medical services.

55. Nonprofit organizations use _____ extensively to reach both their donor and client markets.

56. Other promotional methods include _____ and _____.

57. The service environment is changing, bringing with it a focus on increasing _____ and measuring _____ performance.

58. Probably the greatest problem facing service industries today is _____ and the need to increase _____.

59. Measuring marketing performance in nonprofit organizations is a real _____ _____.

60. It is expected that services will continue to grow for both _____ and _____ services.

61. If nonprofit marketing is to have a future, the people in these organizations must understand what _____ and _____.

PART 19E: True-False Questions

If the statement is true, circle "T"; if false, circle "F."

T F   1. In services marketing, middlemen are never used.

T F   2. The quality of services is defined by the consumer and not by the producer-seller of the service.

T F   3. Quantity discounts are not applicable to the marketing of services.

T F   4. While the concept of product mix may be applied to goods, it cannot be applied to services.

T F 5. Because a tax accountant's service cannot be separated from the tax accountant him- or herself, we label this characteristic "inseparability."

T F 6. Services are highly perishable and cannot be stored.

T F 7. The marketing concept cannot be applied to service marketing.

T F 8. Like the demand for goods, demand for services can be elastic or inelastic.

T F 9. Promotion is the part of the marketing mix nonprofit organizations are most familiar with.

T F 10. While the client of the nonprofit organization often does not pay a monetary fee, he or she often pays a nonmonetary "price."

T F 11. The channels of distribution used in nonprofit marketing ordinarily are quite simple and short.

T F 12. One of the major problems for the nonprofit organization is how to measure its effectiveness.

T F 13. The most frequently used middleman in nonprofit marketing is the full-service wholesaler.

T F 14. Even though nonprofit organizations have two distinct markets, donors and clients, a single marketing program is sufficient.

T F 15. Many nonprofit organizations have elaborate physical distribution systems.

PART 19F: Multiple Choice Questions

In the space provided write the letter of the answer that best fits the statement.

____ 1. The target market for most nonbusiness, nonprofit organizations is:
A. Contributors.   B. Clients.   C. Both A and B.

____ 2. Regarding channels of distribution for services:
A. When a middleman is used, he will most likely be an agent.
B. Middlemen are never used.
C. Merchant wholesalers are used frequently.
D. The inability of some service sellers to use middlemen has no marketing advantage.
E. A seller's location with respect to his market is more important when selling products than when selling services.

328

_____ 3. The explosion in service-related jobs resulted in:
   A. Low-paying jobs.
   B. The elimination of manufacturing jobs.
   C. A great increase in professional, technical, and related jobs.
   D. A smaller share of consumer spending.
   E. Few jobs for business-related services.

_____ 4. A general characteristic of services is:
   A. Intangibility.   D. Heterogeneity.
   B. Inseparability.   E. All of the above.
   C. Fluctuating demand.

_____ 5. The idea that it is impossible for a seller of services to standardize output relates to the following characteristic of services:
   A. Intangibility.   D. Heterogeneity.
   B. Inseparability.   E. Perishability.
   C. Fluctuating demand.

_____ 6. The pricing of services suggests:
   A. A greater need for managerial creativity and skill.
   B. Markets that always exhibit elastic demand.
   C. Markets that always exhibit inelastic demand.
   D. Markets that always exhibit perfect competition.
   E. Markets that always exhibit perfect information.

_____ 7. Almost _____ percent of the new jobs created in the past twenty years have been in supplying services.
   A. 33   B. 50   C. 67   D. 75   E. 90

_____ 8. Distribution for nonprofit organizations involves establishing:
   A. Channels of distribution forward to the client market.
   B. Channels of distribution back to the contributor market.
   C. A physical distribution system to reach both groups.
   D. All of the above.
   E. None of the above.

_____ 9. Nonbusiness organizations have done pioneering work in:
   A. Branding.   D. Product warranty.
   B. Labeling.   E. None of the above.
   C. Market segmentation strategies.

___ 10. The most frequently used middleman in nonprofit, nonbusiness marketing is the:
   A. Agent wholesaler.
   B. Merchant wholesaler.
   C. Drop shipper.
   D. Sales branch.
   E. Truck jobber.

___ 11. In the pricing of services:
   A. Markdowns are frequently used.
   B. Cost-plus pricing is rarely used.
   C. Elasticity of demand should influence the price.
   D. Perfect competition tends to exist in many areas.
   E. Nonprice competition is rarely used.

___ 12. The element of the marketing mix most nonprofit firms are familiar with is:
   A. Branding.
   B. Promotion.
   C. Channels of distribution.
   D. Pricing.
   E. Physical distribution.

___ 13. Although clients do not pay a money price, they often have to pay a price in the form of:
   A. Waiting.   B. Ridicule.   C. Embarrassment.   D. All of the above.

___ 14. The difference between for-profit management and nonprofit management often lies in:
   A. Their implementation of the marketing program.
   B. Their understanding of marketing.
   C. Their attitudes toward marketing.
   D. All of the above.
   E. None of the above.

___ 15. In order to measure the performance of nonprofit organizations to clients, one would measure:
   A. Their market share.
   B. Sales volume.
   C. The contributions they receive.
   D. None of the above.

PART 19G: Matching Questions

In the space provided write the number of the word or expression from column 1 that best fits the description in column 2.

1	2
1. Donor markets	___ a. Those separately identifiable, intangible activities that are the main object of a transaction designed to provide want-satisfaction to customers.
2. Client markets	

330

3. Fluctuating demand

___ b. The service characteristic that points to the idea that services cannot be stored.

4. Heterogeneity

___ c. The service characteristic that points to the impossibility of standardizing output.

5. Inseparability

6. Intangibility

___ d. A customer's interaction with any service employee.

7. Perishability

8. Service encounter

9. Services

PART 19H: Problems and Applications

1. Make a list of services that are created and marketed simultaneously.
   A._____
   B._____
   C._____
   D._____
   E._____
   F._____
   G._____
   H._____

   This assignment will illustrate the inseparability of some services.

2. Talk to someone who manages a service company. What methods does he or she employ to market the service? What are the difficulties in making people aware of the company? Prepare a memo for your instructor.

3. Visit an army, navy, air force, or marine recruiting office. Write a report to your instructor describing their facilities, location, target markets, promotional techniques, and "pricing" used. Are they marketing concept-oriented? Ask if their attitudes have changed since the Middle East crisis.

4. The combination of perishability and fluctuating demand offers product planning, pricing, and promotion challenges to executives in a service company. Present an example of how each of these three marketing-mix variables can be used by executives to creatively meet this challenge.
   A. Product-planning example _____
   B. Pricing example _____
   C. Promotion example _____

5.   List the product mix for a telephone company. Does it have dimensions of both breadth and depth? Write a memo to your instructor on this subject.

6.   Make a list of five industrial marketing service companies. See <u>Fortune</u> or <u>Forbes</u> for lists of the largest retailers, banks, life insurance companies, transportation companies, and other firms selling services. Their annual reports will give you an idea as to their product mix.

	Company	Product Mix
A.	_____	_____
B.	_____	_____
C.	_____	_____
D.	_____	_____
E.	_____	_____

7.   Market demand for services fluctuates considerably by season, day of the week, and hour of the day. Give three examples of each type of fluctuation.

Season	Day of the week	Hour of the day
A. _____	D. _____	G. _____
B. _____	E. _____	H. _____
C. _____	F. _____	I. _____

Can you think of any other types of fluctuation in demand for services?

8.   Your college or university is probably a nonprofit, nonbusiness organization. Is the marketing function centralized or decentralized? To what extent is branding used? How about market segmentation? Is it marketing concept-oriented? Even during registration for classes?

9.   Interview 10 students. Ask them how they feel about the efforts of nonprofit groups toward making them contributors. What medium (direct mail, TV, radio, magazine ad, etc.) would they prefer seeing, hearing, and/or reading? What medium would be most effective?

10.   "Fund raisers for nonprofit organizations require more tact, diplomacy, and social poise than traditional sales people in business." Would you agree with this statement? Why?

11.   Interview the head of your Red Cross office. Do they use local advertising? Is the decision to advertise locally made by higher authority? Do they try to measure their advertising effectiveness? If so, how? Are there any legal restrictions on the ads they run? Write a report to your instructor with your findings.

PART 19I (a): Exercise

The text states that services typically possess distinctive characteristics which "create special marketing challenges and opportunities." The characteristics include intangibility, inseparability, heterogeneity, perishability, and fluctuating demand.

Mason Higgins is an insulation contractor. He blows insulation material into the attics and walls of existing houses. He also does work for contractors on new houses. Explain how the characteristics of services: (1) affect his business, and (2) create a special marketing opportunity for him.

1.   Intangibility:

2.   Inseparability:

3.   Heterogeneity:

4.   Perishability:

5.   Fluctuating demand:

PART 19I (b): Exercise

Visit two blood banks in your area--one nonprofit and the other a for-profit operation. After identifying their target contributor and client markets, explain how each uses its marketing mix elements.

	<u>Contributor</u>	<u>Client</u>
Target market: Nonprofit:		
For-profit:		
Product: Nonprofit:		

For-profit:

Price: Nonprofit:

                For-profit:

Distribution: Nonprofit:

                For-profit:

Promotion: Nonprofit:

                For-profit:

PART 19J: A Real World Case: Report Cards for Hospitals

LIVINGSTON, N.J. -- After pop singer Whitney Houston had a baby at St. Barnabas Medial Center here, she was asked to rate the facility. If she responds, she will help determine the profits for a company that provides dietary and housekeeping services to the big, 620-bed nonprofit hospital. But the weight of Ms. Houston's opinion has nothing to do with her star status. All patients are asked to evaluate quality of food, cleanliness, and staff courtesy, using a questionnaire that provides a measuring stick for a novel contract that links profit to patient satisfaction.

As the health-care industry moves into an era of accountability and cost-cutting, the desire to relate patient feedback directly to the bottom line is likely to grow, say hospitals and management-service companies.

Hospitals that farm out certain hospital services--including St. Barnabas, Faulkner Hospital in Boston, and Park Ridge Hospital in Rochester, N.Y.--are in the forefront of what may be a key operating strategy for the 1990s: share the risk.

Contracts that contain incentives have been around for years, and so have patient surveys. But "partnering" has linked the two formally and raised the ante higher for vendors, who now are sometimes expected to invest in state-of-the-art equipment for use in the hospital they have contracted with. A performance-linked contract "is a vendor's gamble," concedes Ronald Del Mauro, president and chief executive officer of St. Barnabas. But he adds, "If we're successful, they're successful."

The vendor for St. Barnabas and Park Ridge is Seiler Corp., a Waltham, Mass., management-services concern owned by Paris-based Sodexho. Seiler, with about $400 million in annual revenue, ranks behind industry giants like Marriott Corp. and ARA Services Inc. Seiler previously ran only the dietary service at St. Barnabas, and Marriott's management services division provided housekeeping services. Then last year, St. Barnabas bundled the two contracts together, tied payment to patient-survey scores, and opened the pact to bids.

By creating an unusually large ($80 million over its life) and unusually long (seven years instead of one) contract, St. Barnabas built in a reason for vendors to consider a "partnership." For its part, Seiler agreed to invest $1.2 million in equipment to update the hospital's kitchen. It stands to earn as much as 150% of a base amount (the base covers Seiler's overhead and a pretax profit) or as little as 60% of the base, depending on quarterly survey scores. What's more, Seiler has already used the St. Barnabas pact signed last August as a marketing model for its recent pact with Park Ridge Hospital.

Critics say vendors like Seiler may simply be "buying" business. Not so, says Donald Storer, executive vice president of Seiler. "We're interested in structuring long-term relationships where the return on investment is worth it," he maintains. St. Barnabas's scores for its housekeeping and dietary services have been about average in recent years--in the 70s to low 80s. The hospital expects that after a year of using a new kitchen, its dietary services will attain scores above 80 and then steadily increase. A score in the 90s would trigger payments of 10% above the contract's base level. Scoring is weighed so that exceptional courtesy, for instance, doesn't make up for a dirty room.

The survey that St. Barnabas puts so much faith in--and Seiler's success hinges on--is a questionnaire developed eight years ago by Irwin Press and Rodney F. Ganey, two Ph.D.s at Notre Dame University in South Bend, Ind. Today, Press, Ganey Associates Inc. has about 400 clients. While many hospitals use the survey to gauge patient satisfaction, only about 10% tie it in some way to payment. But the trend is growing. "Every vendor in this industry has to be very concerned about patient satisfaction," says Mr. Ganey. St. Barnabas's dietary and housekeeping workers are members of Local 1199J of the National Union of Hospital and Health Care Employees, and their contract is with Seiler, the vendor, not the hospital.

Two other hospitals that are using the Press Ganey survey to help determine incentive pay use doctors and other workers who don't belong to unions. Faulkner Hospital, a Boston-area teaching facility with 204 beds, three years ago tied two tailored Press Ganey surveys to its incentive-compensation pay scale for independently contracted emergency-room physicians. One poll surveys general emergency room patient satisfaction, and one asked solely about physician performance. "Our scores improved dramatically," says Ken Belcher, vice president of ambulatory and special services at Faulkner. In 1989-90, when Faulkner signed a contract with Synergon, a St. Louis-based company that supplied board-certified emergency room physicians, its emergency room scores were around 74%. By 1990-91, scores had risen to 86%, triggering $30,000 in bonuses for emergency room doctors, who earn a total of about $200,000 each a year.

In January, Park Ridge Hospital in Rochester, N.Y., signed an eight-year $28 million contract with Seiler that is similar to the St. Barnabas deal. Seiler "offered us a partnership we couldn't turn down," says Patrick Burns, head of corporate services at Park Ridge. Mr. Burns says the contract represents a $4 million savings from its previous arrangements. And Seiler will also invest some $350,000 in capital equipment, Mr. Burns says.

While number crunchers like the idea of measuring satisfaction, such scores shouldn't replace clinical outcome, the scientific measure of whether changes in therapy, length of stay, and such improve a patient's medical condition, warns Daniel Sisto, president of the Hospital Association of New York State in Albany. Both patient satisfaction and clinical outcome must be measured, Mr. Sisto says. "A patient may have a fine medical outcome and still complain bitterly about how they were treated," he adds.

Of course, none of this cost-quality management is free. The annual fee to get the copyrighted Press Ganey survey and number-crunching services is about $3,100, which includes quarterly scores. Last year, St. Barnabas paid about $6,000 for its inpatient survey, including postage and special reports.

St. Barnabas's Mr. Del Mauro defends the survey's value. "I don't know how you can do business--whether it's a restaurant or a warehouse--without knowing the feelings of your customer. Our business is health care," he says, "and health care in this country is in institutional transition."

____ 1. The patient survey discussed in this article targets:
A. The donor market. B. The client market. C. Both client and donor markets.

____ 2. The patient survey is an attempt to:
A. Expand the service line.   D. Brand the service.
B. Alter the service offerings.   E. Manage the service quality.
C. Manage the service life cycle.

PART 19K: Answers to Questions

PART 19D: Completion
1. profit-seeking company/nonprofit organization
2. media sponsorship/advertising/donations/ coupon use
3. private gain/social responsibility
4. more money
5. tangible-goods/services
6. goods/services
7. identifiable/intangible/want-satisfaction
8. service economy
9. 90
10. low-paying/professional/technical/related work
11. one-half
12. business/consumer
13. administrative expenses
14. social/economic
15. intangibility/inseparability/heterogeneity/ perishability/fluctuating demand
16. benefits
17. visualization/association/physical representation/documentation
18. separated/simultaneously
19. quality/quality control
20. perishable/stored
21. marketing
22. producers/creators/marketers/ marketing/success
23. nonprofit/total marketing
24. slower
25. identify/analyze/marketing-mix/marketing objectives
26. donors/clients
27. two/marketing programs
28. essentially the same
29. offer/service-mix/features/quality
30. consumer want
31. business/client markets
32. feel good/guilt/organizations/tax deduction/status/religious beliefs
33. expanding/contracting/altering/life cycle

34. services/goods
35. branding
36. service quality
37. consumer/producer-seller
38. consumer expectations
39. quality-improvement
40. total quality management/TQM/long run
41. services/perishable/stored/nature of demand
42. donation/contributors
43. pricing situation/same methods
44. Discount strategies/variable
45. price competition/advertising/ segmentation/comparative prices
46. channels of distribution/physical distribution
47. short/simple/creator-seller
48. agent middleman
49. good location
50. donor
51. Promotion
52. Personal selling
53. service encounter
54. professional-services
55. advertising
56. sales promotion/publicity
57. productivity/customer-satisfaction
58. inefficiency/productivity
59. managerial challenge
60. consumer/business
61. marketing is/what it can do for them

PART 19E: True-False Questions
1. F 2. T 3. F 4. F 5. T 6. T
7. F 8. T 9. T 10. T 11. T 12. T
13. F 14. F 15. F

PART 19F: Multiple Choice Questions
1. C 2. A 3. C 4. E 5. D 6. A
7. E 8. D 9. E 10. A 11. C 12. B
13. D 14. D 15. D

PART 19G: Matching Questions
a. 9 b. 7 c. 4 d. 8

337

CHAPTER 20

INTERNATIONAL MARKETING

PART 20A: Chapter Goals

After studying this chapter, you should be able to explain:

- The importance of international marketing to firms and countries
- The impact of the macroenvironmental factors of culture, economics, and political/legal forces on international marketing
- Alternative organizational structures for operating in foreign markets
- Strategic considerations in formulating international marketing programs
- The prospects for the U.S. in international marketing

PART 20B: Key Terms and Concepts

1. International marketing [564]

2. Comparative advantage [564]

3. Technological advantage [565]

4. Exporting [566]

5. Export merchant [566]

6. Export agent [566]

7. Company sales branch [566]

8. Contracting [566]

9. Licensing [566]

10. Franchising [566]

11. Contract manufacturing [566]

12. Direct investment [566]

13. Joint venture [567]

14. Strategic alliance [567]

15. Wholly owned subsidiary [567]

16. Multinational corporation [567]

17. Global marketing [568]

18. Infrastructure [569]

19. Level of economic development [570]

20. Less-developed countries [571]

21. Newly industrialized countries [571]

22. Highly industrialized countries [571]

23. Expropriation [571]

24. Tariff [571]

25. Import quota [571]

26. Local-content laws [571]

27. Boycott [572]

28. General Agreement on Tariffs and Trade (GATT) [572]

29. European Community (EC) [572]

30. European Free Trade Association (EFTA) [573]

31. European Economic Area (EEA) [574]

32. North American Free Trade Agreement (NAFTA) [574]

33. Product extension [576]

34. Product adaptation [577]

35. Invention [577]

36. Dumping [577]

37. Countertrade [578]

38. Cartel [578]

39. Balance of payments [581]

40. Trade balance [582]

339

PART 20C: Summary

Many American firms derive a substantial portion of their sales and profits from their foreign operations. American firms dominated many international markets but now the situation has changed dramatically. European and Japanese firms are providing fierce competition in many of these markets [564].

The development of an international marketing program requires careful consideration of environmental and cultural differences among and within foreign countries and the firm's competitive position at home and abroad. Particular attention to such cultural elements as the family system, social customs and behavior, educational systems, language, and religious systems is important in international market analysis [569-570.It is also necessary to examine the infrastructure of the host country and its stage of economic development [570].

Once the decision is made to deal in international business, a decision must be made as to how the firm will operate. The simplest way is to export through middlemen specializing in foreign trade [566]. Other alternatives include company sales branches in the foreign country, a joint venture, some licensing arrangement, or forming a wholly owned subsidiary [566-567]. The most fully developed organizational structure is the multinational corporation [567].

International product planning, distribution systems, pricing, and advertising must reflect the results obtained from international market analysis [575-581]. The opportunities are great and foreign firms and their respective governments are keenly aware of these aspects of marketing. This interest is manifest in the international balance of trade [581]. America's trade balance has been affected by consumers' preferences for imported products, entry barriers, and many other policies of foreign governments, as well as the technological and marketing capabilities of other nations [582-585].

PART 20D: Completion

1. Marketing becomes international when an organization markets its products in _____ or _____ nations.

2. There are four reasons why firms move into international trade: (1) because of the existence of _____ , (2) because domestic markets become <u>saturated</u> , (3) because some nations have _____ over others, and (4) because of _____.

3. Organizational structures used in foreign markets include: (1) exporting directly to _____ _____ or indirectly through _____, (3) direct _____, and (4) the _____.

340

4. A(n) _____ is a middleman operating in the manufacturer's country who buys goods and exports them.

5. Although the simplest way of operating in foreign markets is through export agents, these people generally are not _____ and normally do not generate a large _____ volume.

6. Bypassing the export-import agent middlemen with its own sales branches enables a firm to promote its products more _____, to exploit its foreign markets more _____, and to control its _____ effort more completely.

7. Contracting involves a(n) _____ relationship that allows a firm to enter a foreign market _____ and quickly establish a marketing presence with a limited amount of <u>risk</u>.

8. A(n) _____ arrangement made by a company is one whereby foreign producers are authorized to manufacture the article.

9. Licensing offers a manufacturer a(n) _____ payment whereby he can still enjoy the advantages of his _____ process, _____, _____, and other _____.

10. _____ overseas combines a proven operating formula with local contacts and entrepreneural skills.

11. _____ is initiated by a foreign company which contracts with a foreign producer to supply products in the producer's country.

12. Through contracting, manufacturers enter markets which otherwise might be closed to them as exporters because of the following trade barriers: _____ restrictions, _____ quotas, or _____ tariffs.

13. A joint venture is a(n) _____ arrangement where the foreign operations are owned in part by the _____ and in part by a(n) _____.

14. A joint venture taken to a higher level is called a(n) _____, a formal, _____ agreement between firms (one domestic, the other foreign) to combine their _____ and _____ .

15. With a wholly owned foreign subsidiary, a company has maximum control over its _____ and _____.

16. Success overseas lies in (1) understanding the _____, and (2) gauging which domestic management practices should be _____ to foreign markets, which ones _____, and which ones _____.

17. Four of the social and environmental elements that must be identified and analyzed for their effect on a firm's marketing program are: _____, social _____ and _____, _____, and _____ differences.

18. Two key elements in a nation's economic environment are its _____ and stage of _____.

19. Levels of economic development include _____ countries, _____ _____ countries, and _____ countries.

20. When analyzing economic ability to buy in a foreign market, management must consider: (1) distribution of _____, (2) rate of growth of _____, and (3) extent of _____.

21. The main political concerns of international marketers are the stability of _____, their attitudes toward _____, and _____.

22. The major trade barriers are _____, _____ quotas, _____ laws, and _____ or _____.

23. The four major trade agreements are the: (1) _____ _____ (GATT), (2) _____ (EC), (3) _____ _____ (EFTA), and (4) _____ _____ (NAFTA).

24. Although the growth of these regional trading blocks is a significant development that will create both _____ and _____ for international marketers, other groups to watch include Asia's "_____," the _____, and _____.

25. Designing an international marketing mix includes investigating _____, _____, _____, _____ systems, and _____, especially _____.

26. The biggest problem in conducting marketing research in some foreign markets may be the scarcity of _____.

27. A key question today in _____ involves the extent to which a company can market the same product in several different countries.

28. The first option in product planning is _____, which describes the situation in which a standard product is sold in two or more nations.

29. A second option is _____, modifying a product that sells successfully in one

market to suit the unique needs of other markets.

30. The third option is _____, the development of an entirely new product for a foreign market.

31. _____ and _____ are another consideration in foreign marketing.

32. Price determination in international marketing is similar to that discussed in earlier chapters except for _____ problems and lack of control over _____ pricing.

33. Sometimes firms engage in _____, selling products in foreign markets below the prices charged for these same goods in their home market.

34. _____ or _____ involves trading domestically made products for imported goods.

35. The _____ allows American firms to join in a trade combination in foreign countries without being charged with a violation of American antitrust laws.

36. A(n) _____ is a group of firms which produce similar products and which have combined to restrain competition in manufacturing and marketing.

37. Four groups of middlemen that need to be recognized in foreign trade are: (1) _____ foreign-trade middlemen, (2) foreign trade middlemen _____, (3) wholesalers and retailers operating _____, and (4) manufacturers' sales branches and offices _____.

38. Physical-distribution expenses account for a(n) _____ of the final selling price in foreign markets than in domestic markets.

39. The _____ had the effect of limiting considerably the competitive position of American companies in international trade.

40. A controversial issue is the extent to which _____ can be standardized in international markets.

41. Standardization of advertising has increased because of an increase in international _____ and _____, and because of increasing advertising _____.

42. People in foreign countries object particularly to American _____-sell advertising.

43. A nation's _____--the difference between what it exports and what it imports-- _____.

44. Throughout the 1980s, the U.S. ran a huge _____ balance of trade.

45. Six other factors affect U.S. balance of trade: consumer _____, _____, barriers to _____ and other _____ policies, _____ structure, relative _____ capabilities, and the price and quantity of _____.

PART 20E: True-False Questions

If the statement is true, circle "T"; if false, circle "F."

T F   1. Branding is especially important in international marketing.

T F   2. Brokers are not used in international marketing.

T F   3. Foreign middlemen usually are very aggressive in their pricing policies and strategies.

T F   4. Most foreign countries prohibit the use of advertising by American firms.

T F   5. Countertrade and barter mean the same thing.

T F   6. Exchange controls and other currency regulations rarely present any obstacles in foreign marketing.

T F   7. Most firms engaged in international marketing devote more funds to foreign marketing research than to marketing research in the U.S.

T F   8. The scarcity of reliable statistical data is the biggest problem in some foreign markets.

T F   9. Cost-plus pricing is probably used to a greater extent in export marketing than at home.

T F 10. A cartel is a group of companies which produce similar products and which have combined to restrain competition in manufacturing and marketing.

T F 11. The cause of America's international trade-balance problems lies somewhere other than in high labor costs.

T F 12. A favorable balance of merchandise trade exists for a nation when its exports exceed its imports.

T F 13. "Dumping" occurs when a government action supports the domestic price at a level below the international market price.

T F 14. There is broad agreement over the issue of global standardization of advertising messages in international marketing.

T F 15. If, in a foreign setting, businesses are expected to bribe officials in order to make a sale, there is nothing to prevent an American firm from doing so.

PART 20F: Multiple Choice Questions

In the space provided write the letter of the answer that best fits the statement.

___ 1. Which of the following countries is not a member of the European Community?
   A. Great Britain. B. Netherlands. C. Poland. D. Italy. E. Germany.

___ 2. In the past decade, which of the following has occurred?
   A. Foreign firms are producing a wide variety of high-quality, low-priced goods.
   B. Foreign firms are investing in the U.S.
   C. U.S. firms are investing in foreign countries.
   D. International trade has grown.
   E. All of the above.

___ 3. Since 1977, it has been illegal for American firms operating abroad to bribe foreign officials under provisions of the:
   A. FCPA. B. FDIC. C. FDA. D. FTCA. E. Webb-Pomerene Act.

___ 4. Gathering marketing data in foreign markets is often difficult because:
   A. Of the suspicion of strangers.   D. Opinion polls are uncommon.
   B. Of the distrust of government.   E. All of the above.
   C. Of strong individualism.

___ 5. An example of a middleman operating in foreign trade is:
   A. American foreign-trade middleman.
   B. Foreign-trade middleman located abroad.
   C. Wholesalers and retailers operating within foreign markets.
   D. Manufacturers' sales branches and offices located in foreign countries.
   E. Any of the above.

___ 6. A boycott in international trade is also known as a(n):
   A. Tariff.   C. Import quota.   E. None of the above.
   B. Local-content law.   D. Embargo.

___ 7. The highest level of international involvement is:
   A. Exporting through importers or export-import middlemen.
   B. Licensing a foreign producer to make the product in exchange for royalties.
   C. Franchising a local investor to represent the domestic company.
   D. A strategic alliance.
   E. The multinational corporation.

___ 8. The benefits of exporting through company sales branches in international marketing include:
   A. Products can be promoted more aggressively.
   B. Its foreign markets can be developed more effectively.
   C. Its sales effort can be controlled more completely.
   D. All of the above.
   E. None of the above.

___ 9. The most likely success regarding global standardization is to be found in the area of:
   A. Durable business goods.
   B. Durable consumer goods.
   C. Wearing apparel.
   D. Food and drink products.
   E. Services.

___10. The easiest and simplest means of operating in foreign markets is by:
   A. Exporting directly to importers, or through export-import middlemen.
   B. Exporting through company sales branches.
   C. Entering into licensing arrangements.
   D. Entering into a joint venture.
   E. Establishing a wholly owned foreign subsidiary.

___11. A partnership arrangement in which the foreign operation is owned in part by the domestic company and in part by a foreign company is known as:
   A. Exporting directly to importers, or through export-import middlemen.
   B. Exporting through company sales branches.
   C. Entering into licensing arrangements.
   D. Entering into a joint venture.
   E. Establishing a wholly owned foreign subsidiary.

___12. Countries such as Burma, Vietnam, Haiti, and Somalia are known as:
   A. Less-developed countries.
   B. Newly industrialized countries.
   C. Highly industrialized countries.
   D. First-world countries.
   E. None of the above.

___13. A situation where a firm's foreign price is lower than its domestic price is known as:
   A. Dumping.
   B. Countertrade.
   C. A tariff.
   D. An import quota.
   E. A boycott.

346

___14. The formal trade agreement that involves more nations than any other is the:
  A. General Agreement on Tariffs and Trade (GATT).
  B. European Community (EC).
  C. European Free Trade Association (EFTA).
  D. European Economic Area (EEA).
  E. North American Free Trade Agreement (NAFTA).

___15. The balance of payments for the U.S. is affected by:
  A. Its military forces stationed overseas.
  B. Foreign aid.
  C. Oil imports.
  D. American tourist travel abroad.
  E. All of the above.

PART 20G: Matching Questions

In the space provided write the number of the word or expression from column 1 that best fits the description in column 2.

1	2
1. Balance of payments	___ a. Selling products in foreign markets below the prices charged in the home market.
2. Balance of trade	
3. Boycott	___ b. The European Community.
4. Cartel	___ c. The means whereby foreign manufacturers are authorized to produce American goods.
5. Contract manufacturing	___ d. Companies that produce similar goods and have combined in an effort to restrain competition.
6. Countertrade	
7. Dumping	___ e. A partnership arrangement in which the foreign operation is owned in part by the American company and in part by a foreign company.
8. EC	
9. EEA	___ f. Another name for an embargo.
10. EFTA	___ g. Another name for barter.
11. Expropriation	___ h. The difference between what a nation imports and exports.

347

12. Franchising

13. GATT

14. Infrastructure

15. International trade balances

16. Joint venture

17. Licensing agreement

18. Multinational corporation

19. NAFTA

20. Wholly owned subsidiary

_____ i. A nation's ability to provide transportation, communications, and energy.

_____ j. Having an investment in a country seized by the host nation.

PART 20H: Problems and Applications

1.   With two other students, talk to a banker about the role that international banking plays in the development of foreign trade. Have questions for him or her on loans, Export-Import Bank, credit guarantees for U.S. exporters, marketing services, etc. Prepare your summary for class discussion.

2.   What are the risks involved in quoting prices in foreign currencies?

3.   Select any one item and explain why it is exported or imported. Do this for a specific industry and firm.

4.   Find out what foreign publications are published by the U.S. Department of Commerce. Evaluate these publications.

5.   Why do nations try to promote their exports?

6.   Does the United Nations seek to aid and promote international marketing?   Prepare a memo on this subject for your instructor.

7.   The U.S. depends on imports in the areas of agriculture, forestry, fisheries, minerals, and manufactures. Consult the *Statistical Abstract of the United States* and find out what percent of the domestic supply of each commodity is imported for consumption in the U.S.

8.   From the latest issue of the *Statistical Abstract of the United States*, find the imports, exports, and total foreign trade for the top ten countries in the world.

Country	Imports	Exports	Total Foreign Trade
1.			
2.			
3.			
4.			
5.			
6.			
7.			
8.			
9.			
10.			

9.   Consult the <u>Statistical Abstract</u> and complete the following table for U.S. imports..

Commodity Group	Percent of New Supply Imported		
	1970	1980	199__
Agriculture	___	___	___
Coffee	___	___	___
Tea	___	___	___
Minerals	___	___	___
Bauxite and other aluminum ores	___	___	___
Manganese and other concentrates	___	___	___
Manufacturers	___	___	___
Pulp-mill products	___	___	___
Rubber footwear	___	___	___
Sewing machines and parts	___	___	___

What can you conclude about the need of the U.S. for foreign trade?

PART 20I (a): Exercise

Tom and Lorene Maxwell founded Tolovino, a small winery in the northern San Joaquin Valley of California, shortly after Tom's discharge following the Korean War. Over the years, low prices coupled with quality products have made Tolovino a preferred name in premium jug wine throughout California and the West. Their son, Phillip, a viticulture and wine making graduate, has been interested in international business for a long time. He is anxious to embark on his long-held dream of marketing Tolovino brands in Mexico. After becoming established there, he plans to expand throughout the rest of Central and South America.

Phillip's plan is to:
1.   Use the same successful U.S. advertising theme.

2.   Initially ship the product in jugs--four one-gallon or eight half-gallon per cardboard carton--and later make an arrangement for a Mexican vintner, where the wine would be shipped from the U.S. in refrigerated tank trucks for bottling locally under the brand name "Tolovino."

3.   Phillip plans on hiring an American knowledgeable in the wine business.   That person would initially operate a sales office in Mexico City and solicit orders locally and later be the liaison between the local vintner and the home office.

As Tom Maxwell, you have been thinking about Phillip's plan for some time. He has been pressing you for an answer.

1.   What do you think of selling Tolovino wines in Mexico?
2.   Do you foresee any problems with advertising?
3.   Are you satisfied with the proposed channels of distribution?
4.   Do you foresee any other problems? Do you need any additional information?

PART 20I (b): **Exercise**

Many American companies, most notably Wal-Mart, have pursued a "Buy America" campaign. But how much does the average person know about the actual ownership of American companies? The following is intended to test that question.

List whether you think these companies' products or services are:	U.S.-Owned	Foreign-Owned	Don't Know
1. Airborne Express			
2. Benetton (Clothes)			
3. BIC (Pens)			
4. Canada Dry (Beverages)			
5. Capitol (Records)			
6. Carnation (Foods)			
7. Dannon (Yogurt)			
8. Eveready (Batteries)			
9. Firestone Tire and Rubber			
10. Heineken (Beer)			
11. Kentucky Fried Chicken			
12. Lever Bros. (Soaps, toothpaste, etc.)			

13. Nestle (Foods)
14. Nike (Shoes)
15. Norelco (Appliances)
16. Panasonic (Electronic products)
17. Pillsbury (Foods)
18. Polaroid (Film)
19. Reebok (Shoes)
20. Seagram and Sons (Liquors)
21. Shell Oil (Petroleum products)
22. Sohio Petroleum
23. Timex (Watches)
24. United Parcel Service
25. Wal-Mart (Retail stores)

PART 20J: A Real World Case: Going Global

Pink diapers for girls and blue ones for boys? The idea prompted snickers at first, but no one's laughing now. The sex-typed diapers are a hit on three continents. Their universal success is also the latest sign that Procter & Gamble Co. has learned a lot about marketing overseas.

P&G wasn't always so nimble abroad. For years, it was something of an Ugly American, taking products developed for the U.S. market and trying to push them into foreign markets with American-style marketing and ads. Such efforts to standardize worldwide marketing techniques were fashionable in the early 1980s, under the banner of "global marketing." But P&G has learned that the trick to going global is acting like a local.

BIG LOSSES. Take P&G's experiences in Japan. A homogeneous society, Japan remains in many ways a classic mass market. Still, for P&G, it is a fragment of the worldwide market, and one for which it has carefully tailored its marketing. But it learned to do so only after some bitter lessons--and more than $200 million in losses from its arrival in 1971 to 1987. "P&G had a very hard time accepting that Japan was not going to be like the U.S.," says an American marketing executive in Tokyo.

P&G won an early lead in disposable diapers after introducing Pampers in Japan in 1977, for example. But it quickly lost market share when competitors Uni-Charm Corp. and Kao Corp. introduced fitted, thin diapers that won over mothers who had resisted disposables. "We really didn't understand the consumer," says Edwin L. Artzt, P&G's vice-chairman, who acknowledges that P&G was slow to improve its bulky, rectangular Pampers.

Now, things have turned around dramatically. P&G's sales in Japan grew 40%, to $1 billion, in the fiscal year ended June 30 [1989]. Overall international profits grew by 37%, to $417 million. Says P&G's Artzt: "We want to be the No. 1 consumer-products company in Japan." To help

351

reach that goal, P&G has hired more Japanese staff and attuned its ways to local styles. "It's more Japanese than some Japanese companies," says Noriko Sakoh, an analyst at SBCI Securities (Asia) Ltd.

TALKING DIAPERS. For example, P&G's ads now prominently mention the company's name as well as the product's. That's something P&G's ads in the U.S. rarely do, but such corporate identification is important to the Japanese. And while a U.S. ad might show a diaper absorbing a cup of liquid, a popular Pampers ad in Japan used an indirect approach: A talking diaper promised toddlers that the brand wouldn't leak or cause diaper rash. P&G finally introduced a superabsorbent thin diaper, and then it surprised rivals with the pink and blue Pampers. After sinking to less than 10% of the market, P&G's share is up to 20.5%, challenging Kao for the No. 2 spot.

Worldwide, P&G is rolling out new products more quickly, partly because it has built strong local operations that are closer to the market. "P&G used to be bloody slow," says Michael R. Angus, chairman of Unilever PLC, P&G's global archrival. "They were so thorough, the world changed between the origination of an idea and the product actually appearing on shelves."

P&G now tries to develop what Artzt calls "big edge" products, with a technology than can be applied worldwide but in forms tailored to local needs. Its Japanese sanitary pad, Whisper, for example, is smaller and thinner than its U.S. counterpart, Always. "We've made it right for the Japanese woman, and we've made it right for the American woman," Artzt says. P&G's foreign performance has been so torrid that there is even talk that Artzt, who is in charge of international, could become P&G's next chief executive. The very idea speaks volumes about the globalization of the Cincinnati colossus.

Source: "P&G Goes Global by Acting Like a Local," *Business Week*, August 28, 1989, p. 58. Reprinted from August 28, 1989 issue of *Business Week* by special permission, copyright © 1989 by McGraw-Hill, Inc.

____1. Contrary to what the text says, P&G has found its greatest success regarding global standardization in the area of:
   A. Durable business goods.
   B. Durable consumer goods.
   C. Wearing apparel.
   D. Nondurable consumer goods.
   E. Services.

____2. According to the article, in what organizational stage in the evolution of an international business is P&G?
   A. Wholly owned subsidiary.
   B. Joint venture.
   C. World or global enterprise.
   D. Licensing arrangement.
   E. Use of export-import middlemen.

PART 20K: Answers to Questions

PART 20D: Completion

1. two/more
2. foreign markets/saturated/comparative advantages/technological advantages
3. foreign importers/import-export middlemen/investment/multinational corporation
4. export merchant
5. aggressive marketers/sales
6. aggressively/effectively/sales
7. legal/indirectly/risk
8. licensing
9. fee or royalty/production/patents/ trademarks/assets
10. Franchising
11. Contract manufacturing
12. exchange/import/prohibitive
13. partnership/domestic company/foreign company
14. strategic alliance/long-term/capabilities/ resources
15. marketing program/production operations
16. foreign environment/transferred directly/ modified/eliminated
17. family/customs/behavior/education/ language
18. infrastructure/economic development
19. less-developed/newly industrialized/highly industrialized
20. income/buying power/available financing
21. governments/free trade/expropriation
22. tariffs/import/local-content/boycotts/ embargoes
23. General Agreement on Tariffs and Trade/ European Community/European Free Trade Association/North American Free Trade Agreement
24. opportunities/challenge/Four Tigers/CIS/ China
25. marketing research/product planning/price/ distribution/advertising/standardized advertising
26. reliable statistical data
27. product planning
28. product extension
29. product adaptation
30. invention
31. Branding/labeling
32. currency conversion/middlemen's
33. dumping
34. Countertrade/barter
35. Webb-Pomerene Act of 1918
36. cartel
37. domestic/located abroad/within foreign countries/located in foreign countries
38. larger share
39. Foreign Corrupt Practices Act of 1977
40. advertising
41. communications/entertainment/costs
42. hard
43. trade balance/must balance
44. negative
45. preferences/technology/entry/ government/tax/marketing/oil

PART 20E: True-False Questions
1. T 2. F 3. F 4. F 5. T 6. F
7. F 8. T 9. T 10. T 11. T 12. T
13. F 14. F 15. F

PART 20F: Multiple Choice Questions
1. C 2. E 3. A 4. D 5. E 6. D
7. E 8. D 9. A 10. A 11. D 12. A
13. A 14. A 15. E

PART 20G: Matching Questions
a. 7 b. 8 c. 17 d. 4 e. 16 f. 3
g. 6 h. 2 i. 14 j. 11

353

PART EIGHT

MANAGING THE MARKETING EFFORT

CHAPTER 21

MARKETING IMPLEMENTATION AND EVALUATION

PART 21A: Chapter Goals

After studying this chapter, you should be able to explain:

- The role of implementation in the management process
- Organizational structures used to implement marketing
- The tasks of staffing and operating in the implementation process
- The role of a marketing audit in evaluating a marketing program
- The meaning of misguided marketing effort
- Sales volume analysis

357

PART 21B: Key Terms and Concepts

1. Planning   [598]

2. Implementation   [598]

3. Evaluation   [598]

4. Organizational structures for implementing strategic planning

     a. Geographical specialization   [601]

     b. Product specialization   [602]

     c. Customer (market) specialization   [603]

     d. Major-accounts organization   [603

5. Importance of good selection   [603]

6. Delegating authority and responsibility   [604]

7. Coordinating marketing activities   [604]

8. Motivating people   [605]

9. Communicating inside a company [605]

10. Marketing audit   [607]

11. Misdirected marketing effort   [607]

12. 80-20 principle   [607]

13. Iceberg principle   [608]

14. Sales volume analysis   [609]

15. Market-share analysis   [610]

16. Marketing cost analysis   [611]

17. Direct costs   [614]

18. Indirect costs   [614]

19. Contribution-margin approach   [615]

20. Full-cost approach   [615]

21. Small-order problem   [616]

PART 21C: Summary

The management process in marketing may be defined as the planning, implementation, and evaluation of a firm's marketing effort. The implementation stage is the operational stage in which the company attempts to carry out its strategic plan. Without the will to implement plans, they are useless [599].

The implementation stage includes three broad areas of activity: organizing, staffing, and operating. In the organizing phase, it is wise to coordinate all marketing efforts into one department whose top executive reports directly to the chief executive officer. Within the marketing department, the firm should utilize some form of specialization based upon geographical territories, products, or customers. According to the authors, staffing is the most important step in this management process [603]. In order to operate effectively, management must concern itself with delegation, coordination, motivation, and communication [603-605].

358

The evaluation stage measures performance results against predetermined goals. This process enables management to determine the effectiveness of its implementation efforts and to plan future corrective actions as needed [605-609].

One of the most often overlooked aspects of marketing management is that of evaluating marketing results. A major evaluation tool for appraising marketing activities is the marketing audit [607]. The auditing concept, long used in the area of accounting, provides a systematic and critical review of a company's entire marketing system, including goals, objectives, personnel, and plans. The marketing audit seeks to provide a current status report of market activities to uncover problems and to point out marketing opportunities.

Although the marketing-audit concept is extremely sound, workable, and valuable in the evaluation of a company's marketing efforts, it has not enjoyed widespread use in actual business practice.

There are many reasons for misdirected marketing efforts, which an effective program of evaluation seeks to uncover [608]. Often, the reasons cannot be found because accounting data are not available in sufficient detail. To pinpoint problem areas, there are two general types of analysis of marketing effort. One is an analysis of sales volume. This involves a detailed study of a company's net sales section of the operating statement [609]. On the other hand, a marketing cost analysis is a detailed study of the operating and expense section of the operating statement. Ideally, both of these means of analysis should be used when one studies a firm's marketing activities, for each complements the other.

The analysis of marketing cost has, in recent years, become more than just good business practice. In many instances it has become a necessity because of the possibility of having to justify price differentials to various customers in a court of law. Unlike volume analysis, cost analysis derives information on the profitability of sales. It helps pinpoint cost items that are out of line or excessive [610-615].

PART 21D: Completion

1. The implementation stage of the management process in marketing is the _____ stage--the one in which the company tries to carry out its _____.

2. The _____ stage involves determining how effectively the organization achieves the goals set in the strategic planning phase of the management process.

3. Good planning cannot overcome poor _____, while effective implementation very often can overcome _____.

4. The implementation stage includes three broad activities: (1) _____ the marketing

359

effort, (2) _____ the organization, and (3) _directing_ the workers as they carry out the _____ .

5. After establishing a company's _____ , an early activity is to organize the people who will be _____ it.

6. Firms are streamlining their organizational structures by _____ the number of executive levels between the _____ and the _____ .

7. In a marketing-oriented enterprise, all marketing activities are coordinated under one _____ who typically is a(n) _____ .

8. The organization of the sales force within the marketing department is by _____ _____ , by _____ , or by _____ .

9. A territorial organization usually ensures better implementation of _____ in local markets and better control over the _____ .

10. The major advantage of organizing by _____ sales organization is the specialized attention each product line can get from the _____ .

11. When organizing by type of customer, customers are grouped either by _____ or by _____ .

12. This organizational form is likely to increase as more companies fully implement the _____ .

13. In an effort to deal with large, important customers, many firms are adopting a variation of customer specialization called _____ organization.

14. The second important task of management, _____ , in the authors' opinion, is the most important stage in the management process.

15. The third broad activity included in the implementation stage of the management process involves actually _____ a marketing program.

16. The key to success in this activity is to put into practice four concepts involving the management of people: _____, _____, _____, and _____ .

17. Delegation means to give a person a job to do (_____) and the tools to do it with (_____).

18. Effective coordination sometimes is difficult to achieve because of differences in _____ , _____ , and _____ among the groups involved.

19. Successful leaders in any field use <u>economic</u> motivate as well as _____ motivation.

20. Two guidelines to successful internal communication are to adopt a "_____ " management style and to bring a problem _____ as soon as management is aware that one exists.

21. Shortly after a firm's plans have been set into motion, the process of _____ should begin.

22. A(n) _____ is a comprehensive review and evaluation of the marketing function in an organization--its philosophy, environment, goals, strategies, organizational structure, human and financial resources, and performance.

23. The well-known "80-20" principle has often been found to be true when evaluating a firm's marketing efforts. Under this principle, ____ percent of the firm's sales come from ____ percent of its customers. On the other hand, ____ percent of its sales comes from ____ percent of its customers.

24. The "iceberg" principle illustrates the major reason why firms misdirect their marketing effort--that is, they lack sufficiently _____ data.

25. Firms also lack information on exact marketing _____ with which to compare their actual performance.

26. The evaluation process involves trying to: (1) find out _____ happened, (2) find out _____ it happened, and (3) decide _____ about it.

27. A(n) _____ is a detailed study of the Net Sales section of a firm's operating statement.

28. Management should analyze its _____ volume, and its volume by _____ and by _____.

29. But this is not enough: company sales must be analyzed by _____ or by _____ , for example.

30. In a _____ analysis, the company's sales are compared to the industry's sales, thereby telling the company how it is doing relative to its competitors.

31. A marketing cost analysis is a detailed study of a firm's _____ section of the operating statement.

32. In the analysis of ledger expenses, actual marketing costs taken from the firm's accounting ledger are compared with the firm's _____ or with _____ data.

33. An analysis of the cost of the marketing activities such as advertising or warehousing gives executives _____ than they can get from an analysis of ledger accounts alone.

34. Marketing cost analysis is expensive in _____, _____, and _____.

35. Moreover, the job of allocating _____ or _____ costs is a difficult problem encountered in marketing cost analysis.

36. The two ways of handling the allocation of indirect expenses are: (1) the _____ or _____ method, and (2) the _____ method.

37. In the contribution-margin method, only _____ are allocated to each marketing unit being analyzed.

38. In the full-cost approach, all _____ , whether _____ or _____ , are allocated among the marketing units under study.

39. The identification of strong or weak territories is a major benefit of _____ and _____ analysis. Sometimes, changes in the _____ can bring them into line with current sales potential.

40. When the relative profitability of products is known, management may do a number of things to improve the standing of less profitable items. For example, it may simplify a(n) _____ , change _____ compensation , or alter _____.

41. Analysis often shows management that the firm is losing money in servicing certain customers who buy _____ at a time.

PART 21E: True-False Questions

If the statement is true, circle "T"; if false, circle "F."

T F   1. The answer to the small-order problem is simple: accept no order for less than $500.

T F 2. A marketing audit is able to spot problems in a marketing plan.

T F 3. A marketing audit is merely an after-the-fact review of a business structure and includes no evaluation of the effects of alternatives before a decision is reached.

T F 4. Direct marketing costs are usually difficult to allocate.

T F 5. Under the contribution-margin system, an attempt is made to allocate all direct costs.

T F 6. The "iceberg" principle does not exist in well-managed companies.

T F 7. There is a close relationship between planning and implementation in the management process.

T F 8. The first major job in implementing a firm's strategic planning is to organize the people who will be doing the actual implementation work.

T F 9. In marketing-oriented enterprises, all marketing activities are usually coordinated under the chief executive officer of the company.

T F 10. The most widely used method of organizing the sales force is by territory.

T F 11. A company selling thousands of items, such as a drug wholesaler, would be well advised to organize its sales force by product category.

T F 12. As the marketing concept is more fully implemented, organizing sales forces by product line will become more pronounced.

T F 13. According to the text, the most important stage in the management process is the selection of staff.

T F 14. The management task is really simple: all a manager has to do to get the job done is to depend on himself.

T F 15. It is not enough to have a good strategic plan. It is useless if it cannot be carried out in action.

PART 21F: Multiple Choice Questions

In the space provided write the letter of the answer that best fits the statement.

_____ 1. Which of the following best describes a total evaluation program?
    A. Synergism   D. Marketing cost analysis
    B. Marketing audit   E. The management process
    C. "80-20" principle

_____ 2. A sales volume analysis is a detailed study of the _____ section of a firm's operating statement.
    A. Operating Expense   C. Gross Sales   E. Extraordinary Income
    B. Net Sales   D. Cost of Goods Sold

_____ 3. Most of the problems in cost allocation arise in connection with _____ costs:
    A. Direct   B. Indirect   C. Variable   D. Out-of-pocket   E. Separable

_____ 4. Which of the following best illustrates the "80-20" principle?
    A. 72% of our customers account for 12% of our sales volume.
    B. 80% of our products are sold in 80% of our territories.
    C. Sales increased 15% last year.
    D. Sales volume increased 27% but sales territory A decreased 6%.
    E. Volume increased 8% but profit increased only 20%.

_____ 5. A marketing cost analysis is LEAST likely to be used as an aid in:
    A. Selecting the most profitable order size.
    B. Determining the minimum profitable order size.
    C. Determining the market potential.
    D. Deciding what products to drop from the line.
    E. Handling the small-order problem.

_____ 6. Which of the following is the best example of expenses classified by activity groups?
    A. Storage, order filling, sales promotion.   D. Office supplies, postage.
    B. Sales persons' salaries and expenses.   E. Sales managers' salaries.
    C. Rent, taxes.

_____ 7. Organizing the sales department in such a way as to implement the marketing concept most fully would lead a company to organize by:
    A. Geographic areas.   C. Customer (market).   E. None of the above.
    B. Product.   D. Product-manager.

_____ 8. According to the authors, the most important job in the management process is:
    A. Planning.   B. Staffing.   C. Evaluating.   D. Organizing.   E. Operating.

_____ 9. All the following are concepts involving the management of people EXCEPT:
    A. Delegation.   C. Intimidation.   E. Motivation.
    B. Coordination.   D. Communication.

_____ 10. A marketing cost analysis is a detailed study of the _____ section of a firm's operating statement.
    A. Operating Expense   C. Gross Sales   E. Extraordinary Income
    B. Net Sales   D. Cost of Goods Sold

_____ 11. The product specialization method of organizing a sales force works best when companies are marketing:
    A. Complex technical products.   D. All of the above.
    B. Unrelated or dissimilar products.   E. None of the above.
    C. Thousands of items.

_____ 12. A cause of misplaced marketing effort is that executives must make decisions based on inadequate knowledge of:
    A. The disproportionate spread of marketing effort.
    B. Reliable standards for determining what should be spent on marketing.
    C. What results should be expected from these expenditures.
    D. All of the above.
    E. None of the above.

_____ 13. The evaluation process includes the following task:
    A. Find out what happened.   D. All of the above.
    B. Find out why it happened.   E. None of the above.
    C. Decide what to do about it.

_____ 14. The implementation stage in the marketing management process involves:
    A. Organizing the marketing effort.   D. All of the above.
    B. Staffing the organization.   E. None of the above.
    C. Directing the operational efforts of the staff.

_____ 15. Marketing efforts are often misdirected because:
    A. Marketing executives often lack detailed sales information.
    B. Marketing executives often lack knowledge of costs.
    C. Marketing executives often lack reliable standards for determining what should be spent on marketing.
    D. All of the above.
    E. None of the above.

PART 21G: Matching Questions

In the space provided write the number of the word or expression from column 1 that best fits the description in column 2.

1	2
1. Contribution-margin approach	____ a. Setting up a sales force using territories.
2. Customer specialization	____ b. Setting up a sales force wherein the marketing concept is most fully utilized.
3. Direct costs	____ c. Also known as contribution-to overhead allocation method.
4. "80-20" principle	
5. Full-cost approach	____ d. A detailed study of the net sales section of a firm's income statement.
6. Geographic specialization	____ e. A systematic, comprehensive, periodic review and evaluation of the marketing function in an organization.
7. Iceberg principle	
8. Indirect costs	
9. Major-accounts organization	____ f. The principle that illustrates the major reason why firms misdirect their marketing effort.
10. Marketing audit	
11. Marketing cost analysis	____ g. An example is the salary of a salesperson being charged to a specific territory.
12. Market-share analysis	
13. Product specialization	
14. Sales volume analysis	

PART 21H

Problems and Applications

1.   Visit a manufacturer or a retailer in your area. What is their procedure for test marketing their product?   If they don't do test marketing, how do they determine product acceptance?

2.   Read several recent articles on test marketing and evaluate the "state of the art" of this marketing tool. (See the *Journal of Marketing Research*.)

3.   Using the buying-power index found in the latest edition of "Survey of Buying Power" (published by *Sales & Marketing Management*), allocate the sales potential for a product on a regional basis.   Assume the product's national sales potential is 15,000,000 units.

4.   *Business Week* periodically reports the findings of surveys of consumer buying intentions, such as the buying of new houses. For some past time period, compare one of these reports on consumer intentions to buy houses with actual house sales as reported in *Business Week*.

5.   Read some recent court cases which involve the use of marketing cost analysis for justifying price differentials. (See the "Legal Developments in Marketing" section in the *Journal of Marketing*). What do you conclude from your reading?

6.   Interview several certified public accountants in your area about the use of marketing cost analysis by local businesses. Write a memo to your instructor.

7.   Discuss the steps you would take in analyzing the marketing activities of a regional cookie manufacturer from a marketing cost analysis point of view.

8.   Talk to a business person. What is his or her opinion of marketing cost analysis? Does her or she use it?

9.   Interview the local sales manager of a large, national firm. How is their sales department organized? In your judgment, is this the most effective plan? What does the sales manager think?

PART 21I: Exercise

Bernardo Jones, Inc., an old-line home water heater manufacturer, has had an unbroken string of ten years of increasing sales with the exception of the recession year of 1991 (see Table 21-1).

Table 21-1. Bernardo Jones, Inc., and Industry Sales for 1991-2000

Year	B.J.Sales ($millions)	Industry Sales ($millions)	B.J. Percentage Share
2000	85.2	600	
1999	82.1	540	
1998	77.4	490	
1997	64	405	
1996	60	370	
1995	53.8	320	
1994	48.2	292	
1993	53.5	304	
1992	46.3	260	
1991	43.2	240	

As the new marketing manager, you have pulled together data on industry trends for the past ten years as well as your territory and product breakdowns (see Tables 21-2 and 21-3).

Table 21-2. Territorial Sales Volume for Bernardo Jones, Inc., 2000

Territory	Sales Goals ($millions)	Actual Sales ($millions)	Performance Percentage	Dollar Valuation ($millions)
A	12.4	16.3		
B	14.2	14		
C	18.6	12.4		
D	20.2	20.4		
E	19.8	22.1		

368

Table 21-3. Product Line Sales Volume for Bernardo Jones, 2000

Product	Sales Goals ($millions)	Actual Sales ($millions)	Performance Percentage	Dollar Valuation ($millions
30 gal. electric	12.4	8.7		
30 gal. powermiser	10.5	13		
30 gal. gas	12.1	13.3		
40 gal. electric	13.2	10.1		
40 gal. powermiser	12.1	14.6		
40 gal. gas	12.5	13.1		
50 gal. electric	4.6	4.1		
50 gal. powermiser	3.1	3.4		
50 gal. gas	4.7	4.9		

1.   Make a market share analysis by completing Table 21-1. What does this analysis show?

2.   Make a sales results versus sales goals analysis for the year 2000 by completing Table 21-2. What does this analysis show?

3.   Bernardo Jones makes three standard tank sizes: 30, 40, and 50 gallon. Water is heated by electricity and gas (both natural and propane or butane). Three years ago, they developed the "Powermiser" model of electric hot water heater. This has twice the normal amount of insulation and a feature for cutting the power to one of the electrodes in the heating cycle so as to conserve energy. It sells for about 28 percent more than the regular electric models. The sales goals and actual sales figures by model are shown in Table 21-3. What do these data indicate?

4.   Do you need any more information to complete the analysis?

PART 21J: A Real World Case: Planning for Success

I love an industry and marketplace that are so exciting, vibrant and tolerant that a couple of engineers who have a great idea can start a company. Unfortunately, these new companies often are like roving mobs rather than armies planning to go out and win on the battlefield. Two years after their formation, fewer than five out of 100 marketplace contenders will still be around. The dazed, battle-worn engineers will walk the scarred landscape wondering what went amiss. These people blow their chances for success because they don't have "the right stuff."

Our engineers assign responsibility and authority without consideration for true capabilities. Just because someone handles the checkbook at home is no reason to believe he can be the finance officer of the company. The best technical guru may not be the best choice for vice president of engineering. The person who had the idea may not be the best person for president, and the most outgoing individual probably is not the one to guide marketing and sales.

Being able to talk technically or having good sales sense has nothing to do with being an outstanding marketer. These people often think that good marketing is belly-to-belly selling. Their marketing plan is to double sales next year. They fail to understand the total marketing concept. Their believe that advertising, public relations, selling and other marketing activities are separate and independent functions.

All parts of marketing activity are interdependent: pricing, packaging, positioning, and service, as well as advertising, selling, literature, and promotion. The successful organization doesn't separate advertising plans from the other parts of its marketing activities. It views each as a necessary and vital building block.

The primary purpose of the marketing plan is [to] make certain all relevant facts are known so you are aware of the obstacles that have to be overcome, and the opportunities that can be exploited. When these are known, you can establish a realistic set of objectives and plan your actions to achieve them. The plan uses all of the marketing tools: advertising, selling, sales-support literature, direct mail, public relations, pricing, packaging, distributor/dealer support, etc.

A lot of attention last year [1985] was given to Apple's event-marketing activities. Unfortunately, many of our new "marketing professionals" will know that this is really the kind of marketing needed to ensure success. They don't realize (and Apple hasn't told other members of the industry) that event-marketing is part of an overall marketing plan and strategy. In addition, as they have found from experience, event-marketing cannot be the major focus of the marketing program but must be used judiciously.

The marketing plan is not an academic exercise. The very act of putting the plan on paper requires a complete knowledge of the facts so that you will have a tighter, more foolproof plan. It will help you size up and structure your market and determine the market's total business volume.

Then you can compare your market's breakdown of sales with spending patterns. Properly done, a marketing plan will allow you to evaluate alternative methods of meeting marketing objectives. It also will provide evidence on which to make recommendations and sound programs. But more important, the marketing plan produces a unified, cohesive program for everyone in the organization to understand, use, and follow. It helps you change the product mix when necessary. It helps show the need for pricing changes and what portion of the market you are penetrating. The plan clearly can show you who the prospective buyers are, where they are located, and what appeals are most likely to affect their purchasing decisions.

Your marketing plan should consist of six elements:

1. <u>Statement of facts</u>. This is the most important because everything else depends on a correct understanding of the facts surrounding the market, business, and products. In general, the plan should include every fact that has any significant relevance to it. This includes an objective appraisal of the product lines, sales history of the products, competitive situation, pricing, and expenditures for past marketing activities. It also should include details on who the purchasers are, their wants and needs, and an analysis of your trade relations.

2. <u>Problems and opportunities</u>. Most of the problems can be solved. At that point, the problem becomes an opportunity. What are the problems? They may be the product lines or their prices. They may be unsatisfactory sales support material. They may be misdirected advertising. Regardless of the problem, recognition is the first step in creating an opportunity.

3. <u>Identification of objectives</u>. Such objectives as "increase sales," "improve share of market," or "increase distribution" don't define the target enough. As far as possible, objectives have to be stated in terms of results. For example, increasing readership of ads is only a desirable intermediate objective. The important thing is the number of specifics, designs, or buyers who receive the message and are informed or persuaded.

The distinction should be clear between objectives and budget forecasts. Although objectives must be realistically attainable, they should be sufficiently conservative so they can be realized. Sales figures are projected from these objectives, marketing expenses are determined, and gross profits are established.

4. <u>The complete marketing plan</u>. If the statement of facts reveals that defects in products or product lines are interfering with the success of your operation, the plan should recommend making corrections. The plan should evaluate alternative marketing and promotional strategies. On the basis of evaluation, it should recommend the particular strategy that appears most likely to succeed. Similarly, with respect to executing promotional strategy, alternatives should be considered. These have to be presented fairly and objectively with the pros and cons clearly spelled out. Only in this way is it possible to make sound business decisions.

5. <u>The recommended marketing appropriation</u>. The plan should include a recommendation on the amount to be spent on marketing, and how to spend it. It also must include the complete supporting rationale for why the amount is correct, based on the needs of the product lines, the activities necessary to meet those needs, and the gross profit to be generated by the estimated sales volume.

6. <u>Forecast of volume and profit</u>. The marketing plan should include a profit-and-loss projection based on a conservative estimate of the sales volumes to be attained, the gross profit to be realized at the proposed prices, and estimated costs. It also should include the deductions that must be made from that gross profit to calculate a profit-before-tax figure.

As you can see, the plan gives management a clear, comprehensive picture of the state of the

371

business, its problems, and opportunities. It spells out the objectives management considers essential, as well as the specific means by which they are pursued. It gives management the opportunity to judge the soundness of the strategic and tactical approach that will be taken. It puts members of the organization on record with marketing and sales objectives, as well as expense and profit budgets that should be considered a commitment on their part to deliver the performance outlined and detailed in the plan. If the plan works--if it is right in its determination of marketing objectives and if events prove that satisfactory progress has been made toward those goals--then we have to assume it was a good plan.

Unfortunately, many people fall into a trap. They assume that because a plan worked in 1985 it will work in '86 and '87. They seem to forget that the market, its wants, and its needs aren't stagnant from one quarter to the next, let alone from one year to another. Another problem is that too many neophyte marketers feel that once they have completed the annual marketing plan they are free from the drudgery for another 12 months. Wrong.

A lot of benefits can be derived from a mid-year review. The obvious reason is that it helps develop the following year's plan. More important, it helps realign and modify the present year's program when necessary. Granted, it requires a little time and effort, but only a total fool follows a battle plan that isn't working. And business is war. Each of us had better be fighting to win.

_____

Source: G. A. (Andy) Marken, "Success Is No Accident: You Need a Plan," *Marketing News*, May 23, 1986, p. 28. Reprinted from *Marketing News*. Published by the American Marketing Association, Chicago, IL 60606.

_____

____1. The most important element in the marketing plan is:
    A. Stating the facts.   D. Recommending the appropriation.
    B. Problems and opportunities.   E. Forecasting volume and profit.
    C. Identifying objectives.

____2. Without specifically saying so, the author would probably maintain that the most important means for organizing for implementation is:
    A. A company-wide plan.   D. Customer specialization.
    B. Geographical specialization.   E. Territorial or product specialization.
    C. Product specialization.

PART 21K: Answers to Questions

PART 21D: Completion
1. operational/strategic plan
2. evaluation
3. implementation/poor planning
4. organizing/staffing/directing/strategic plans
5. strategic marketing plan/implementing
6. reducing/workers/chief executive officer
7. marketing executive/vice-president
8. geographical territory/product line/ customer type
9. sales strategies/sales force
10. product-specialized/sales force
11. type of industry/channel of distribution
12. marketing concept
13. major-accounts
14. staffing the organization
15. directing and operating
16. delegation/coordination/motivation/ communication
17. responsibility/authority
18. interests/priorities/personalities
19. economic/psychological
20. walking around/out in the open
21. evaluation
22. marketing audit
23. 80/20/20/80
24. detailed
25. costs
26. what/why/what to do
27. sales volume analysis
28. total sales/product lines/market segments.
29. market segments/sales territories
30. market-share
31. operating expense
32. past data/trade association
33. more information
34. time/money/manpower
35. indirect/common
36. contribution-margin/contribution-to-overhead/full-cost
37. direct expenses
38. expenses/direct/indirect
39. volume/cost/channels of distribution
40. product line/sales people's/channels of distribution
41. small quantities

PART 21E: True-False Questions
1. F 2. T 3. F 4. F 5. T 6. F 7. T
8. T 9. F 10. T 11. T 12. F 13. T 14. F
15. T

PART 21F: Multiple Choice Questions
1. B 2. B 3. B 4. A 5. C 6. A 7. C
8. B 9. C 10. A 11. D 12. D 13. D 14. D
15. D

PART 21G: Matching Questions
a. 6 b. 2 c. 1 d. 14 e. 10 f. 7
g. 3

CHAPTER 22

MARKETING: APPRAISAL AND PROSPECTS

PART 22A : Chapter Goals

After studying this chapter, you should be able to explain:

- A societal perspective for evaluating marketing performance
- The major criticisms of marketing
- Consumer, government, and business responses to consumer discontent
- Consumerism and its effect on marketing
- The ethical responsibilities of marketers
- Trends influencing future marketing activity
- Some strategic adjustments necessary to cope with change

374

PART 22B: Key Terms and Concepts

1. Basis for evaluating performance	[622]	7. Social responsibility [632]
2. Nature of marketing criticisms	[624]	8. Green marketing [636]
3. Responses to marketing problems	[626]	9. Market fragmentation [638]
4. Consumerism	[626]	10. Niche marketing [638]
5. Ethics	[630]	11. Reconsumption [641]
6. Reasons for ethical behavior	[630]	12. Trade loading [642]

PART 22C: Summary

Since businesses and their marketing methods have become pervasive and more identifiable in our society, their mistakes and shortcomings are easier to recognize. As a result, they have received a proportionally larger share of criticism regarding the manner in which they conduct their operations. These social and economic criticisms are directed at all elements of the marketing mix--product, distribution structure, pricing system, and promotional activities [624-626].

Marketing has been attacked for being exploitative, inefficient, and even illegal, and for stimulating unwholesome demand [624]. Several of the criticisms stem from the complex question: "Does marketing cost too much?" While it is not possible to objectively answer this question, for organizations adopting the marketing concept, costs are not unreasonable. Certainly, while many of the objectives to marketing are valid, the offensive behavior is confined to a small minority of all marketers [626].

Responses to critics have come from consumers, government (federal, state, and local), and business itself [626-630]. Consumerism--protests against perceived institutional injustices, and the efforts to remedy them--has had a marked effect on marketing behavior [626].

Consumer responses to marketing problems have included protests, boycotts, political activism, and the support of special-interest groups. Businesses have responded to criticism by improving communication, providing more and better information, upgrading products, producing more sensitive advertising, and enhancing customer service [629-630].

The best answer to marketing criticism is ethical behavior by business [630]. Besides being morally correct, there are practical reasons to do right: it can restore public confidence, avoid government regulation, retain the power granted by society, and protect the image of the organization. Another method of judging the ethics of a particular act is to ask three questions:

Would I do this to a friend?   Would I be willing to have this done to me? Would I be embarrassed if this action were publicized nationally [631]?   While business could act more ethically, consumers could do the same by stemming the tide of shoplifting, credit-card misuse, check fraud, and coupon misredemption [633].

The numerous criticisms of marketing suggest the broadened marketing concept has not been widely adopted. If the concept is to be generally implemented, it is essential that marketers change their notion of consumer orientation [639].

While the prospects for marketing in the 1990s are difficult to predict, strong current trends are likely to continue into the near future. These include consumer demographic and value changes, continued fragmentation of the market, a continuance of the explosion in information, and renewed efforts in global marketing [639-643].

PART 22D: Completion

1. The objective of an organization is to accomplish its goals through the determination and satisfaction of _____.

2. Management must also strike a balance among the wants of _____, the objectives of the _____, and the welfare of _____.

3. The criticisms of marketing can be categorized as follows: (1) _____--taking unfair advantage of a consumer or situation, (2) _____--a waste of resources, (3) stimulating _____--encouraging consumers to buy products that are detrimental to the individual, and (4) _____.

4. These charges can be grouped according to the _____ components: product, price, distribution, and promotion.

5. Criticisms of products center on how well they meet customers' _____.

6. Complaints against prices stem from the idea that the seller is making a(n) _____ _____ or that the buyer has been _____about prices.

7. _____ is the least understood and least-appreciated marketing mix element.

8. The most common accusations against marketing focus on promotion   --especially in _____ and _____.

9. Most of the complaints against personal selling are focused at the _____ level, allegedly poor quality of _____ and _____.

10. There are _____ and _____ criticisms of advertising.

11. The social criticisms of advertising are: (1) there is an overemphasis on our _____ _____ and underemphasis on our cultural and moral values; (2) advertising manipulates impressionable people, especially _____; and (3) advertising is often _____, _____, and in _____, (4) making _____ claims for products and (5) overusing _____ and _____ appeals.

12. The economic criticisms of advertising are: (1) some critics charge that advertising simply shifts _____ from one _____ to _____ therefore raising marketing costs _____; and (2) large advertisers, through effective product differentiation, build the impression in consumers' minds that their brand is better than other brands, thus creating a(n) _____ to market entry, resulting in _____ and _____.

13. Before steps can be taken to remedy criticisms of marketing, one must find out the cause of the criticism. In a firm, is the cause the marketing department or is it _____ _____; and in the economy, is the cause the marketing system or is it the U. S. _____?

14. Consumerism can be defined as: (1) a consumer protest against the perceived injustices in the relationships between _____ and _____, (2) efforts to remedy those _____.

15. President Kennedy identified four rights of the consumer: right to _____, right to be _____, right to _____, and the right to be _____.

16. Consumerism covers three areas of consumer dissatisfaction and remedial efforts: (1) discontent is generated in marketing activities of direct buyer-seller relationships between _____ and _____; (2) consumerism is not limited to discontent with business alone, but with any organization in which there is a(n) _____; and (3) consumerism includes the indirect effect that an exchange relationship between _____ social units has on a(n) _____ party.

17. Consumer reaction's to marketing problems have ranged from _____ registered with offending organizations to _____.

18. Cultural conditions that provided impetus to the 1960s consumerism movement are again coming into place because consumers are more sensitive to _____ and _____ concerns.

19. Given society's sensitivity, it has become _____ to support consumer concerns.

20. At the federal level, many _____ protecting consumers have been passed while several _____ have been empowered to do the same.

21. In _____ there has been considerable interest in consumer-support laws.

22. Business has responded with: (1) better _____ with consumers, (2) more and better _____ for consumers, and (3) more carefully prepared _____.

23. Ethics are _____.

24. Marketing executives must balance their own interests (recognition, pay, promotions) with the best interests of _____, their _____, and _____.

25. In setting ethical guidelines, many firms have formal _____ for their employees that identify specific acts as unethical.

26. Honest answers to the following questions will help solve ethical issues: (1) Would I do this to a _____? (2) Would I be willing to _____? and (3) Would I be embarrassed if this were _____?

27. But there are also four practical reasons for behaving ethically: (1) to reverse declining _____ in marketing, (2) to avoid increases in _____, (3) to retain the _____ granted by society, and (4) to protect the _____ of the organization.

28. _____ involves improving the well-being of society.

29. _____ also have a responsibility to behave ethically in exchange relationships.

30. Changes in the future include: (1) changes in _____, (2) changes in _____, and (3) the development of _____.

31. Some demographic changes include a(n) _____ population, greater _____ diversity, and an increase in _____ households.

32. As the population ages, changes in values include broadened _____, increased _____, and balanced _____.

33. Efforts by marketers to respond to environmental concerns with new and altered products are known as _____.

34. Increasing market information has led to the identification of smaller and smaller market segments. This is known as _____.

35. The development of fragmented markets in turn has led to the tailoring of goods and services to very small market segments. This is called _____.

36. The net effect of fragmented markets is a shift in promotional spending from _____ to _____ and _____ publications.

37. Five proactive efforts to improve market performance are: (1) instilling a(n) _____ orientation, (2) adopting a(n) _____, (3) emphasizing _____ and _____, (4) designing _____ strategies, and (5) building _____ .

38. Describing the _____ and implementing it in an organization are two different things.

39. To be successful in the future, marketers must adopt a _____ toward markets, products, and marketing activity.

40. In a push toward increased quality, U.S. industries have adopted a technique called _____ (_____).

41. In the future, environmental acceptance of a product will be based on its entire _____, from _____ through _____.

42. Making products so that they can be used longer and reused either in part or whole is called _____.

43. Forms of reconstruction include: _____, _____, _____, and _____.

44. In an effort to build relationships, some marketers are moving away from _____, a practice that induces wholesalers and retailers to buy _____ products than they can _____ in a reasonable length of time.

PART 22E: True-False Questions

If the statement is true, circle "T"; if false, circle "F."

T F 1. A marketing executive should act in a socially responsible manner because this will help minimize government intervention.

T F 2. Advertising has been attacked on economic grounds but not on social grounds.

T F 3. According to the text, the major goal of marketing management should be satisfaction of the needs of the consumer, as the consumers perceive these needs.

T F   4. The goal of social responsibility on the part of marketing executives is not compatible with the business goal of long-run profit maximization.

T F   5. Some of the charges made against marketing really are criticisms of America's general economic system.

T F   6. It is easier to evaluate the effectiveness of marketing in an individual firm than its role in the economy as a whole.

T F   7. The strongest indictments leveled against marketing usually are in the area of promotional activities.

T F   8. A firm may be able to reduce its total costs by increasing its marketing costs.

T F   9. Trade loading is a practice that tends to build favorable long-term relationships between buyers and sellers.

T F 10. An exchange relationship between two persons will sometimes create a consumer problem for a third.

T F 11. One of the four "rights of the consumer" identified by President John F. Kennedy was the right to sue.

T F 12. In niche marketing, one version of a product is replaced by several.

T F 13. A marketing executive should be socially responsible only to his customers.

T F 14. Consumerism began in the 1960s.

T F 15. Deceptive advertising is a violation of our basic right to be informed.

PART 22F: Multiple Choice Questions

In the space provided write the letter of the answer that best fits the statement.

____1. Some marketers engage in unethical behavior--but so do some consumers by:
    A. Engaging in shoplifting.
    B. Writing forged checks.
    C. Engaging in credit card fraud.
    D. Vandalizing places of business.
    E. All of the above.

___ 2. Criticisms of marketing center on actions that can be categorized as:
   A. Exploitation.
   B. Inefficiency.
   C. Illegal behavior.
   D. Stimulating unwholesome demand.
   E. All of the above.

___ 3. The most common accusation against marketing focuses on:
   A. Product.
   B. Price.
   C. Distribution.
   D. Promotion.
   E. Channels.

___ 4. The right to _____ was NOT one of the rights of the consumer as identified by President Kennedy.
   A. Safety
   B. Be informed
   C. Choose
   D. Be heard
   E. Sue the government

___ 5. A marketing executive should act in a socially responsible manner because:
   A. This will help minimize government intervention.
   B. This will retain the power granted by society.
   C. This will protect the image of the organization.
   D. All of the above.
   E. None of the above.

___ 6. All of the following are criticisms of products EXCEPT:
   A. Adequate repair services.
   B. Deceptive packaging.
   C. Heavily promoted product improvements are often trivial.
   D. Planned style obsolescence.
   E. Products fail or break under normal use.

___ 7. If we are successful in reducing distribution or marketing costs in the U.S., it will probably be due to:
   A. Eliminating certain marketing functions from the marketing process.
   B. A reduction in the number of different types of middlemen.
   C. A reduction in the number of middlemen who are competing on the same level of distribution.
   D. The discovery of more efficient methods of performing the various marketing functions.
   E. The more general use of shorter channels of distribution.

___ 8. Business has responded to consumer problems by:
   A. Communicating better with consumers.
   B. Getting more and better information to consumers.
   C. Making product improvements.
   D. Establishing customer service departments.
   E. All of the above.

____ 9. All of the following are social criticisms of advertising EXCEPT:
   A. There is an overemphasis on a material standard of living.
   B. There is an overemphasis on cultural, spiritual, ethical, and moral values.
   C. Advertising makes people buy things they should not have, cannot afford, and do not need.
   D. Advertising is often deceptive.
   E. Advertising is often in bad taste.

____10. All of the following are economic criticisms of advertising EXCEPT:
   A. Advertising costs too much, thus increasing the cost of marketing.
   B. Since marketing costs so much, the prices of products are raised.
   C. It leads to a concentration of business by allowing large advertisers, through effective product differentiation, to obtain a large share of the market.
   D. Advertising is often false and in bad taste.
   E. Advertising can create a barrier to market entry, resulting in a high level of market concentration, further resulting in high prices.

____11. Consumerism includes the following broad area of dissatisfaction:
   A. Discontent with direct buyer-seller exchange relationships.
   B. Discontent with nonbusiness, nonprofit organizations.
   C. Discontent with government agencies.
   D. Discontent of those indirectly affected by the behavior of others.
   E. All of the above.

____12. Reconsumption includes all of the following EXCEPT;
   A. Refilling. B. Repairing. C. Restoring. D. Remaking. E. Reusing.

____13. A strategic proactive effort that marketers can initiate is:
   A. Instilling a market-driven orientation.
   B. Adopting a global orientation.
   C. Emphasizing quality and satisfaction.
   D. Designing environmentally sound strategies.
   E. All of the above.

____14. All of the following demographic changes are likely to take place in the next twenty years EXCEPT:
   A. An increase in household size.
   B. An aging population.
   C. Greater ethnic diversity.
   D. An increasing value placed on time.
   E. Increasing opportunities in travel and tourism.

____15. All of the following changes in consumer values are likely to take place in the 1990s EXCEPT:
   A. An increase in volunteerism.
   B. An increase in self-orientation.
   C. Heightened interest in the future quality of life.
   D. An increased demand for good service.
   E. An increased focus on the home.

PART 22G: Matching Questions

In the space provided write the number of the word or expression from column 1 that best fits the description in column 2.

	1		2
	1. Consumer Bill of Rights	___a.	A protest against perceived business injustices and the efforts to remedy those injustices.
	2. Consumerism		
	3. Ethical behavior	___b.	Four rights stated by President John Kennedy.
		___c.	Replacing one version of a product with several.
	4. Ethics	___d.	Conforming to an accepted standard of moral behavior.
	5. Fragmented markets		
	6. Niche marketing	___e.	Designing materials, components, and packages so that they can be used longer or reused either in part or whole.
	7. Reconsumption		
	8. Social responsibility		
	9. Trade loading		

PART 22H: Problems and Applications

1.   From a study of periodicals in your school's library, write a memo to your instructor on what the U.S. economy and society will be like at the turn of the century. Consider such factors as population, income, and life-style patterns.

2.   Based upon your conclusions in question 1, write a memo discussing what you believe marketing will be like at the turn of the century. Evaluate marketing activities into the following

elements of the marketing mix: products, promotion, channels of distribution, and pricing.

3.   Interview several business people on their views of the place of marketing activities in the coming years. What changes do they see? What has created these changes? Compare your findings with those of others in your class.

4.   Assume you are the sales manager for a manufacturer of electrical appliances. How would elements of the marketing mix be affected by another nationwide energy shortage?

5.   Interview the manager of a manufacturing company. How has his or her company become more "socially responsible" in the last few years?

6.   Interview a local minister, priest, or rabbi and the manager of the Chamber of Commerce or Better Business Bureau on the subject of social responsibility and business ethics. Report your conclusions in a memo to your instructor.

7.   Make a list of public and private organizations within your community that have as a purpose to protect, inform, or lobby for consumers.

8.   Based upon your understanding of the consumerism movement, what would you advise the marketing manager of a small video store to do in designing his or her annual marketing plan?

9.   What evidence can you find to support the premise that business people *do* have a degree of social responsibility and are concerned with maintaining or improving the "quality of life"?

10.   Talk to the manager of a manufacturing company. Has installation of pollution-abatement equipment had any effect on their sales? What importance is this equipment given in their annual budget?

11.   Cut out advertisements for pollution-control systems. Whom do these companies appeal to and what themes do they use to promote their systems?

PART 22I: Exercise

In Chapter 1, we started this section of the Study Guide with an exercise to see if you could identify marketing-concept orientation. Now that you know the marketing concept in all its aspects, see if you can do the following exercise. Write "MCO" for the firms having the marketing concept orientation in its broadest aspects as discussed by the authors in this chapter.

1.   Firm A   "I'll give them any color car they want so long as it's black."
       Firm B   "I'll give them any color car they want."

2. Firm A   "By adding plastic carrying handles, we can make it give better service."
    Firm B   "By adding plastic carrying handles, we can cut our costs."

3. Firm A   "If we can get you to sign this contract today, we can easily fit it into our factory schedule."
    Firm B   "If we can get you to sign this contract today, you can get the products in time to meet your sales goals."

4. Firm A   "We offer you a means for gathering, processing, and analyzing business data."
    Firm B   "We make computers."

5. Firm A   "We make pumps."
    Firm B   "We deliver usable water into people's homes at the right pressure and in the right volume."

6. Firm A   "The first product my grandfather made when he started this furniture factory is this Shaker love seat. We'll always make it."
    Firm B   "The simplicity of this classic Shaker furniture design is continuing to enjoy wide acceptance."

7. Firm A   "Please donate blood. Your hospital needs it."
    Firm B   "Please donate blood. You will never know when you or one of your loved ones will need it."

8. Firm A   "Perhaps we had better get back to taking Visa cards. A lot of customers seem to be using them."
    Firm B   "We'll continue with MasterCard as long as they give us a better deal than Visa."

9. Firm A   "Profits are down. Let's look around to see if we can do a better job of meeting the needs of our customers."
    Firm B   "Profits are down. Let's initiate a cost-reduction program."

10. Firm A   "No way I'm going into that new shopping center. The rents are outrageous."
    Firm B   "No way I'm going into that new shopping center. Our customers are better served if we stay right here."

PART 22J: A Real World Case: Through the Glass Darkly

Last year [1988] was a good one for the supermarket industry judging by responses to the

385

Progressive Grocer Annual Report, and 1989 is expected to continue in the same vein. Retailers, wholesalers, and manufacturers all are optimistic about the general state of the economy, the retailing climate and particularly about the prospects of their companies.

Of course, nagging problems still exist, and there are some new, or accentuated, concerns. The primary one is availability of employees, particularly qualified ones. That has been a problem in recent years, but now it has shot to the top of the worry chart. And well it might. Barring a deep recession that is virtually at a depression level, there is little likelihood that the situation will improve for generations; rather, it will worsen.

Since there is more concern about the effect of heightened inflation than of recession, it is clear that executives do not expect a lessening of the labor crunch.

Another matter that troubled industry executives last year was the accelerated pace of mergers and acquisitions. Will that boon (or bane) of the 1980s, the leveraged buyout, continue at its present pace in the next decade? It might, unless Congress is impelled to take action to curb this practice, or the regulatory agencies become more interested in regulating than they have been, or all the attractive targets have already been LBOd. In any event, where executives in the past were not overly upset by the rash of corporate mergers and LBOs, they now consider them a definite threat to the well-being of the industry.

There are several viewpoints on the effect of these big deals. One is that all's well that ends well. In that scenario, a well-managed company will benefit from an LBO or a major acquisition, despite the debt burden, because it will shed some fat and emerge as a healthier company. According to that theory, the end result also will benefit the industry--and consumers. But then there's the question of companies that are not well managed. In the words of one retailer, "The bad ones will go down in flames and will hurt innocent bystanders."

Not everyone agrees that the consolidations will benefit consumers. Some feel that they will suffer in the near term if pricing becomes less aggressive. But there's also the viewpoint that, as one retailer put it, fewer and larger entities will not serve customers well in the long run either because "all the oligopolies are not going to beat each other up. They're going to survive together."

Other possible industry negatives in 1989 include increased competition from wholesale clubs and other nonfood retailers, as well as the possible impact of hypermarkets. Meanwhile, as food consumed away from home continues to eat away at supermarkets, albeit at a slower rate, food retailers realize they must step up their efforts to attract purchasers of prepared food.

As always, rising costs constitute a perceived problem for retailers and wholesalers. Wages are going up, and despite the lack of good employees, retailers need more of them to staff the many additional service departments. But more an issue than wages are the continuing increases in the cost of benefits. If Congress succeeds in enacting legislation calling for mandatory benefits, with

386

or without a presidential veto, the cost could be even higher.

Then there's the environment. Retailers would like the problem of what is euphemistically referred to as solid waste to go away, but they realize that it won't. Gone are the days when this country could accumulate and dump waste with impunity. There is a growing realization in the supermarket community that it is better to be part of the solution than part of the problem.

In line with that is the question of food safety. How much of this problem is real and how much is perceived is problematical. But since perception can wreak a great deal of havoc, this is another area where the members of the industry must continue to move positively this year.

And underlying all these concerns is the trade relations bugaboo. All facets of the industry, when questioned by Progressive Grocer, gave poor grades to the current state of trade relations.

Even more pertinent than the grades themselves is the degree to which executives are obsessed with the chasm between retailers and suppliers and the level of mistrust they feel exists between the two parties.

When asked to comment on the industry issues that disturb them, both sides harkened time and again to trade relations. Suppliers used such strong words as "extortion," "graft," and "rape" to characterize actions by the trade.

Retailers and wholesalers denied these charges and, in turn, railed against class of trade favoritism. They claimed that suppliers, by raising list prices and increasing deals, cast the first stone and therefore are responsible for the contretemps.

Said one chief executive, "The basic problem is lack of trust. Manufacturers ask too much for their products. As a result, retailers don't know what the bottom line is on price, so they continue to push for price. Sometimes they push unfairly," he conceded.

So it appears that despite the relatively good overall outlook, something is rotten in the state of supermarketing. The basic problem is not competition, a labor shortage, inflation, environmental concerns or the myriad of other very real problems that will continue to appear--and be dealt with--as inevitably as night follows day.

Rather the problem is a state of mind. Industry factors must decide whether they are going to operate in a constructive manner, with long-term benefits to their consumers, their companies and the industry in mind, or whether they will nickel-and-dime themselves to death. The latter course may bolster bottom lines and preserve product franchises in the short run, but it cannot succeed over the long haul.

As one executive put it, "The retailer today is so geared toward deals and allowances that many times we forget what got us where we are--merchandising. We merchandised our shelving; we

387

merchandised our ends; we priced competitively; we looked at what our competition was doing. Today, many retailers are working on their bottom lines strictly based on what deals they can get. And deals are not going to hold us together. We've got to get back into merchandising for profit and for consumers." Equally valid criticisms can be levied against suppliers.

There is no easy prescription for constructive engagement. In fact, it's a difficult task. But it obviously is within the power of all facets of the industry to take concrete steps that will move us from our present non-productive course to one that can work over the long haul.

As Pogo said, "We have met the enemy, and he is us." It's time we acknowledged that and began to take some constructive action.

_____

Source: Steve Weinstein, "Commentary: The Enemy Is Us," *Progressive Grocer*, April, 1989, pp. 4-5. Reprinted with the permission of Progressive Grocer magazine, Division of Maclean Hunter Media Inc.

_____

____ 1. According to the article (and without saying so directly), the thing that will save the supermarket industry in the future is:
   A. More aggressive pricing.   D. Better employees.
   B. The marketing concept.   E. More LBOs.
   C. Biodegradable packaging.

____ 2. In order to reduce distribution costs we must:
   A. Eliminate certain marketing functions from the marketing process.
   B. Reduce the number of different types of middlemen.
   C. Encourage more LBOs.
   D. Discover better methods of performing marketing functions.
   E. Generally use shorter channels of distribution.

PART 22K: Answers to Questions

PART 22D: Completion

1. consumer wants
2. consumers/organization/society
3. exploitation/inefficiency/unwholesome demand/illegal behavior
4. marketing mix
5. expectations
6. excessive profit/misled
7. Distribution
8. promotion/selling/advertising
9. retail/retail selling/service
10. social/economic
11. material standard of living/children/false/deceptive/bad taste/exaggerated/fear/sexual
12. demand/brand/another/marketing costs/barrier/high prices/greater profit
13. some other department/economic system
14. business/consumers/injustices
15. safety/informed/choose/heard
16. consumers/businesses/exchange relationship/two/third
17. complaints/boycotts
18. social/environmental
19. politically popular
20. laws/regulatory agencies
21. state legislatures
22. communications/information/advertisements
23. standards of moral conduct
24. consumers/organizations/society
25. codes of ethics
26. friend/have this done to me/publicized nationally
27. public confidence/government regulation/power/image
28. Social responsibility
29. Consumers
30. demographics/values/market information
31. aging/ethnic/single-parent
32. perspectives/skepticism/lifestyles
33. green marketing
34. market fragmentation
35. niche marketing
36. mass media/consumer/trade
37. market-driven/global orientation/quality/satisfaction/environmentally sound/relationships
38. marketing concept
39. global orientation
40. Total Quality Management/TQM
41. life cycle/design/disposal
42. reconsumption
43. refilling/repairing/restoring/reusing
44. trade loading/more/resell

PART 22E: True-False Questions

1. T   2. F   3. T   4. F   5. T   6. T
7. T   8. T   9. F   10. T   11. F   12. T
13. F   14. F   15. T

PART 22F: Multiple Choice Questions

1. E   2. E   3. D   4. E   5. D   6. A
7. D   8. E   9. B   10. D   11. E   12. D
13. E   14. A   15. B

PART 22G: Matching Questions

a. 2   b. 1   c. 6   d. 3   e. 7